No Accident, Comrade

No Accident, Comrade

CHANCE AND DESIGN IN COLD WAR AMERICAN NARRATIVES

STEVEN BELLETTO

OXFORD
UNIVERSITY PRESS

UNIVERSITY PRESS

Oxford University Press, Inc., publishes works that further
Oxford University's objective of excellence
in research, scholarship, and education.

Oxford   New York
Auckland   Cape Town   Dar es Salaam   Hong Kong   Karachi
Kuala Lumpur   Madrid   Melbourne   Mexico City   Nairobi
New Delhi   Shanghai   Taipei   Toronto

With offices in
Argentina   Austria   Brazil   Chile   Czech Republic   France   Greece
Guatemala   Hungary   Italy   Japan   Poland   Portugal   Singapore
South Korea   Switzerland   Thailand   Turkey   Ukraine   Vietnam

Copyright © 2012 by Oxford University Press, Inc.

Published by Oxford University Press, Inc.
198 Madison Avenue, New York, New York 10016

www.oup.com

Oxford is a registered trademark of Oxford University Press

All rights reserved. No part of this publication may be reproduced,
stored in a retrieval system, or transmitted, in any form or by any means,
electronic, mechanical, photocopying, recording, or otherwise,
without the prior permission of Oxford University Press.

Library of Congress Cataloging-in-Publication Data
Belletto, Steven.
No accident, comrade : chance and design in Cold War American
narratives / Steven Belletto.
    p. cm.
Includes bibliographical references and index.
ISBN 978-0-19-982688-9 (acid-free paper) 1. American fiction—20th
century—History and criticism. 2. Cold War in literature. 3. Chance
in literature. 4. Political fiction, American—History and criticism.
I. Title.
PS374.C57B45   2012
813'.54—dc22   2011010928

1 3 5 7 9 8 6 4 2

Printed in the United States of America
on acid-free paper

Contents

Acknowledgments   vii

1. Chance, Narrative, and the Logic of the Cold War   3

2. Aesthetic Responses to Political Fictions: Pynchon and the Violence of Narrative Chance   35

3. The Zemblan Who Came in from the Cold: Nabokov's Cold War   61

4. Accidents Going Somewhere to Happen: African-American Self-Definition at Mid-Century   80

5. The Game Theory Narrative and the Myth of the National Security State   101

6. Their Country, Our Culture: The Persistence of the Cold War   129

Coda: Cold War Meaning   147
Notes   155
Bibliography   185
Index   199

Acknowledgments

Earlier versions of chapters 3 and 5 appeared in *ELH* 73 (Fall 2006) and *American Quarterly* 61.2 (June 2009), respectively. I am grateful to these journals for permission to reprint portions of those essays here.

First thanks go to the person who first taught me that there could be some connection between books and the Cold War, Tom Schaub. Way back when, I pleaded with him to admit me to his overbooked grad seminar; from the moment he relented to his directing me through a dissertation, I have come to appreciate Tom's remarkably comprehensive knowledge of American literature and culture—and his example of remembering always that there is more to life than the academic life. I would not have survived graduate school, let alone advanced in my career, without the guidance of Rebecca Walkowitz, who truly embodies professionalism in the best sense of the word—I have followed her example and advice for many years, and I owe much of whatever success I have to knowing her. Since I met him, David Zimmerman has been generous both with his archive of theoretical knowledge and his bag of pedagogical tricks, and I remember having long conversations with him about chance and risk that first got me thinking about the topic of this book. I am grateful also to Russ Castronovo and Jeremi Suri for reading parts of this argument in very different forms—many changes, which I hope are for the better, are due to their suggestions.

I have also been quite fortunate to have many friends strangely willing to neglect other things in order to engage my work. Dennis Britton and Amy Johnson have been reading and rereading parts of this book since I first began to formulate its scope, and I thank them for slogging through my bouts of incoherence, and helping me to straighten them out. Chris Scalia, between thinking up diversions in both Wisconsin and in the hills of Virginia, commented with rigor that would make Jacob Dousterswivel proud. David LaCroix, my go-to expert on all things pertaining to African-American literature, helped me immensely with chapter 4. At various times and in various places, Krista Kauffmann, Mike LeMahieu, Kristin Matthews, Will Rogers, Kim Rostan,

Michelle Sizemore, Hilary Teynor, and Caroline Willis all offered incisive criticisms that have benefited this book in untellable ways. Dan Grausam and I have had an on-going conversation about the field of Cold War literary studies for years now, and he has read almost this entire manuscript and offered insight that has made it immeasurably richer, and I am glad to have this opportunity to thank him again for his generosity.

I also owe much to my friends and colleagues at Lafayette College who have read and commented on parts of this book. Paul Cefalu, a one-man cottage industry of scholarly production, has read many chapters, and has offered veteran advice about negotiating academic publishing. Joe Shieber has dissected this book's logic more than once, and the whole is better for his scalpel. As a Russian historian, Josh Sanborn offered much appreciated insight into the other side of the story. Carrie Rohman has listened to me hash out ideas in my office and then read dubious first results, and yet has remained convinced that someone somewhere may find the end result interesting. It is also my great pleasure to thank Lafayette College for granting me a midterm research leave, which allowed me to finish this book. I would also like to express my appreciation to all the members of the English department for their encouragement, particularly the two department heads since I have been there, Suzanne Westfall and David Johnson.

And I am, of course, very much indebted to Brendan O'Neill, my editor at Oxford University Press, for seeing merit in this book. Andy Hoberek and an anonymous reader commented on the manuscript for the press, and their suggestions and criticisms have improved the final product in numerous ways.

Thanks also to my oldest friend, Travis Grosser, for continuing to distract me with good ideas like camping sans supplies in remotest Bihar, and to my parents, Owen and Nancy Belletto, and my brother, James, for all their humor and support. Finally, if any traces of warmth or creativity are detectable in this book, it is thanks to the example of Shirin Vazir, who has these attributes to spare, and who shares them with me on a daily basis.

No Accident, Comrade

1

Chance, Narrative, and the Logic of the Cold War

It was a Friday in late December 1957, and a light rain fell on Idlewild. Those were the days before the airport could boast Eero Saarinen's ultramodern TWA terminal, so the most arresting feature for the freshly disembarked was perhaps the massive Alexander Calder mobile dangling from the ceiling of the International Arrivals Building, which had just opened earlier that month. For one new arrival in particular, a 24-year-old student from Poland who wandered into immigration with a mere $2.80 in his pocket, the sheer scale of that building must have represented the potential of his new life in the United States. Although he was already accepted by Columbia University's doctoral program in sociology, it still seems remarkable that this young man, who had only a working knowledge of English, could have in eight months managed to secure a contract with Doubleday for a book explaining Soviet life to American audiences. The book was serialized in *The Saturday Evening Post* and condensed in *Reader's Digest*, and when it was published in 1960, it caught the attention of readers as eminent and far-flung as Konrad Adenauer and Bertrand Russell, who wrote the author a letter of admiration.[1]

The young man, Jerzy Kosinski, would go on to write such classic novels as *The Painted Bird* (1965) and *Being There* (1971) but that first book, *The Future Is Ours, Comrade*, was billed as a nonfiction blend of sociological analyses and reportage.[2] That Kosinski came to publish the book so quickly is explained by the special position he occupied, somewhere between the cultural norms of the world's two superpowers. As he soon discovered, the Cold War had its own peculiar logic and strange obsessions, and Americans were bent on exploring their grim fascination with their remote rivals. Kosinski was a Russian speaker with detailed notes from a research trip he had taken to the Soviet Union in the mid-1950s, and he found that he could exploit such a position to help explain why the two political and economic systems clashed. The prospects for peace at that time were indeed tenuous: earlier the very week Kosinski arrived in the States, there had been a NATO conference in Paris; before flying back home, Dwight

Eisenhower led a silent prayer before the present heads of state. Eleanor Roosevelt, in a column she had written daily since 1936, urged NATO to convince "the Soviets that a Communist world is not possible."[3] Had the young Kosinski scanned the front page of the *New York Times* on his way into the city, he would have seen a nation trying to make further sense of its protracted competition. Amidst the NATO conference coverage, headlines reported that industrial production in the Soviet Union had increased 10 percent over the past year; that Soviet scientists were anxious to best their American counterparts; that the Pentagon was requesting another billion dollars for weapons development.[4]

Given such uneasy curiosity about the Soviet Union, it seems almost natural that Kosinski would publish a book like *The Future Is Ours, Comrade*—after all, his very presence in the United States had shades of Cold War politics. As part of a Polish exchange program, he was awarded a Ford Foundation Fellowship through the Institute of International Education, an organization whose ostensible aim was to promote international education, but whose tacit goals were to expose foreign nationals to the charms of American democracy. Although Kosinski always denied it publicly, his biographer, James Park Sloan, thinks it likely that *The Future Is Ours, Comrade* was given the imprimatur of the United States Information Agency (USIA), a CIA-sponsored program that promoted books sympathetic to the American democratic system.[5] Whatever Kosinski's specific involvement with the CIA (in later years he would joke about his supposed connections with the intelligence community), we do know that in 1958–59, he recorded broadcasts in Polish for Radio Free Europe, that he applied for a job at the USIA, and that, as Sloan puts it, *The Future Is Ours, Comrade* "is everything an American propaganda agency, or the propaganda arm of the CIA, might have hoped for in its wildest dreams."[6]

One reason that Kosinski's book was so suited to its Cold War environment is that it verified the popular American sense that the Soviet system, totalitarian in both theory and practice, sustained itself by crushing individual will and manufacturing its own idiosyncratic version of reality.[7] Through his various "conversations with the Russians," Kosinski argued that while the average Russian was not all that different from the average American, the Soviet command were masters of social regimentation who demanded utter obedience. Among the more striking ways that he illustrated the extent of such control was to show that in the Soviet Union, what passed for objective reality was managed so completely that even chance itself seemed not to exist.[8]

Kosinski's work is thus a good starting place for *No Accident, Comrade* because it is a clear example of how the concept of chance became politicized during the Cold War. In fact, examining Cold War literature and culture through the prism of chance allows us to see the emergence of a new kind of relationship between aesthetics and politics during the period. The next several pages will explain how Kosinski associated chance with American democratic freedom and the denial of chance with Soviet-style totalitarianism, an idea found in a surprising number of places in Cold War culture. I begin with this perceived opposition and argue that because it was unique to the Cold War, the era put pressure on the idea of narrative itself—the designed nature of which seems fundamentally at odds with chance—and especially on the work of so-called literary fiction. This chapter explains first how the concept of chance circulated in Cold War culture, and then shows how the use of chance in fictional narratives took on a political cast. Throughout this book, I argue that in the Cold War frame, chance became a complex, elastic concept whose self-reflexive use by fiction writers and other cultural producers generated questions about freedom, control, and narrative's fundamental ability to represent or otherwise engage objective reality.

The Future Is Ours, Comrade is particularly illustrative in this regard: there Kosinski includes an anecdote about Aliosha, a Soviet military officer, who explains what happened when one of his charges, Private First Class Usbakhov, slipped out for a night of carousing. When Usbakhov does not return for morning call, Aliosha is faced with a dilemma. Although he is obliged to report immediately this breach in the rules—resulting in severe punishment for Usbakhov—he tries to be humane by bringing in another private to take the absentee's place at roll call. On the third day of Usbakhov's absence, as Aliosha is beginning to panic about his own rule breaking, he receives a call from battalion headquarters informing him that a "control commission" is coming to inspect selected units, including his platoon. Poor Aliosha curses his luck: "My legs buckled under me. I had never thought that fate, or chance, or so-called objective reality could be so cruel, so unbelievably malicious. Of all the platoons, it had to be mine selected for inspection."[9] He sweats his way through the inspection, hoping that the imposter will go undetected, but then chance deals him another crippling blow: of all the soldiers present, it is the fake Usbakhov who is singled out for special questioning, and the ruse soon unravels. After the whirlwind of punishment that follows, Aliosha, still not quite believing what has happened, learns the truth, that a few days prior Usbakhov had been plucked from recess by "officers of the counterintelligence" who sequestered him off-post to see whether the commanding officers would follow protocol for reporting missing personnel.[10] The lesson is clear: so profoundly has the Soviet system infiltrated everyday life that "so-called objective reality" itself—which would contain chance occurrences, however improbable—has been replaced by a vision of the state so pervasive that even chance becomes evidence of planning.[11]

It is tremendously suggestive that this lesson is illustrated by a purportedly chance event turning out to be actually a product of design. As implied by the conflation of concepts in Aliosha's exclamation (fate, chance, and objective reality), chance can be viewed as a signal or marker of "objective reality" precisely because it is not subject to human planning and lies outside of design. Chance, as the concept is commonly understood, is that which has not been intended. And yet under Soviet control, chance scarcely has room to maneuver: Aliosha learns that given enough knowledge, chance events can be explained as part of a larger design, a design that Kosinski suggests is an arbitrary and artificial narrative order that he and his interlocutors refer to as "Soviet reality."[12] In an interview years later, Kosinski would put a finer point on this idea: "[P]lot is what a totalitarian state inflicts upon any of its citizens."[13] Aliosha's tale is thus revealing because it suggests that "Soviet reality" has a narrative quality—it is not something that exists outside the will of human beings, but something that has a legible "plot." From this point of view, chance becomes especially significant because it has potential to disrupt design, to expose Soviet reality as a fiction. In *The Future Is Ours, Comrade*, chance is aligned with objective reality, and so the Soviet Union is represented not only as brutal and nakedly power-mad but also as philosophically misguided because it excludes, denies, or otherwise attempts to manipulate chance.

Kosinski's book is but one example of the recurring criticism found in numerous works written in the United States during the Cold War, that Marxism could not objectively or scientifically describe reality because it denied the existence of chance. One way to illustrate this criticism is to look at the writing of history, since there one could choose either objective facts or the ideological manipulation of these facts. This is why Richard Evans, writing on the treatment of causation in history, can refer to "Isaiah Berlin and others who argued, in the style of Cold War attacks on Soviet historical 'determinism,' that history was governed by chance, accident."[14] Evans is alluding to the determinism evident in sentences such as these, written by Friedrich Engels: "Historical events thus appear on the whole to be likewise governed by chance. But where on the surface accident holds sway, actually it is always governed by inner, hidden laws and it is only a matter of discovering these laws."[15]

It was this sort of thinking, examined by Americans with varying degrees of rigor in countless works of fiction and nonfiction, that seemed to prove that Soviet citizens were living in a fiction written for them by a handful of humorless, power-obsessed authoritarians. For orthodox Marxists, this story went, chance is a result of ignorance; perceiving chance is an index of one's incomplete knowledge of the universe. Nikolai Bukharin, intellectual darling of the Bolsheviks before Stalin had him executed, wrote in 1921, "If at bottom all things proceed in accordance with law, and if there is nothing that is accidental—causeless—it is clear there can be no such thing as accident in history. . . . historical accidentalism also simply means the intersection of certain causal series of which only one series is known."[16] For those already skeptical of Marxist dialectics, statements like this were taken to mean that Marxists denied the existence of chance, a proposition so patently false that it exposed Marxist "law" as a fiction disguised as objective reality.[17]

In his own later fiction, Kosinski became even more resolute in his criticism of the scientific line that Marxist theorists were thought to take. In discussing his novel *Blind Date* (1977), for example, he remarked that his protagonist "is dissatisfied with Marxism because he feels betrayed by the Soviet society that preaches 'objective destiny,' proclaiming, in a travesty of scientific discourse, that Marxism offers access to the 'scientifically' established 'objective' laws of history which man has no choice but to obey, and that the State and the Communist Party have a moral duty to enforce at any cost to the population."[18] As he did in *The Future Is Ours, Comrade*, Kosinski attacks Soviet Marxism by insisting that while it claims to identify "'objective' laws of history," it actually creates a fiction that is then fit imperfectly onto objective reality. This idea percolated through American culture and is found distilled to the point of parody in the phrase "no accident"—as, for example, in Randall Jarrell's comic novel *Pictures from an Institution* (1954), in which one character remarks that the decor in a friend's living room is deliberate: "[T]hese colors were, as Marxists say, 'no accident,' they were a scheme."[19] Writing on William F. Buckley's book *God and Man at Yale* (1952), Dwight Macdonald likewise speculated about why Buckley had decided to attack Yale's faculty as being anti-Christian and pro-collectivist: "A Freudian," he writes, "might mutter 'father fixation'; a Marxian might note it is 'no accident' that a rich young man . . . has such views."[20] Some twenty-five years later, Vivian Gornick ended her journalistic account of American Communism with a quip from an old-school Party organizer, who ironically reanimates this phrase while taking the long view of history: "'[Socialism] will come [to the United States]. After all,' [he] finishes with a mocking grin, '[I]t is no accident, comrade, that you and I are sitting here today, talking about these things.'"[21]

Kosinski's own thinking had by the 1970s been clarified by the ideas of Jacques Monod, a Nobel Prize-winning biologist and Kosinski's close friend. Monod's best-selling book, *Chance and Necessity: An Essay on the Natural Philosophy of Modern Biology* (1971), makes the case that "[p]ure chance, absolutely free but blind, [is] at the very root of the stupendous edifice of evolution."[22] Throughout *Chance and Necessity*, Monod argues that "natural selection operates *upon* the products of chance and can feed nowhere else; but it operates in a domain of very demanding conditions, and from this domain chance is barred."[23] Such a description means that while it is possible to analyze and understand the "demanding conditions" in which evolutionary processes operate, the universe as a system is ultimately indeterminate and therefore unpredictable—a notion that would be unsettling to any Soviet apparatchik.

In his later, meditative chapters—the "natural philosophy" of the subtitle—Monod reflects on the human need for order and pattern, and what this means for contemporary politics. We all share, he writes, a "very human tendency to believe that behind everything real in the world stands a necessity rooted in the very beginning of things. Against this notion, this powerful feeling of destiny, we must be constantly on guard.... The universe was not pregnant with life nor the biosphere with man. Our number came up in the Monte Carlo game. Is it any wonder if, like the person who has just made a million at the casino, we feel strange and a little unreal?"[24] In this turn from biology to philosophy, Monod's political agenda becomes clearer: he is arguing against those theories that describe a biological or historical destiny. Monod's ideas were of particular interest to Kosinski—and are relevant to a discussion of Cold War cultural studies—because as the book vacillates between biology and philosophy, it does so to offer proof that the putative science of Marxist dialectical materialism is fundamentally flawed.

According to Monod, a cardinal sin of orthodox Marxists is their belief that the universe bends to any human construct, including dialectical materialism: "The immense influence of Marxist ideology does not derive alone from its promise of liberation for man, but also, and probably mainly, from its ontogenic structure, the explanation it provides, sweeping and in detail, of past, present, and future history.... human history connects with that of the cosmos to obey the same eternal laws."[25] The argument here is that "Marxist ideology" is among the more pernicious examples of the "anthropocentric illusion" that a universe of chance conforms to anything but physical laws.[26] Drawing philosophical and political conclusions from his understanding of biology, Monod closes his book with a dismissal of historical materialism, the very language of which Kosinski would later poach to explain the philosophical underpinnings of *Blind Date*: "[H]istorical materialism rests upon a total confusion of the categories of value and knowledge. This very confusion permits it, in a travesty of authentic discourse, to proclaim that it has 'scientifically' established the laws of history, which man has no choice or duty but to obey if he does not wish to sink away into nothingness."[27] For Monod as for Kosinski, in a Marxist, purportedly scientific view of history, reality becomes subject to a prescribed set of conditions and possibilities, and free will itself is absorbed in the larger tide of historical inevitability. Far from delivering on its "promise of liberation for man," dialectical materialism straitjackets both choice and chance so that the universe is distorted to fit the Party Line. When Monod and Kosinski call such thinking a "travesty" of "authentic" or "scientific" discourse, they do so to emphasize how consequential it can be when this distorted reality comes to take the place of "objective reality." The result, Monod thinks, is a profound confusion of "value and knowledge"—so deeply has "Marxist ideology" penetrated the Soviet Union that their definition and understanding of reality itself has transformed. Objective reality becomes subject to Marxist value, and all the while this value is trumpeted as mere knowledge, as a manifestation of scientific law. Monod counters this notion by citing chance itself as evidence of the falseness of Marxist ideology. In other words, where one looks for chance and finds none (or discovers, as Aliosha does in *The Future Is Ours, Comrade*, the presence of hidden design), one will find ideology rather than objective reality. *Chance and Necessity* begins in pure science and ends with a sober denunciation of Marxism, and chance is crucial in both cases because it marks objective reality.

Whereas Monod saw Marxist claims to objective, scientific analyses of the universe as an urgent problem for those who considered themselves members of the legitimate scientific community, Kosinski was interested in how fiction writers might function in ways similar to the severe control commission in Aliosha's tale. In *Blind Date*, Monod himself makes an appearance in Kosinski's fictional world. As a reader of *Chance and Necessity* might expect, Kosinski's Monod is critical of a Russian character, Romarkin, because he denies the chance nature of the universe. Although Romarkin was skeptical enough of Soviet authority to have been sentenced to three years of hard labor in Siberia for raising his hand at a rally and asking how Stalin came to be qualified to write a treatise—an instant classic!—on linguistics, he is still unable to conceptualize a reality rooted in chance.[28] Monod says to the novel's hero, Levanter:

> Even now, . . . your friend Romarkin doesn't dare to admit that blind chance and nothing else is responsible for each random event of his life. Instead, he is searching for a religion that, like Marxism, will assure him that man's destiny is spelled out in the central plot of life. Meanwhile, believing in the existence of an orderly, predetermined life scheme, Romarkin bypasses the drama of each unique instance of his own existence. Yet, to accept a notion of destiny, he might as well believe in astrology, or palm reading, or pulp novels, all of which pretend that one's future is already set and needs only to be lived out.[29]

This echoes *Chance and Necessity*, but with a significant difference: Kosinski's fictional Monod conceptualizes the Marxist dismissal of chance in narrative terms. The problem is that Marxism describes a "central plot of life"—it is this "plot" that seems false and arbitrary to those outside the system. Such a plot is dangerous because, to borrow again from *Chance and Necessity*, it confuses value and knowledge. Kosinski's Monod links the scientific assurance of human destiny to pseudo-science (astrology), the occult (palm reading)—and, importantly, bad fiction (pulp novels). This grouping suggests why Monod's critique was of interest to a fiction writer: pulp novels are fictional narratives which would, like astrology or Marxism, present a disingenuously coherent design behind each "random event" in life. Rather than affirming randomness itself, which would, according to Monodian logic, be an affirmation of objective reality, pulp novels flaunt their own design, and are enjoyable because they conform to recognizable templates. Kosinski suggests that by acknowledging the play of chance in the universe, a fiction writer can create a narrative representation of reality that does not have the constrictive effect of a totalitarian plot. The problem, of course, is that chance is at odds with the ordered nature of narrative design, a fact that occupied numerous writers of the Cold War.[30]

Kosinski's and Monod's books are comparatively straightforward examples of how the concept of chance was mobilized during the Cold War, a conflict as much about language and the strategic deployment of rhetoric as it was about atomic bombs and the strategic deployment of missiles. A character like Romarkin, hopeless because he denies "blind chance" in favor of a "central plot of life," is suggestive of the issues that fiction writers would encounter when creating their own central plots. *Blind Date* and *Chance and Necessity* are but two instances of a widespread cultural interest in chance found in a range of material, from novels and scientific treatises, to works of sociology, political science, philosophy, history, and even mathematics. Although *No Accident, Comrade* primarily concerns the presence of chance in literary fiction, it touches on some of these other contexts to explore the circulation of chance in Cold War culture: some people did conceive of the global conflict as neatly as Kosinski did, placing chance squarely on the side of American democratic freedom and the denial of chance on the side of Soviet totalitarianism, but many others criticized American claims of democratic freedom by suggesting that domestic cultural narratives controlled or otherwise manipulated chance in ways reminiscent of "Soviet reality." The following chapters demonstrate the various ways that writers and other cultural producers dealt with the narrative use of chance in a Cold War frame; before moving on to these specific examples, a sketch of the current state of Cold War literary studies will clarify the importance of exploring chance during the era.

Cold War Literary Studies Now

As may be clear from the preceding discussion of how Kosinski's aesthetic use of chance contained a political critique, for the purposes of this book, the Cold War will be conceptualized primarily as a rhetorical field that shaped the way that reality was understood.[31] As I have shown elsewhere, the Cold War has been of interest in literary studies because it required language to bear an enormous political weight, and as such was suggestive of the ways that language is always political.[32] By focusing on chance as a privileged if conflicted cultural signifier, this book recalibrates our sense of the political during the period, and in turn what can count as Cold War literature.

Cold War literary studies is at something of a crossroads as scholars propose different theories about how best to understand "Cold War literature." The term itself implies there is a politics always somehow embedded in the literature. The most obvious way to categorize Cold War literature is as work that thematizes politics—in this category one thinks of Richard Condon's *The Manchurian Candidate* (1959) (and the great film it spawned) or John LeCarré's *The Spy Who Came in from the Cold* (1963). Such books count as Cold War literature because characters are caught in the side effects of the U.S.–Communist rivalry and the author wants to make a point about how this abstracted global conflict levels real damage on individual lives. And yet, despite some notable exceptions, this category does not account for the majority of consequential work that has been done in Cold War literary studies.[33]

Since people began to look at Cold War literature as such, there has been a tendency to focus not on work that explicitly engages politics—Irwin Shaw's anti-McCarthyite *The Troubled Air* (1951) or Allen Drury's dramatization of U.N. infighting, *A Shade of Difference* (1962)—but rather on aesthetic objects that can be read as "political" in less conventional or obvious ways. Recent work in Cold War literary studies has yielded readings of cultural artifacts like *Mad* magazine, the Elvis film *King Creole* (1958), Allen Ginsberg's *Kaddish* (1959), the production of kabuki theater in the West; and of novels like Sylvia Plath's *The Bell Jar* (1963), Jack Kerouac's *Doctor Sax* (1959), James Dickey's *Deliverance* (1970), and Patricia Highsmith's crime thriller *The Blunderer* (1954).[34] How might such works, which do not at first blush seem political at all, reflect the Cold War? Why have they been understood not simply as being written *during* the Cold War, but rather as *of* the Cold War?

The reason that such seemingly apolitical texts have been read as part of Cold War culture is that they all say something about the subtle ways that language was tied to "so-called objective reality," and how this reality was circumscribed by large cultural narratives and their impact on individual lives. There have been various models for thinking about this impact; since about the mid-1980s, the dominant model was containment—which focused on the domestic echoes of American foreign policy and how the encouragement of consensus played out across a range of cultural artifacts.[35] As Alan Nadel writes: "[T]he story of containment had derived its logic from the rigid major premise that the world was divided into two monolithic camps, one dedicated to promoting the inextricable combination of capitalism, democracy, and (Judeo-Christian) religion, and one seeking to destroy that ideological amalgamation by any means."[36] This "major premise," authorized by the power of the atomic bomb, informed the containment narrative, which, as Nadel and others have shown, permeated many aspects of American life during the Cold War.[37]

Perhaps because of the containment model's power in describing the relationship between cultural and personal narratives in the United States, literary studies has been slow to conceptualize the Cold War as a global phenomenon. As recently as 1993, Amy Kaplan could lament what she called the "absence of empire in the study of American culture."[38] Since then, there has been an expanding body of work about American empire and imperialism, and Cold War literary studies has begun a turn to what Leerom Medovoi has called the "three worlds imaginary," which views U.S. cultural and aesthetic production within the dynamic of complex global relations.[39] In both the containment and three-worlds models, "the Cold War" offers a frame for tracing the circulation of dominant cultural narratives—whether national or transnational in nature—with the hope of understanding how individuals conceptualized their relationship to these narratives. *No Accident, Comrade* likewise assumes, as Nadel has put it, that "the American cold war is a particularly useful example of the power of large cultural narratives to unify, codify, and contain—perhaps *intimidate* is the best word—the personal narratives of its population."[40] Although the scope of this book ranges to the post–Cold War period, much of the work discussed dates from the early Cold War (from the late 1940s to the early 1960s) because it was then that competing cultural narratives became the center of American civic life—and, by extension, of private lives yoked to public narratives.[41]

It is in this interplay between public and personal that I understand Cold War fiction as having the potential to be political.[42] My use of chance as an organizing principle will help demonstrate this because chance—as I show in the next sections—must be interpreted differently in narrative fiction and in real life, an observation that is a starting point for my discussions in the following chapters about how varieties of narrative innovation can expose the ways that "objective reality" was stabilized by cultural and political narratives. By emphasizing the Cold War rhetorical frame, *No Accident, Comrade* suggests that when language itself is interrogated in ways that turn on questions of freedom and control, we can call this political engagement. Because politics were during the Cold War often viewed as being fictions, and the conflict itself betrayed its narrative quality again and again, the act of literary fiction making became laden with political significance, as did the use and theorization of chance within these narratives. Thus what are called "politics" in this book do not name direct action like organizing protests or lobbying for legislation, but rather an acknowledgment of the idea that "objective reality" is shaped by language, and that this shape does have real consequences for the ways that power could either subjugate or ennoble people. To recognize that, during the Cold War, the act of fiction making itself became associated with political regimes (and vice versa) is to recognize that novels have potential to be authoritative sites for theorizing the nature of narrative and the attendant ways that stories structure individual and civic lives. As we will see, chance exposes the limits of narrative and therefore highlights the imperfect relationship between narratives—whether cultural, explicitly political, or avowedly aesthetic—and real life, which in turn allows us to understand more fully the ways lives, both personal and civic, are structured by stories, an understanding that is, contextually speaking, political.

Senses of Chance

For reasons that will become clear, the senses of "chance" most useful for our purpose cannot really be divorced from the context of the Cold War, but we can begin with some preliminaries. Chance can mean a number of things: if I hit my hop bet at the craps table, I am over the moon because it was statistically unlikely for me to do so; if I say that I accidentally wiped out on an icy sidewalk before my big meeting, it was because I did not intend to; if I say that I was in Bhutan, of all places, and I ran into an old friend by chance, I am drawing attention to two independent causal chains (the events in my life and the events in his) coming together in an unexpected—and therefore remarkable—way. In each sense, chance means that which is unplanned and unintended; true to its etymological roots in the idea of falling, the word "chance" marks the absence of design.

Genealogies of chance often begin in the first century B.C.E., with Roman poet and philosopher Lucretius's treatise, *De Rerum Natura*.[43] In Book II, Lucretius famously articulates an atomic theory that views the universe as chance-based: "Though atoms fall straight downward through the void / by their own weight, yet at uncertain times / and at uncertain points, they swerve a bit—/ enough that one may say they changed direction."[44] This originary sense of the atomic swerve is relevant to a discussion of the Cold War because, as implied by my brief treatment of Jacques Monod's work, the idea that chance plays a fundamental role in the universe was becoming more and more widespread in the twentieth century. As Ian Hacking has argued, "The most decisive conceptual event of twentieth century physics has been the discovery that the world is not deterministic. . . . A space was cleared for chance."[45] For Hacking, American philosopher Charles Sanders Peirce was emblematic of a profound shift in Western thinking about chance. In work such as "The Doctrine of Necessity" (1892), Peirce attempted to refute as naive or impudent those theories that deny the existence of chance: "Try to verify any law of nature, and you will find that the more precise your observations, the more certain they will be to show irregular departures from the law. We are accustomed to ascribe these, and I do not say wrongly, to errors of observation; yet we cannot usually account for such errors in any antecedently probable way. Trace their causes back far enough, and you will be forced to admit they are always due to arbitrary determination, or chance."[46] This idea Peirce elsewhere calls "absolute chance," a concept affinitive with what Monod means when he writes of "pure chance" and what Lucretius means when he writes of the atomic swerve.

By the mid-twentieth century, Anglo-Austrian philosopher Karl Popper, responding to advances in quantum physics, argued that the universe is fundamentally indeterminate and a product of "absolute chance." Like Monod, Popper develops observations drawn from science (for him physics rather than biology) into a political philosophy repudiating Marxist determinism. Contrasting absolute chance to other kinds of chance, which are products of "the incompleteness of our knowledge," Popper writes:

> Quantum mechanics . . . introduced chance events of a second, and much more radical kind: absolute chance. According to quantum mechanics, there are elementary physical processes which are not further analyzable in terms of causal chains, but which consist of so-called "quantum jumps"; and a quantum jump is supposed to be an absolutely unpredictable event which is controlled neither by causal laws nor by the coincidence of causal laws, but by probabilistic laws alone. Thus quantum mechanics introduced, in spite of the protests of Einstein, what he described as "the dice-playing God." Quantum mechanics regards these absolute chance events as the basic events of World 1 [the physical world]. Although I do not believe that quantum mechanics will remain the last word in physics, I happen to believe that its indeterminism is fundamentally sound.[47]

While one may have to look to the quantum realm to find events that are truly examples of absolute chance—Popper's quantum jump or Lucretius's uncertain swerve—functionally, many events in life can be said to be absolute chance. As Hacking has shown and as Popper implies, quantum theory has been important to nonspecialists for its suggestion that absolute chance could operate in the universe at all. The existence of absolute chance in the quantum realm thus functions as a metaphor for the ways that larger events could be seen as chance-based and therefore indeterminate—even if technically, unlike quantum jumps, they have causes that are theoretically discernable. Therefore, in this book, *absolute chance* does not name the absence of causality strictly speaking, but rather the absence of planning or intention; it is an abstract concept that cannot be predicted or determined by laws or theories, and it cannot be a result of a person's purpose or intention.[48] As we will see in the next section, during the Cold War many Americans, taking a cue from developments in the physical sciences, argued that the Soviet insistence on historical laws ignored the existence of absolute chance—in 1957, Popper himself applied his ideas to a book-length explanation of why "the belief in historical destiny is sheer superstition."[49]

Chance and American Perceptions of the Soviet System

I have suggested that as a rhetorical field, the Cold War encouraged Americans—and those sympathetic to American democratic norms—to mobilize the concept of chance in order to underscore the naturalness of American democratic freedom as opposed to Soviet-style totalitarianism. Jacques Monod delivered the lectures on which *Chance and Necessity* were based at Pomona College in 1969, but the fundamental suggestion of the book's philosophical portion—that Soviet reality was an all-encompassing fiction visible as such because it denied the operation of absolute chance—was evident in numerous works dating from the late 1940s to the mid-1960s. Thus, Monod's basic thesis and Kosinski's poaching of this thesis are extensions of ideas that had been circulating for two decades.[50]

As Sovietology became a lucrative and important area of study, sociologists, historians, and political scientists consistently returned to the concept of chance when describing the Soviet system to both specialized and lay readers.[51] In one of the most influential works of political sociology to emerge from the 1950s, *The End of Ideology: On the Exhaustion of Political Ideas in the Fifties* (1960), Daniel Bell analyzes the Soviet system by looking at "ten theories in search of reality."[52] Although Bell claims he is interested only in comparing various approaches to understanding the Soviet system, when he touches on Soviet attitudes toward chance, he cannot help but betray his sense that Marxist logic does not always hang together:

> The characteristic fact about Bolshevik mentality is its refusal to admit of accident and contingency. Everything has a reason, a preordained motive. Hence the sinister refrain in Bolshevik rhetoric: "It is no accident, comrade, no *mere* accident, that . . ." or, "Why at this time, why at *this particular moment*, does the enemy choose . . .?" And so all such questions lead, with insidious intent, to the ultimate question: *kto-kovo*, who is using whom? One is reminded of the episode some years back when two Ukrainian delegates to the UN wandered into a small New York delicatessen during a holdup and, failing to understand the command of the robbers, one of them was shot in the thigh. Vishinsky [a Soviet diplomat], either to embarrass the United States, or because he was truly suspicious, rejected the explanation of the New York police department that, since it was a holdup, the shooting could not have been political. "How could it have been a holdup?" he asked. "It was a *small* delicatessen." In wealthy, capitalist America, who would bother to hold up a *small* store? [italics and ellipses in original][53]

Bell implies that objective reality is characterized by chance—in real life, things can happen accidentally and cannot necessarily be explained by political agendas or historical laws. His example is a minor political flap that occurred in 1946, when Ukrainian delegate Gregory Stadnik was shot in the thigh during a Manhattan robbery. *Pravda* described the incident as a "terroristic" attempt on Stadnik's life, while the American press insisted, as a *New York Times* editorial put it days later, that Stadnik was simply in the wrong place at the wrong time: "[I]f a fanatic had actually had intentions on Mr. Stadnik's life he would, as Secretary [of State] Byrnes contends, have chosen a different place. He would not have stationed himself in a delicatessen store on the mere chance that a Ukrainian delegate would walk in."[54] For Bell, the incident is illustrative of the ways that Marxist ideology clouds rather than clarifies one's perception of reality. It is safe to assume that most Americans would have agreed with Secretary of State Byrnes that the incident was aligned with "mere chance" rather than political design so the response of *Pravda*—or, as Bell reports it, Andrey Vishinsky, one of the legal architects of Stalin's purges—seems absurd to the point of being comical. While Stadnik's run-in offers a telling example of Paul Virilio's claim that "the mass media of the old Soviet Union never gave out information about accidents," even more significant is how the incident demonstrates that what counts as chance is a matter of interpretation.[55] For an American interpreting the "Bolshevik mentality," focusing on the ways that chance and accident were conceptualized by the Soviets was a way to prove that Marxist orthodoxy was flawed because it was built not on scientific objectivity, but on ideologically-inflected interpretation.[56]

The idea that chance helps one see Soviet conceptions of reality as suspect interpretation—rather than quantifiable fact—was present in numerous studies aiming to explain or analyze the workings of the Soviet system. In describing the prevailing theories being used to understand the sometimes-inscrutable Soviet character, Bell suggests that one of the more influential ones was the psychoanalytic approach, favored in the early 1950s by the RAND Corporation, a think tank funded by the U.S. Air Force and responsible for helping guide American nuclear strategy. Emblematic of this approach is the work of Nathan Leites, whose book, *A Study of Bolshevism* (1953) attempted, as Bell put it, "to define 'Bolshevik character' as a type distinct in social history."[57] Leites's earlier book, *The Operational Code of the Politburo* (1951), had been a resource for the American military during the Korean War; *A Study of Bolshevism* proved likewise valuable because it attempted to unlock the inner workings of the Bolshevik mind.

A Study of Bolshevism proceeds by looking at important quotations from Party leaders past and present and then extrapolating a psychology of what Leites calls the Bolshevik mentality. Since part of the purpose of Leites's work is, as he puts it, to "enhance the skill of Western policy-makers," he begins with one signal difference between the antagonistic sensibilities: chapter 1, "The Range and Limits of Prediction," starts with the subheading: "The Denial of Accidents."[58] Leites takes as a motivation a suggestive remark Stalin made in 1950: "It is Bolshevik doctrine that 'History never does anything of moment without some particular necessity.'"[59] This basic idea we have already seen in the snapshots from Engels and Bukharin, and Leites takes it as a fundamental characteristic of the Bolshevik psychological makeup:

There is in Bolshevik doctrine an emphatic and recurring denial that important events can be "accidental." . . . If an event that is important for the Party—and what event is not, directly or indirectly?—is predictable by the Party, or at least can be explained after it has happened, it is felt in some measure as controlled by the Party—even if on analysis the event was caused by factors outside the Party's control. . . . The feat of intellectual mastery, of knowing the event before it happens, or knowing its roots and how it emerged from them, where others simply have to take it as given, may console one for the lack of real mastery. . . . If, on the other hand, an event were viewed as "accidental," one would feel dominated by an unintelligible outer force—a feeling particularly dreaded by the Bolsheviks.[60]

Here again chance is tied to interpretation: as Leites notes that all *important* events can be explained by laws or even foretold by those with the correct philosophical orientation, he also emphasizes that these events need only be *important for the Party*. Therefore, the seemingly objective sense that historical events conform to larger, predictable patterns is actually an example of subjective, selective interpretation. Like Bell, Leites is dismissive of such an interpretation; just as *Pravda*'s reading of the Stadnik affair seems feeble, when Leites frames the Bolshevik psychology in terms of its "emphatic and recurring" denial of accidents, it too seems feeble, and as Leites himself puts it, a poor substitute for the "lack of real mastery."

For Margaret Mead, Leites's colleague on the Studies in Soviet Culture research team at the American Museum of Natural History, the Bolshevik denial of chance was tied to the Soviet compulsion for total control. In her analysis *Soviet Attitudes Toward Authority* (1951), she writes: "The need for eternal watchfulness is enhanced by the Bolshevik refusal to admit that anything is accidental. . . . The appropriate behavior for the Party leadership faced with such grave dangers [of accidents and political opposition] within and without is to watch over everything and control everything. This demand for total responsibility, total control is reiterated again and again."[61] As Mead understands it, the Bolshevik "refusal to admit that anything is accidental" is not only an academic folly, but is indeed a motivation for the practical subjugation of individual will.[62]

Probably the bluntest expression of such ideas is a 1956 polemic called *The Chance Character of Human Existence*. This work, by a little-known philosopher and social critic writing under the name John Brill, was a broad defense of Darwinian thought framed explicitly by Cold War politics. As a cultural document about chance's conceptual elasticity, Brill's book is of interest because it lays bare the cultural preoccupations with chance encouraged by the Cold War logic already described. Brill assumes the universe is subject to absolute chance; if in the struggle between the United States and the Soviet Union, American democracy both acknowledges and embodies chance, it must be natural. If, by contrast, the Soviet system erases chance to legitimate an all-encompassing totalitarian narrative, it must be unnatural.

Brill's book may thus be read as a comparatively crude distillation of the interlocking ideas about chance, design, and politics already discussed, and that were becoming increasingly prominent in early Cold War cultural rhetoric.[63] As Brill works through the idea that evolutionary theory offers a narrative powerful enough to account for the history of human existence, he insists, as Monod would years later, that at the center of this theory is "blind chance." He writes: "From an evolutionary viewpoint we are born, live and die in a world of chance. . . . To those who contend that there is a directive purpose in the universe we can only say that from the evolutionary standpoint there is not a slightest ground for a belief in any direction or control behind the forces of nature, that these forces are impersonal, are uncontrolled and are the result of blind chance."[64] This passage is both a reiteration of a theory that recognizes and allows for the operation of absolute chance in the universe and the foundation for Brill's subsequent denunciation of Communism.

For Brill, as the Soviet regime denies the operation of absolute chance, it likewise denies the possibility for individual expression. "The totalitarian type of Government," he writes, "which subjugates the individual and makes him subservient to the state does not conform to the fundamental principle of evolution, namely that the individual must have the fullest opportunity for the fullest expression of its own individuality."[65] Here is perhaps the most straightforward expression one is likely to find of the connections among chance and freedom, on the one hand, and determinism and subservience, on the other. From Brill's perspective, the freedom embodied by absolute chance is tied to nature, whereas totalitarian governments attempt to deny the operation of absolute chance, thereby controlling individual freedom and resulting in an unnatural ideology fitted imperfectly onto objective reality.

In a range of disciplinary frameworks, then, Sovietological studies of the early Cold War found the Soviet system flawed in part because it denied the existence of accidents and the operation of absolute chance in the universe. Even thinkers more favorably disposed to Marxist theories criticized the Soviet corruption of such theories. In 1954, American Slavicist Ernest Simmons organized an interdisciplinary conference on Soviet thought, the proceedings of which were published in 1955 as *Continuity and Change in Russian and Soviet Thought*. In his contribution, Herbert Marcuse—who had long-standing Marxist sympathies and few kind words for the capitalist system—argued that the Soviets had perverted orthodox Marxism when it came to their attitudes toward chance. For Marx and Engels, Marcuse wrote, the "objective laws" of history are at bottom governed by "man himself."[66] In this view, Marx maintained an objective determinism that still preserved the "subjective factor" of human agency. Soviet-style Marxism, on the other hand, attempted to erase this agency because it could threaten the regime. "Soviet Marxism," Marcuse argues, "subjugates the subjective to the objective factors in a manner which transforms the dialectic into a mechanistic process."[67] In Marcuse's critique, a characteristic of Soviet Marxism is its attempt to remove any chance factors in order to "protect and justify the established regime."[68] Marcuse would thus seem to confirm Leites's sense that the most terrifying things for the Bolshevik (and then later, Soviet) mentality are chance factors themselves.

These varied Sovietological analyses tell us not only that the concept of chance became an important point on which criticisms of the Soviet Union turned, but they also begin to explain why chance—as a marker, in this context, of objective reality—became a feature of American democratic freedom. The few contemporary scholars who have touched on the concept of chance in the Cold War have tended to view it only as a negative force, embodied by the looming threat of an accidental nuclear exchange. Chance was a rough cognate of contingency, the argument goes, a notion fearsome to many Americans because it symbolized the crumbling systems of traditional order. Historian Jackson Lears suggests, for instance, that for the "intellectual generation" represented by Paul Tillich's influential *The Courage to Be* (1952), "chance was a source of anxiety."[69] This is what I would call the "Dr. Strangelove/Fail-Safe" view of chance during the Cold War: accident was predominately a source of fear because with the exponential proliferation of atomic arsenals, an accident could conceivably lead to unprecedented destruction, as happens in films such as *Dr. Strangelove* and *Fail-Safe* (both 1964).[70] In *Fail-Safe*, chance is the wild card in a global nuclear game: "I think," says an American general after a nuclear bomb has been sent by mistake to obliterate Moscow, "we have to assume it is our accident and not their plan." The menace in this case is the accident, not the plan.

Tony Jackson has proposed a relationship between chance and what he terms the "nuclear ending": "With nuclear weapons the one certainty is the form of annihilation, and the great uncertainty is whether the event will actually happen.... For the certainty of the kind of destruction and the uncertainty of whether destruction will actually happen made the idea of chance more generally and potently present for more people than ever before."[71] Jackson's and Lears's work document another important dimension of chance at mid-century; but what my account helps explain is that if chance could be a source of anxiety, it could also mark notions of democratic freedom.[72] This is what I take Arthur Schlesinger, Jr., in his widely read *The Vital Center: The Politics of Freedom* (1949), to mean when he writes that the Soviets could not brook indeterminacy: "The principle of indeterminacy ... and the western emphasis on the observer as a factor in the experiment, are unacceptable to the Soviet version of Marxist materialism."[73] When Schlesinger refers to "the principle of indeterminacy," he is counterpointing the historical determinism posited by dialectical materialism, a determinism that, as we have seen, was embodied in the Soviet system.

Schlesinger's remark that the West has a claim on indeterminacy is telling: if it is true that the Soviets were viewed as totalitarian puppet masters who dreamt of leaving nothing to chance, then it helps explain why Americans, committed at least in principle to individual agency, began to see chance as a symptom of democratic freedom. In the concept of chance, democratic freedom was united with objective reality. As suggested by those Sovietologists who focused on "the plan," so powerful was the perceived reach of Soviet control that even the concept of planning itself could be seen as suspect. This idea became a theme of the inaugural symposium of the New York University Institute of Philosophy on "Determinism and Freedom in the Age of Modern Science" (February 1957). Although the participants tended to discuss the guiding concepts in the abstract, moderator Sidney Hook framed the urgency of the symposium in frankly political terms:

> Whereas in the past the extension of the deterministic philosophy in the natural sciences was hailed as a support of human freedom because it increased man's power of control over nature, today belief in determinism in the social sciences and social affairs is feared by many because it increases the power of men to control other men.... In some quarters this reaction has gone so far that even the term "planning" and the notion of a "planned society," which a short generation ago was the hallmark of a rational social philosophy, are viewed with suspicion as suggesting, if not evidencing, a conspiracy against human freedom.[74]

In the 1930s, Hook had written several books on Marxist thought, but like many left-leaning intellectuals, by the late 1930s he had come to repudiate Stalinism and what was considered a corruption of Marxist ideals.[75] Statements such as this demonstrate another dimension of this shift—just as Marcuse was critical of the Soviet attitude toward chance, which he contrasted to the orthodox Marxist view—Hook suggests the menace of totalitarian control manifested specifically in "social planning," which could no longer be politically innocent.[76]

Given this presumption that even the "planned society" could be evidence of the Soviet lust for power, broader questions of determinism versus free will became proxies for debates about Soviet planning versus Western freedom. As William Barrett, another contributor to the symposium, put it, Hook's own work discredits the notion that the universe is determinate: "[T]he introduction of human personality multiplies the factors of chance beyond the determinist's ability to press them into any one of his ready-made schemes."[77] Barrett ties individual human agency to chance, a conceptual connection meaning that Americans, committed as they are to individualism, are likewise committed to engaging objective reality: "[The] historical future is thoroughly problematic and uncertain.... we encounter a vast, shaggy, amorphous mass of unpredictability on which our knowledge has made very little impression. . . . Of course this final litany of contingency is not intoned as proof—only as a reminder to the determinist that the spheres in which determinism has so far been established are restricted."[78] While Barrett's invocation of "factors of chance" carries the note of anxiety suggested by Lears and Jackson, I hope that the foregoing discussion has also pointed to chance as something potentially generative. For Barrett, the very existence of chance proves the restrictions of Soviet design. The special rhetorical demands of the Cold War allowed a range of thinkers to dismiss Soviet totalitarianism as conceptually flawed because it operated from the premise that absolute chance did not exist, or was manageable enough to be irrelevant. Yet the very context in which such a dismissal operates suggests that chance itself is a fluid concept that needs to be stabilized by narrative and interpretation. After all, were chance a phenomenon or concept that all people agreed upon—like gravity—there would be no cause for American anti-Marxists to insist on its existence. This suggests that what counts as chance can only be understood in context, which emerges when one considers the claims various kinds of narratives make on objective reality.

Chance in Fictional Narratives

Thus far I have described chance as though it is a stable, easily digestible concept (as merely marking the absence of planning or intention). Although this view is a necessary product of the service to which chance was put in the various Sovietological analyses already discussed, it is an oversimplified one. As we have seen, one suggestion common in these works was that the Soviet Union perpetuated a vast fiction on its subjects and the world; and yet when we start talking about fictional narratives as such, we find that the role and operation of chance becomes far more subtle and complex. Part of the work of this book, in fact, is to demonstrate how Americans writing during the Cold War developed sophisticated responses to the question of chance as it was deployed in political discourse. For these writers, the idea that the Soviet denial of chance pointed to a pernicious fiction generated an awareness of the new political stakes of incorporating moments of chance into their writing. In order to understand the complex ways in which chance operates in fictional narratives of the Cold War, I want to pause over how chance in narrative is tied to interpretation.[79]

The notion that chance depends on and demands interpretation is a starting point for Ross Hamilton in his recent literary and intellectual history of accident. Hamilton traces a genealogy of accident in Western culture that begins with Aristotle's related theories of accident and substance. For Aristotle, substance constitutes the essence of an object or a human being, whereas accident is that which is mutable and inessential.[80] Hamilton demonstrates various engagements and amplifications of Aristotle's theories in key moments in Western culture, from the ways in which Christian theologians assimilated accident to its modern uses in Freudian and Darwinian theory. One abiding theme in Hamilton's work is that whatever the particular service it has been asked to perform, the very notion of accident depends always on interpretation. As Hamilton notes in his introduction, when discussing the accidental event in particular, Aristotle

> defines an accidental event not merely as an exceptional, rare, or unlikely occurrence—what happens "not for the most part"—but adds the further qualification that the outcome must differ from the one intended. Therefore, just as subtle distinctions define the nature of the relationships among inessential qualities, his definition of the accidental event is predicated on an interpretive analysis of the purpose for which the act was undertaken . . . because chance applies only to outcomes linked to actions chosen and performed with a specific purpose in mind, the term requires a clear understanding of initial intent.[81]

There are two things of note here: first, that accidents always require "interpretive analysis" to be understood as such; second, that in order to successfully perform this interpretive work, one must have a sense of the intention that began the chain of events. In this way, an accidental event is that which is unplanned, or that occurs despite someone's intentions. This means that in order for an accident to exist, there must also be a purpose or intention to be deviated from.

This may seem to pose a special problem for creative writers (for Aristotle, poets or playwrights), since artistic forms are necessarily a product of purpose and intention. But Aristotle thinks that with the proper incorporation, accidents can be made to serve the larger aesthetic design of the work. Hamilton shows that in *Poetics* and elsewhere, Aristotle thinks that accident has a "greatly expanded" role in tragedy:

> "Tragedy, [writes Aristotle,] is an imitation not only of a complete action, but also of incidents arousing pity and fear. Such incidents have the very greatest effect on the mind when they occur unexpectedly and at the same time in consequence of one another; there is more of the marvellous in them then than if they happened of themselves or by mere chance" (9.1452a2–6). . . . In this sense, the actions that make up a tragic plot form a series of unexpected occurrences designed to compel the audience to perceive causal relationships between them. Of course, the spectators of a Greek tragedy possessed the prior knowledge required for accurate interpretation. What moved them was partly seeing the seemingly accidental event turn out to be necessary and

partly seeing how grasping the same realization affected the characters. In other words, by fostering interpretation, Aristotle imbued the literary mode of the accident with significance.[82]

For Aristotle, then, accidents in tragedy assume "significance" when they can be made to serve as logical or necessary aspects of the plot. Put in these terms, the accidental event in a tragedy is hardly accidental—far from being set *against* a notion of "intent" or "purpose," Aristotle argues that when it comes to art, an accidental event must *confirm* artistic purpose. Hamilton's phrase "the seemingly accidental event" is thus suggestive; it implies that for Aristotle, there are no truly accidental events in a tragedy, since the play writ large is a product of purpose and intent. So long as the play is being lavished with "accurate interpretation," then accidents in the world of the tragedy become ironically the best illustrations of the playwright's skillful design: although they may occur unexpectedly, they are ultimately satisfying because they seem necessary given the formal structure of the play as a whole. As Hamilton writes: "[T]he playwright must present narrative accidents as probable or necessary events and purge them of ambiguity or chance in order to reach the heights of his art."[83]

Narrative Chance

Hamilton's reading of Aristotle suggests that there is an important difference between an accidental event and narrative accident, an idea implied when he writes that in Aristotle's schema narrative accidents are purged of chance. In this section, I would like to develop the implications of the term "narrative accident" to think more broadly about what "narrative chance" might mean. As Hamilton writes, Aristotelian logic dictates that chance events in a good tragedy are only "seemingly accidental" because they conform to a larger design; building on this idea, I want to point out that "narrative chance" must be fundamentally (and ontologically) different from absolute chance because a narrative world is designed.

Here I want to make a crucial distinction between fictional and historical narratives. It is true that chance can exist in a historical narrative in the sense that a writer can describe a real-life accidental event: "I saw the car hit the tree." This is narrating chance in the same way a writer might narrate the color blue or the abstract concept of love. When it comes to a fictional narrative, however, chance becomes problematic in ways that other abstract concepts do not because chance, by definition, marks that which is beyond planning, intention, and purpose. Thus, whenever an accident or other chance event occurs in a fictional narrative, it is always an example of "narrative chance"—that is, chance which is tied to planning, intention, and purpose. Writers exhibit varying degrees of awareness of this phenomenon—which is why it is possible for, say, a car accident in a novel to remain unremarked upon by the implied author. But the fictional narratives discussed in this book all register this phenomenon, and thematize its problems in different ways. As mentioned previously, many Cold War writers began noticing the very existence of narrative chance because the absorption of absolute chance was being cited as evidence of Soviet ideology, which was in turn being dismissed as a fiction. For writers committed even vaguely to anti-Soviet notions of democratic freedom, narrative chance became a significant issue for the questions it raised about interpretation, and for the ways that it could help one conceptualize issues of planning, control, and design—issues critical to both fiction writers and to the architects of Cold War states.

In this book, *narrative chance* will name a concept distinct from absolute chance: because a fictional narrative is necessarily designed, and chance is necessarily not designed, narrative chance suggests that narrative alters the concept of chance because it occurs as a component of a design. In the world of a fictional narrative, then, no events are "really" products of absolute chance, since the author has planned them with some intention. Thus, while accidents may occur for the characters within the fictional world, they are not, from an objective perspective, chance events. As William Paulson has put it, "Narrative . . . entails or even imposes a priori pattern, rather than either revealing an intrinsic structure of events or accepting their contingency."[84] Paulson's emphasis on narrative's a priori pattern reminds us that such pattern would exclude absolute chance, since any accident or chance occurrence in a narrative must always conform to the structures that make the pattern possible.

In his book on chance and the modern British novel, Leland Monk has argued "the oxymoronic nature of the phrase 'chance in narrative.' . . . it is in the nature of narrative to render chance as fate so that 'what happens' in a story becomes indistinguishable from the more evaluative 'it was *meant* to happen.'"[85] Another way of articulating this observation is to say that narrative chance is always interpretable—to register the collapse of what happens with what is *meant* to happen is to register that narrative chance is, as I have said, a product of intention and purpose. Monk ultimately goes so far as to say that "chance marks and defines a fundamental limit to the telling of any story: *chance is that which cannot be represented in narrative.*"[86] If we take this to mean that absolute chance and fictional narrative are fundamentally at odds with each other, then Monk's statement makes sense. While it is certainly possible to represent chance in narrative form ("I saw the car hit the tree"), it is impossible for chance in a narrative to *be* absolute chance (although, as I discuss later, there are examples from writers who have tried). The fact that narrative chance is not absolute chance is in and of itself important because it serves as a starting point for writers concerned with exploring the differences between objective reality and narrative representations of that reality. Much of this book concerns writers who notice that narrative chance cannot be absolute chance, and who then use this notion as a way to start thinking more complexly about their own narratives, and about the cultural and political narratives guiding American civic life.[87]

Gary Saul Morson helps us see how the distance between narrative chance and absolute chance could become a political or ethical problem for writers. Morson identifies a phenomenon that parallels the way that narrative turns chance into narrative chance; for him, the nature of narrative is problematic for writers wishing to represent the temporal freedom of real life: "The need for a literary work to possess structure and closure works against the project of representing freedom. Because structure itself imposes a pattern, any structured description of freedom may be tacitly self-contradictory. The shapes of the work and of the world it represents are likely to differ, thereby creating temporal anisomorphism and the constant threat of unwanted irony."[88] Morson discusses various works that he sees as creating a more open sense of temporality using a technique he calls "sideshadowing," which "names both an open sense of temporality and a set of devices used to convey that sense. . . . In Tolstoy's hands, [for example,] it conveyed a sense of the contingency of events."[89] Although he focuses specifically on concepts of temporality, Morson's argument, that writers have found foreshadowing problematic because it implies a backward causation nonexistent in real life, might apply also to notions of chance in fiction. In fact, when describing why a writer like Tolstoy employs sideshadowing rather than foreshadowing, Morson speaks in terms of chance events, because absolute chance marks that which is outside causal explanation:

> Life as Tolstoy imagines it does not fit a pattern, as art does. Our lives tend to no goal; neither are they destined to be shaped into a story. They are filled with chance events that nevertheless have lasting effects and are shaped by incidental causes that need not have happened. Events filled with promise lead nowhere. Everything that the essential surplus provides in art—structure, closure, the assurance of significance—is usually absent from life. But people sometimes imagine that life is more or less like novels in this respect. Tolstoy's paradoxical method is to use the essential surplus to make us aware of its pure artifice.[90]

Morson notes an ontological difference between life and art—or, as I put it above, objective reality and fictional narrative. Chance makes this difference visible: in real life, absolute chance is unplanned and divorced from intention, but may be nonetheless significant; in art, on the other hand, chance events are there for a reason, and thus signal "structure, closure, the assurance of significance." This is another way of describing what I term narrative chance. If, as I have argued, absolute chance can function as a litmus test for objective reality, and as a measure of freedom as Morson argues, then narrative chance is marked always by its inability to achieve the same sort of freedom possible in real life.[91]

Narrative Chance at Mid-Century

The idea that narrative chance can signal a kind of literary authoritarianism has been of interest to many writers over the years, but it will be one task of this book to show that the Cold War rhetorical field made this interest more widespread and consequential.[92] Kosinski's work offered a clear example of the political work chance could do, but numerous other writers have been so subtle with their use of narrative chance that even the period's most sensitive readers have remarked its presence only in passing.[93] Read through the lens of chance, for example, one of the most well-known short stories of postwar America, Flannery O'Connor's "A Good Man Is Hard to Find" (1952), becomes about the nature of narrative itself, and demonstrates its own vexed relationship to objective reality by drawing attention to the concept of chance. Unlike thinkers such as Jacques Monod or Karl Popper, O'Connor, a devout Catholic, believed "the natural world contains the supernatural," by which she meant that what we think are examples of absolute chance are actually evidence of providential design.[94] In "A Good Man Is Hard to Find," she creates a narrative world in which chance moments are meant to be evidence of her own fictional design, just as putative chance in real life is actually evidence of providential design.

In the story's opening sentences, the grandmother reads a newspaper account explaining that "this fellow that calls himself The Misfit is aloose from the Federal Pen and headed toward Florida."[95] The grandmother points this item out to her son, Bailey, as a reason for not going to Florida—after all, she says, "I wouldn't take my children in any direction with a criminal like that aloose in it." The argument is weak, almost laughable, to both Bailey and the reader, and it tests credulity when the family does indeed encounter The Misfit, who does indeed murder the grandmother and her family. The encounter seems improbable because O'Connor uses the newspaper account to introduce The Misfit long before he appears in person. The narrative structure of the story makes the encounter, the vindication of the grandmother's harebrained protestations, a striking coincidence, so the chance encounter serves to remind us of the story's artifice. When I teach this story, my students invariably want to know why O'Connor would do this, since it would be "more believable" if there had been no mention of The Misfit in the opening paragraph.

One answer is that she does this to introduce the tension between absolute chance and narrative design that she develops throughout the story. The coincidence of the grandmother's encounter with The Misfit is made possible by the chance event of a car accident, which leaves the family stranded on a country road. O'Connor takes pains to emphasize this event, which could be considered both absolute chance in the world of the story, and an example of narrative chance as part of the short story as a whole. First, the accident itself conforms to the grandmother's private logic, for her overly fancy clothes prove functional as well as aesthetic: "In case of an accident, anyone seeing her dead on the highway would know at once that she was a lady."[96] Second, after the accident occurs, the grandchildren are giddy with excitement and scream, "We've had an ACCIDENT!"—a sentence repeated twice more in the story.[97] The fully capitalized word "ACCIDENT" draws attention to itself typographically and conceptually; as an example of narrative chance, it demands to be interpreted both as the unexpected, unintended accident, and as a key part of the story's design, the event that allows The Misfit and grandmother to come together.[98]

When O'Connor draws the reader's attention to the central chance event in the story, she is demonstrating the divergence between her fiction and her idea of objective reality. For O'Connor, this reality included Cold War politics (recall that her characters share their negative opinions of the Marshall Plan) but was framed predominantly by her orthodox Christian beliefs.[99] When she remarked that "the Christian novelist lives in a larger universe" than one who is "merely a naturalist," she meant that the former sees providential laws at work when something like a car accident occurs, while the latter does not.[100] So far, it might seem odd that "A Good Man Is Hard to Find"—written by a staunch anti-Communist—actually shares with orthodox Marxists the sense that absolute chance does not exist. What matters, though, is their respective motivations for so doing, and the important difference is that in O'Connor's story, readers are meant to notice the strident repetition of ACCIDENT as evidence of the story's artifice. In other words, O'Connor's use of narrative chance is meant to create a true representation of objective reality that does not pass for or replace this reality.[101]

The car accident in "A Good Man Is Hard to Find" represents in fact a stock device writers have used to work through a paradox of fiction: even though car accidents of course happen all the time in real life, they often sound pat or unbelievable in fiction, and so the moment of greatest verisimilitude is also the moment where artifice can be most noticeable.[102] Vladimir Nabokov, always one to have fun with fictional conventions, uses a car accident to toy with the difference between absolute chance and narrative chance in his most famous novel, *Lolita* (1955). In that novel, Humbert Humbert deigns to marry Charlotte Haze with the purpose of getting closer to her young daughter, Dolores. After his marriage to Charlotte, Humbert records his lust for Lolita—his imagined version of Dolores—in his diary; when Charlotte discovers these entries, she writes several letters and rushes across the street to mail them. This is the moment when Humbert's secret is about to be exposed, but fortunately for him, chance intervenes and a car hits Charlotte and kills her.[103] Rather than letting this key plot point pass unremarked, however, Nabokov uses the accident as an opportunity to muse on the ordering tendencies of fictional narrative: "No man can bring about the perfect murder," Humbert observes, "[C]hance, however, can do it."[104] But as he continues to think about the fatal accident, Humbert shifts his interpretation of the event from "smiling Chance" to "coincidence." This definitional shift has a point: whereas chance implies a lack of intention or control, coincidence suggests a meaningful convergence, that someone has interpreted the chance event as significant or consequential. When Humbert thinks that "it was the long hairy arm of Coincidence that had reached out to remove an innocent woman," readers are meant to see Nabokov's control of Humbert's universe, a control emphasized through narrative chance.[105]

Flaunting the car accident as narrative chance in *Lolita* is thus a way for Nabokov to announce that chance events in fiction are always disingenuous because the author plans them. This idea reaches comic heights when the driver of the car calls on Humbert to prove the accident was not his fault: "[M]y grotesque visitor unrolled a large diagram he had made of the accident.... [It had] all kinds of impressive arrows and dotted lines in varicolored inks. [Charlotte's] trajectory was illustrated at several points by a series of those little outline figures ... used in statistics as visual aids."[106] The joke here is that the accident being accounted for by the diagrams and arrows was already planned by Nabokov, since it is the author who has converted chance into coincidence by including it within the design of his novel. Humbert's reflections on the matter point both to the limits of representing absolute chance in narrative, and to chance's power to expose an artificial world as such (in chapter 3 I discuss at length Nabokov's most complex engagement with questions of chance, *Pale Fire*, which uses chance to lampoon mid-century ideas about homosexuality).

A decade after *Lolita*, British novelist Nicholas Mosley built a whole novel around the symbolic resonance of the car accident in *Accident* (1965), which stands as a metaphor for the unbridgeable distance between the representation possible in fictional narratives and objective reality. As was the case for many critics of the Soviet system already described, for Mosley absolute chance is an elusive marker of objective reality that can never quite be captured through narrative. Although the novel is set in the claustrophobic world of Stephen Jervis, an Oxford don who spends his days meditating on philosophical problems, the larger cultural backdrop is dominated by the insistently insolvable problem of the atomic bomb, with its potential to unleash an accident far deadlier than a car crash. "We are all gone," writes Stephen, "One mistake and the world is over."[107] The incomprehensibility of death caused by the plot's central car accident thus becomes a writ small example of the incomprehensibility of a large-scale nuclear disaster, which seems to Jervis increasingly real, but which cannot be represented in a fictional narrative. As Steven Weisenburger has written of the novel, "*Accident* argues that what is 'real' is *not* a text—for it is essentially non-narrative, accidental."[108]

If, in the Cold War context I have sketched, chance took on a more urgent political cast, then when American writers experimented with chance in more sustained and complex ways, it tended also to have a political dimension. Although, as I have said, there was a recurring claim that Americans acknowledged chance whereas the Soviets denied it, there was simultaneously the sense that American visions of reality could be authored in ways reminiscent of Soviet reality. This is what Tony Tanner meant when he made the now much-repeated observation that "there is an abiding dream in American literature that an unpatterned, unconditioned life is possible, in which your movements and stillnesses, choices and repudiations are all your own; and . . . there is also an abiding American dread that someone else is patterning your life, that there are all sorts of invisible plots afoot to rob you of your autonomy of thought and action."[109] This perspective attends to the more familiar aspects of Cold War domestic culture: the paranoid sensibility characteristic of writers like Thomas Pynchon and Don DeLillo, and the recurrence of the phenomenon Timothy Melley calls "agency panic"—the sense that the demands of large cultural narratives had foreclosed the possibility of personal agency.[110]

By remarking on the presence or absence of chance in America, writers and cultural observers could in fact argue that the domestic situation might yield stories rivaling anything found in the pages of *The Future Is Ours, Comrade*. For example, William S. Burroughs, among the more prolix if somewhat mystifying critics of the American government and the realities it sponsored, offered this story in an essay about coincidence:

> It is related that a freelance journalist with papers and pictures in his possession proving CIA involvement in the Bay of Pigs was on his way to keep an appointment with an editor and show him this material. Now it just happened that the freelance youth was hitchhiking, and it just happened that a CIA man picked him up. The CIA man did everything he could to dissuade the boy from publishing the material. He failed and called a special number in Washington. On the way to the editor's office that boy was hit and killed by a laundry truck. So that cleaned that up. Murder by car perpetrated during a ten-minute walk through city streets? . . . The Company must have had a way of *pushing* the target in front of the truck.[111]

Although Burroughs does not quite argue that under the U.S. Cold War regime there was no such thing as absolute chance, his paranoid sensibility does depend on the belief that there is, as Tanner puts it, "all sorts of invisible plots afoot," which manipulate accident in the direct service of Cold War politics. Burroughs's ironic repetition of "it just happened that" indicates his sense that nothing could "just happen" to someone who posed a threat to U.S. power. The CIA, America's own homegrown secret police, could orchestrate something that looked like accident in order to further its own agenda, a system of hyper-control functionally similar to the underground world of drug addiction that Burroughs is famous for chronicling; as he once wrote, "There are no accidents in the junk world."[112]

Burroughs responded to his sense that the modern world was subject to increasing social control with innovative work like *Naked Lunch* (1959). Just as Kosinski explicitly worried about the imposition of plot in his work, Burroughs wrote of *Naked Lunch*, "I do not presume to impose 'story' 'plot' 'continuity.'"[113] Instead, he applied his infamous cut-up method, devised in the late 1950s with painter Brion Gysin, which meant that, as he explained, "You can cut into *Naked Lunch* at any intersection point."[114] As Burroughs and Gysin cut phrases and sentence fragments from newspapers and other sources, only to be assembled again at random, they challenged the notion that narrative sensibility is located only in syntactic regularity. By deploying chance, Burroughs thought he was accessing a better or more complete type of reality that conventional narratives could not articulate and that large cultural narratives merely obscured.[115]

The most radical attempt to subject narrative to absolute chance may be found in a collaboration between visual artist La Monte Young and poet Jackson Mac Low. In 1963, Young and Mac Low published *An Anthology of Chance Operations*, a collection of writings, artwork, and musical scores that would lay the foundation for Fluxus, an association of experimental artists from a variety of media that gained traction in the 1960s.[116] The graphic layout of the title page reflected the volume's interest in chance: it was printed in different fonts shooting off at various angles so it is difficult to discern the order of the items in the subtitle ("concept art," "anti-art," "meaningless work," "improvisation," etc.). Like cut-up experimentations, *An Anthology of Chance Operations* suggests that narrative can have meaning regardless of syntax.

Mac Low's work demonstrates a particular interest in exploring how chance disrupts conventional forms, an interest that Ellen Zweig suggests is "part of his political philosophy which he describes as 'pacifist-anarchist' or as a kind of push toward an 'enlightened and anarchistic society.'"[117] For Mac Low at least, formal experimentation could amount to a political critique insofar as it repudiates the notion that linguistic meaning can arise only from syntactic regularity. In one piece, "Score," Mac Low attempts to let absolute chance rule his production, and he dispenses with all units of semantic meaning except the letters themselves. The piece is prefaced by the statement: "The text on the opposite page may be used in any way as a score for solo or group readings, musical or dramatic performances, looking, smelling, anything else &/or nothing at all."[118] Readers are then confronted with absolute chance on the page (see figure 1).

While there is lots to say about this anthology in general, from a narrative point of view, "Score" represents a conceptual dead-end because the only way to interpret this spattering of letters is as absolute chance. If absolute chance rules a creative work, then the composition itself is trumped. This is a problem that some critics have noted with the aleatory music of John Cage, the most well-known contributor

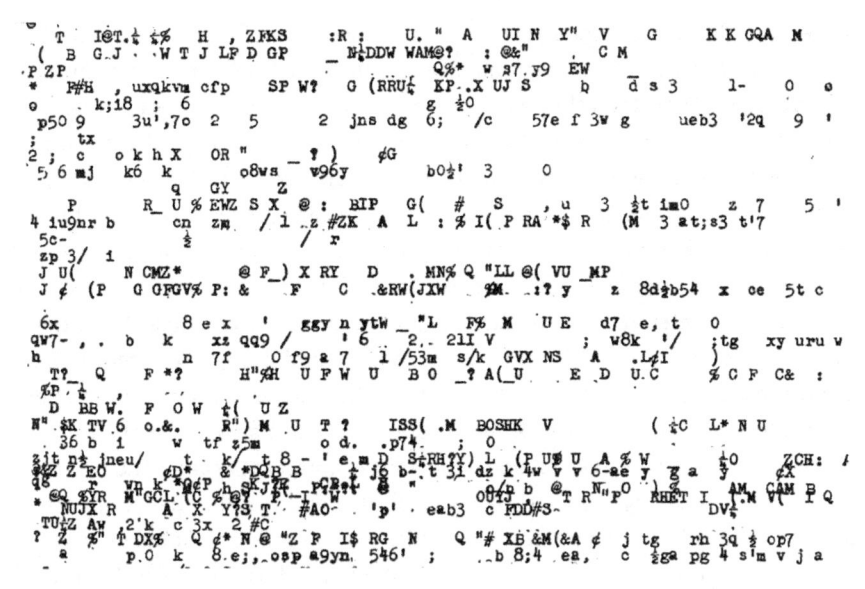

Figure 1. Jackson Mac Low, from "Score," in *An Anthology of Chance Operations* ... (1963)

to *An Anthology of Chance Operations*. Konrad Boehmer writes that because Cage thinks that "the organization of sound according to chance frees the listener from the compulsion that the composed work imposes on him," it is easy to forget that "in its totality, chance is a rigorous system."[119] Mac Low's "Score" demonstrates this totality in a different way: it is true that a reader could follow Mac Low's instructions on the facing page and use these random symbols to score a musical composition or other performance, but such scoring would have to be imposed by the reader ("GFGV%" equals middle C). Thus, while "Score" appears compelling insofar as seems to confirm, say, the broad conclusions of post-structuralist theory by emphasizing the arbitrariness of the sign, because the primary intention is to reproduce absolute chance, all other interpretations are foreclosed because absolute chance cannot be interpreted as part of something else. So one cannot call "Score" a narrative that includes absolute chance, but perhaps a work of visual art composed using the random placement of letters but having no narrative function.[120]

The following chapters, then, do not concern work like "Score" that abandons narrative in favor of absolute chance, but focuses rather on work that uses chance to negotiate the relationship between narrative and objective reality, as inflected by Cold War rhetoric. Building on the cultural context and critical vocabulary offered in this chapter, chapter 2 looks in detail at an important test case of the political dimensions of chance in fiction. After a brief comparison of Ian Hacking's intellectual history *The Taming of Chance* to William Gaddis's novel *The Recognitions* (1955), that chapter analyzes Thomas Pynchon's first novel, *V.* (1963), and argues that its sophisticated use of narrative chance creates an aesthetic response to totalitarian political fictions. One of the first big postmodern novels (and thus a looming presence for many postwar writers), *V.* merits sustained analysis in the context of chance's role in Cold War culture because it thematizes the function of narrative chance in the framework I have described throughout this chapter. It is organized around a series of key historical moments that may or may not be connected to the mysterious Lady V, and thus may or may not be products of chance. As Herbert Stencil roams the globe chasing down references to the Lady V (and even the letter V itself), the novel begins to explore the differences between chance and design. For Stencil, there is no such thing as absolute chance because he interprets everything as connected to V; the novel, on the other hand, tries to open a space for chance even though it is itself designed. In one important chapter, set against the backdrop of a proto-fascist regime that, like Stencil, denies absolute chance, Pynchon suggests a novelist's own potential complicity in creating a fictional universe in which putative moments of chance are actually products of authorial design. *V.*'s innovative form is a way to work out the inclusion of chance in a novel and to level a critique of both totalitarian political systems and also of Cold War norms back in the States, a comparison that became widespread in American fiction in the latter half of the twentieth century.

After chapter 2's tour of the various uses to which chance can be put in fiction with a broadly postmodern sensibility, chapter 3 tests the conceptual power of chance to expose the limits of Cold War cultural narratives. Vladimir Nabokov, a giant of twentieth-century literature, has been taken by many readers to be pugnaciously apolitical in his work—indeed, until very recently, few critics have thought of Nabokov as engaging political questions at all. This chapter shows, by contrast, how attention to chance changes our sense of Nabokov's aesthetic project as it demonstrates a politics folded into the very texture of his writing. Reading *Pale Fire* (1962) in a Cold War context, the chapter suggests that far from being only an apolitical novel of wordplay, it in fact intervenes in midcentury controversies about Communism and homosexuality. The novel's famous formal structure evinces an interest in chance and design reminiscent of some themes discussed in the second chapter: the first part of the novel is a lengthy poem by Nabokov's invented poet John Shade; the second part consists of over two hundred pages of annotations on the poem by Charles Kinbote, a mentally unstable scholar. Kinbote twists the words in Shade's poem so that they seem to allude to Kinbote's own tenure as King of Zembla, a tiny country that has been taken over by Communist-like Extremists who have forced Kinbote into exile. As Kinbote tells his story, he often refers to accidents and other chance events pertaining to the Zembla story, but he does so to emphasize his own control over these accidents; in the "real world" of the novel, we learn that Kinbote has little control, and that he is of course not an exiled king but rather an abrasive, self-important professor subtly ostracized by his community at least partly because of his homosexuality. By focusing on the way Kinbote treats chance versus its presence in the novel as a whole, chapter 3 argues that *Pale Fire* demonstrates the absurdity of what I term the homophobic narrative—the tendency to equate homosexual people with everything from perverts to political traitors—which works by foreclosing chance in ways that echo the denial of chance by those totalitarian regimes haunting Kinbote's fevered tale.

If chapter 3 shows that Nabokov's seemingly apolitical wordplay should actually be read as political critique, then chapter 4 reverses this idea to resist the notion that African-American fiction of the Cold War was only or primarily political. Attention to chance once again allows us to think about the Cold War frame in a new light by explaining how many African-American authors were more reflexive about the problems of design than is generally acknowledged, and that numerous writers negotiated the relationship between the individual and the state by pointing to chance as integral to self-definition. Beginning with a discussion of Colson Whitehead's more recent novel *The Intuitionist* (1999), which revisits the ways that chance was tied to race during the Cold War, the chapter covers a range of works, from the most influential African-American novels of mid-century, Richard Wright's *Native Son* (1940) and Ralph Ellison's *Invisible Man* (1952), to less frequently discussed works such as Wright's own second novel, *The Outsider* (1953), and John A. Williams's *The Man Who Cried I Am* (1967). The chapter demonstrates how African-American writers dramatized a sense of being caught between the competing systems of control represented by Communism on the one hand, and the promise of American democratic freedom on the other. Tracing an arc from *Native Son* to *The Man Who Cried I Am*, the chapter demonstrates the ever-changing relationship between the individual and political rhetoric by showing how the denial of chance was first attributed to Communists, who in *Invisible Man* simply want to control African Americans for their own purposes, and then moves finally to *The Man Who Cried I Am*, which shows that, from a black perspective, American democracy masks a fantasy of complete control.

The idea that the Cold War encouraged a fantasy of state control in the United States runs throughout *No Accident, Comrade*: thus when Pynchon compares a nose job to genocide, or when Nabokov implies a similarity between the homophobic narrative and the operation of a police state, or when African-American writers saw the prospects for equality equally bleak in the United States and the Soviet Union, they identify some continuities among domestic norms and ideas about the totalitarian state. Chapter 5 takes up this theme, but does so from a different perspective. It turns from a primary focus on fictional narratives to explore other ways chance became a privileged cultural signifier during the Cold War by describing a widespread cultural narrative that I term the game theory narrative. The development of game theory was intimately linked to the military demands of the Cold War, but the game theory narrative does not concern a technical understanding familiar to mathematicians or economists, but rather a popularized story about what game theory could do for Americans playing a global game of Cold War. It was touted as a scientific theory that would help the United States win this game by incorporating random strategic moves in order both to outplay the Soviets and to manage the threat of an accidental nuclear exchange. The chapter describes how this story was promulgated by journalists and others in the early 1950s, then how it was engaged, amplified, or challenged in a range of literary and cultural materials, including Philip K. Dick's novel, *Solar Lottery* (1955), about a future world governed by the dictates of the game theory narrative, Robert Coover's novel *The Universal Baseball Association* (1968), Stanley Kubrick's film *Dr. Strangelove* (1964), Richard Powers's novel *Prisoner's Dilemma* (1988), and the political novels of Joan Didion, which range from the 1970s to the 1990s. In many of these works, there is the sense that while game theory is the product of supreme rationality, when applied to the realities of the Cold War, it becomes supremely irrational, and the myth of state control is dangerously reminiscent of totalitarian fantasies of control.

The concluding chapter explores how many of the themes and concerns that preoccupied thinkers during the Cold War persist after 1989, a persistence made visible both in the ways the conflict is explicitly thematized, and in the ways that chance is tied to the sorts of narrative concerns it animated. The chapter begins with a discussion of Paul Auster's writing, which as many readers know has been perennially concerned with questions of chance and coincidence. But by reading Auster in light of the preceding chapters, it becomes clear that his preoccupation with chance and his metafictional tendencies are actually related, for his frequent meditations on chance demonstrate a tension between freedom and control that would be familiar to many other writers discussed throughout this book. From Auster's writing, the chapter analyzes Chang-rae Lee's immediately canonized novel *Native Speaker* (1995), which brings tropes of accident and espionage into the post-1989 present in order to analyze causal systems underwritten by the Cold War. Chapter 6 ends with a look at *My Life in CIA* (2005), by Harry Mathews, a longtime expatriate and American member of the French avant-garde literary group, Oulipo. The book announces itself as a memoir of 1973, when Mathews pretended to be an undercover CIA agent, but then subsequently became accidentally entangled in a real assassination plot complete with covert drops, front companies, and secret agents of various countries. But as readers make their way through Mathews's aesthetic game, facts become hopelessly mixed with fiction, and the book turns on questions of chance and coincidence to show, in retrospect, that their thematization was of a piece with the fabric of Cold War logic.

2

Aesthetic Responses to Political Fictions

Pynchon and the Violence of Narrative Chance

> Science assures us that it is getting nearer to the solution of life, what life *is*, that is ("the ultimate mystery"), and offers anonymously promulgated submicroscopic chemistry in eager substantiation. But no one has even begun to explain what happened at the dirt track in Langhorne, Pennsylvania about twenty-five years ago, when Jimmy Concannon's car threw a wheel, and in a crowd of eleven thousand it killed his mother.[1]
> —William Gaddis, *The Recognitions* (1955)

> During the nineteenth century it became possible to see that the world might be regular and yet not subject to universal laws of nature. A space was cleared for chance. . . . A new type of law came into being, analogous to the laws of nature, but pertaining to people. These new laws were expressed in terms of probability. They carried with them the connotations of normalcy and deviations from the norm. . . . Such social and personal laws were to be a matter of probabilities, of chances. Statistical in nature, these laws were nonetheless inexorable; they could even be self-regulating. People are normal if they conform to the central tendency of such laws, while those at the extremes are pathological.[2]
> —Ian Hacking, *The Taming of Chance* (1990)

These two passages tell different stories about the relationship of chance to narrative explanation. In the first passage, taken from William Gaddis's massive postmodern novel, absolute chance marks the unknowable and inexplicable. Throughout *The Recognitions*, Gaddis sees scientific inquiry as an analogue to religious faith because both phenomena erase chance. Whether one looks to theology or submicroscopic chemistry, the effect is the same: to offer a definitive "solution" to life. But for Gaddis, as for many thinkers discussed in chapter 1, absolute chance is an essential feature of objective reality, and so to explain it as an example of something else is to reduce life's mysteries and complexities to principles and prescriptions. Chance is thus important precisely because it cannot be brought under the control of science or religion—nor can it appear, as I argued in the previous chapter, in fictional narrative without becoming narrative chance.[3]

The second passage is from the opening of Ian Hacking's intellectual history, *The Taming of Chance*, in which he shows that a hallmark of twentieth-century scientific thinking was a more systematic attitude toward chance. Even while the universe was coming to be seen as indeterminate, chance could be "tamed" by expressing it in terms of probability. According to Hacking, chance became important to contemporary Western culture as it was made knowable and explicable. Whereas chance has historically been seen as antithetical to the ideals of reason and culture (Hacking points out that Hume thought it vulgar to believe in chance), by the late nineteenth and early twentieth centuries, chance was systematized and made to work for culture rather than against it. With the creation of "social and personal laws," which depend on probability and statistical inquiry, something as improbable as Mother Concannon's death could be seen as abnormal—"pathological"—because it does not conform to statistical averages. The thrown wheel in *The Recognitions* is, as the narrator remarks, a chance event that cries out for explanation because it lies beyond so many standard deviations. What fascinates is not the death itself, but the improbability of the thrown wheel killing the driver's own mother, something of material importance to human beings, but which is unimportant to—and unaccounted for by—scientific inquiry. The sort of statistical analysis described by Hacking could only explain the event by defining it as wildly improbable, a freak occurrence, thereby excluding it from the normal range of human activity. In *The Recognitions*, by contrast, this perceived abnormality is what comprises the ineffable texture of life.

These divergent views on something like the Langhorne incident raise questions about the relationship among chance, narrative, and interpretation. Hacking's book is about the way reality is interpreted by cultural observers, from philosophers and astronomers to mathematicians and bureaucratic functionaries. For the purpose of his intellectual history, chance is conscripted by a cultural and scientific narrative about the nature of objective reality: the universe is indeterminate, but chance can be systematized if one relies on the proper methodologies. According to this narrative, the universe seems less beholden to absolute chance, even while it is indeterminate. For Gaddis, on the other hand, absolute chance names precisely that which is not accounted for by narrative explanation. As suggested in chapter 1, chance is a marker of objective reality, however elusive—and yet it is always deferred by the act of narration. When the thrown wheel is included in the design of the novel, it ceases to function as an example of absolute chance and becomes instead a phenomenon that invites interpretation. With instances such as this, Gaddis identifies a problem that chance can pose to narrative (are there ramifications to ordering what is by definition not ordered?). Although his work does not offer a "solution" to this problem any more than submicroscopic chemistry solves the unfortunate event at the Pennsylvania racetrack, *The Recognitions* demonstrates a profound interest in such questions, which were likewise taken on by many other postwar writers concerned with the role of chance in their writing.

In order to illustrate how the Cold War frame inflected the use of chance in fictional narratives, this chapter relies on Thomas Pynchon's first novel, *V.* (1963). Pynchon is among the most consequential writers to emerge from the postwar period, and *V.* is an ideal test case for our purposes because it stages the structural similarities between designing chance in fiction and the denial of chance by those modern political systems that attempt to control individuals through all-encompassing fictions. I want to begin with a sustained analysis of Pynchon's work because it shows the extent to which chance became political during the Cold War, and how it could be used by writers to generate critique. In a novel saturated by political history and cultural arcana, it is unsurprising to find examples of the Cold War intellectual context presented in terms much like the ones described in the previous chapter. One minor character, for example, a "huge and homicidal" Russian fond of reading "Bakunin, Marx, Ulyanov [Lenin]," has faith in the inevitable march of history, even if it means the erasure of his own subjectivity. As he says, "I . . . may fall by the wayside. No matter. The Socialist Awareness grows, the tide is irresistible and irreversible. It is a bleak world we live in . . . atoms collide, brain cells fatigue, economies collapse and others rise to succeed them, all in accord with the basic rhythms of History."[4] In *V.* as in many Cold War texts, orthodox Marxism, with its "irresistible and irreversible" sense of history, is the clearest example of a narrative that denies absolute chance.[5]

But *V.* is illustrative not merely for its participation in this familiar rhetoric, but rather for the ways that, against this backdrop, it becomes about the nature of fictional narrative. The book works through a novelist's own role in crafting representations of objective reality, a role politically and ethically urgent given the uniquely rhetorical nature of the Cold War. For Pynchon, figurative violence can be enacted when chance is denied by a narrative, whether fictional, political, or cultural; just as the homicidal Marxist's views can be considered violent, so too might a novelist's representation of the world, insofar as it erases chance in the name of a larger design. Given this premise, the novel's innovative form attempts to retain a sense of the freedom implied by a universe rooted in absolute chance by gesturing toward events or other moments unnarrated, thereby according them the potential to be absolute chance.[6]

A typical opening move for understanding *V.*'s complexities in fact suggests Pynchon's investment in exploring the tension between chance and design in a fictional narrative. From the initial reviews, readers have noticed that the novel's two principal characters, Herbert Stencil and Benny Profane, have strikingly different relationships to chance.[7] As Tony Tanner put it in his influential introduction to Pynchon's work, "If [Stencil's] V. is connected to the actual or hallucinated (imagined, projected) world of plot and cabal apocalypse, then Benny is distinctly a creature of the realm of 'accident.'"[8] As is apparent from a first reading of the novel, Tanner leaves "accident" in quotation marks for good reason. In *V.*, readers are never quite sure about a great many things, but particularly whether the events in the world of the novel are unconnected, chance-based events given meaning retroactively by characters' interpretations, or whether such events are indeed evidence of a conscious conspiracy.[9]

Much of *V.*'s plot is driven by Herbert Stencil, the son of a British intelligence officer who finds a cryptic reference to the letter V in his father's notebooks: "'There is more behind and inside V. than any of us had suspected'" (49). Stencil roams the world looking for clues as to who or what V might be, chasing the illusive shimmer of the titular letter V and the glimmer of its bodily instantiation, the Lady V—variously called Veronica Manganese or Vera Meroving or Victoria Wren or someone else—thereby imposing an idiosyncratic order onto history that another character calls "Stencilization" (246). For the conspiracy-minded Stencil, there is no such thing as absolute chance, for things that appear fortuitous or otherwise uncontrolled are actually evidence of the V conspiracy. Stencil's plotting counteracts chance, as suggested by the idea that his "random movements before the war had given way to a great single movement from inertness to—if not vitality, then at least activity. Work, the chase—for it was V. he hunted" (51). Paul Celmer reads Stencil's "activity" of meaning-making as emblematic of the conspiratorial logic invited by the Cold War; he sees Stencil's elaborate conspiracy theory as an example of the "Communist-plot genre" (Communist agents are conspiring in secret to overthrow the U.S. government; these Communists could be *anyone*!), but he thinks that ultimately, the novel "undermine[s] the Communist-plot genre."[10] Quoting Richard Hofstadter's seminal book, *The Paranoid Style in American Politics* (1965), Celmer notes conspiracies like Stencil's "make no allowance for accidents: the world they depict 'is nothing if not coherent—in fact, the paranoid mentality is far more coherent than the real world, since it leaves no room for mistakes, failures, or ambiguities.'"[11] Thus, in his intolerance of absolute chance, Stencil seems a good Cold Warrior while also being reminiscent of someone like the "huge and homicidal" Marxist in that he finds it inevitable that V should be somehow connected to important historical events.

The novel registers these tensions in numerous ways, but perhaps the most vivid critique of Stencil's method comes from another character, Dudley Eigenvalue, surely the only "psychodontist" or soul dentist in recent fiction. Eigenvalue, using a professionally apt analogy, illustrates how Stencilization "makes no allowance for accidents": "Cavities in the teeth occur for good reason, Eigenvalue reflected. But even if there are several per tooth, there's no conscious organization there against the life of the pulp, no conspiracy. Yet we have men like Stencil, who must go about grouping the world's random caries into cabals" (162). Throughout *V.*, Eigenvalue's idea of "conscious organization" is reflected in various instances of "pattern" or "design" or "engineering," all of which are figured as antagonists of absolute chance—accidents and other random occurrences are such precisely because they do not conform to a particular pattern, nor are they products of engineering or design. In *V.*, chance is emblematic of an absence of conscious organization.

How then to avoid behaving as the paranoid Stencil does when conceptualizing chance's place in a fictional narrative? After all, fiction is itself a result of conscious organization, and therefore excludes the possibility of absolute chance. One obvious strategy is to draw attention to the problem as Eigenvalue does when he notes that Stencil's quest is predicated upon the faulty assumption that certain phenomena cannot be products of chance. For Stencil, any correspondence of detail or appearance of V becomes a meaningful coincidence, and so through interpretation he erases the palpable workings of absolute chance in the universe. This is what Stencil intuits when he muses that "V.'s is a country of coincidence" (500). As Eigenvalue points out, however, this is wrongheaded because some things in the universe do occur by chance—for chance itself can be a "good reason." But for those who seek pattern, who rely on design as the only source of significant meaning (as readers do), chance is threatening because it lies outside the system. Stencil recognizes this tension throughout the novel; when he happens upon someone who may be a potential piece of the V conspiracy, he thinks that it occurs "apparently by accident." Later, when he comes across the name again, he concludes that it was presented to him "by what only could have been design" (500). Although Eigenvalue is talking about Stencil's dubious questing after V when he notes the danger of turning "random caries into cabals," the charge could also apply to the work of a novelist, who incorporates chance for the purposes of a fictional design.

A Slapstick Routine So Violent

The counterpoint to Stencil's obsessive meaning-making is Benny Profane, a character who conforms to no seeming pattern, who does not much bother to look for meaning in life, and who is consistently subjected to chance and accident. In Profane, Pynchon offers an antihero who is acted upon by chance that is not chance, since events that are for him absolute chance are in fact products of the narrative's design. A sometime sailor and road worker, Profane is a self-described "schlemihl" who bounces from job to job, woman to woman, and has a conflicted relationship with inanimate objects. *V.* opens as Profane "happened to pass" through Norfolk, Virginia, on Christmas Eve, 1955. This association with the accidental or fortuitous persists until the end of the novel, when we learn that Profane winds up on Malta, where the action closes, "by accident" (407). Whatever else has changed in the tumultuous twentieth century, Profane remains more or less the same, for he is content to "drift" through life without purpose or plan: "He came back to the ship that morning in the fog knowing that Fortune's yo-yo had also returned to some reference-point, not unwilling, not anticipating, not anything; merely prepared to float, acquire a set and drift wherever Fortune willed. If Fortune could will" (407).

Pynchon begins to develop an aesthetic response to the figurative violence that can attend narrative chance by subjecting Profane to the violence that comes with the choreographed chance of slapstick comedy, which in turn serves as a metaphor for the fantasies of complete state control characteristic of totalitarian regimes. Although readers at first may find it disingenuous to compare slapstick to totalitarianism (and offensive to equate them, which the novel does not do), *V.* nevertheless does want readers to notice that the two aesthetic and political phenomena share a similar relationship to chance, which in turn raises questions about the effects of their respective tendencies toward design.

Viewers of a Charlie Chaplin or Buster Keaton film normally do not let the hero's multiplying injuries overshadow the acrobatic fun, but the nature of slapstick—a plot driven by accidents run amok—does imply questions about the relationship among chance, design, and violence. Consider, for instance, an imaginary outline of a generic slapstick film: a man steps on a rake and it hits him in the face. Minutes later, recovering in his apartment, he trips, falls from a fifth-story window and bounces from awning to awning, only to land in a wheelbarrow full of cement left by careless workers on their lunch break. Perhaps the wheelbarrow frees from its blocking and rolls down a steep hill, narrowly missing cross-traffic. Such is the stuff of classic slapstick comedy—funny because it surprises, visually compelling because of the complexity and ingenuity of the arranged stunts. Chance events proliferate to form a larger design that reveals its own special logic: it would be as improbable for someone in real life to survive a chain of accidents like these as it would be for Jimmy Concannon's thrown wheel to kill his own mother, and yet in the case of slapstick, viewers take comfort in knowing that the hero will make it through unscathed. This is what Larry Langman means when he remarks that slapstick is pervaded by "a sense of unreality" because of "the improbability of the stunts."[12] Such "unreality" is comforting when compared to chance events in real life, which are not managed or controlled, and so have potential to do us harm. The paradox of slapstick, then, is that accidents are arranged so carefully that they form the core of the plot, and are therefore far from accidental. In this light, Pynchon as cultural critic shares an insight offered by Max Horkheimer and Theodor Adorno in their influential 1944 critique of the "culture industry" when they called slapstick "organized cruelty."[13] For Horkheimer and Adorno, slapstick film is emblematic of a debased culture that distracts people from real emotion by giving them a prescribed range of options that substitutes for real choice. Slapstick is thus organized cruelty both because it subjects its protagonists to injury and because it legitimates such violence in the name of fun.

Pynchon focuses in particular on how the designed chance inherent in slapstick represents a figurative violence on the part of the director. From scenes explicitly borrowed from cinematic slapstick to apparently random occurrences that are read by characters as evidence of far-flung conspiracies, V. emphasizes the tendency of humans to want to account for or use chance in some way. But in V., to overengineer—that is, to rely on types of design, whether engineering, patterning, or indeed fictional narratives that leave no room for absolute chance—is to create the potential for violence. In the case of slapstick, the violence (the injuries sustained by the protagonist) is visible but strangely immaterial.[14] With respect to its attitudes toward chance, then, slapstick functions like novel writing; just as the pratfalls and banana peel slips in slapstick are carefully planned, so too are all the moments of ostensible chance in a novel actually products of design. In a novel, as in slapstick, it is not the chance event itself that threatens, but rather the designed event that is meant to *look* like chance.

As Profane's adventures increasingly conform to the logic of slapstick, readers begin to sense the violence underwriting the apparently throwaway moments of comedy. In one job he has fallen in to, for example, Profane is asked to make a salad, but somehow "managed to get frozen strawberries in the French dressing and chopped liver in the Waldorf salad, plus accidentally dropping two dozen or so radishes in the French fryer (though these drew raves from the customers when he served them anyway, too lazy to go after more)" (21). In another scene, Profane's attempts at lovemaking on a billiard table degenerate into slapstick as his would-be lover's "sudden movement dislodged an avalanche of pool balls on his stomach. 'Dear God,' he said, covering his head. . . . Profane creaked to his feet, zipped his fly up again, blundered out through the darkness. He got out to the street after tripping over two folding chairs and the cord to the jukebox" (152). Like an early Keaton two-reeler, the comedy comes from what is unplanned or uncontrolled taking over the plot; it is not the events themselves that are important, but their unexpectedness and proliferation.

Profane has many such moments that demonstrate he is "[a]ccident prone" (128), and while the notion of accidentally deep-fried radishes is relatively innocuous, as Pynchon develops the slapstick theme, it is worth pausing over the violence of seemingly humorous actions like an "avalanche of pool balls" crashing onto Profane's stomach. This other, violent side of slapstick humor is alluded to by "Girgis the mountebank," a minor character who is a street performer by day and a thief by night. Girgis thinks, "[T]he clowning—that took it out of him. . . . Falling off the top of a motley pyramid of Syrians, making the dive look as near-fatal as it actually was; or else engaging the bottom man in a slapstick routine so violent that the whole construction tottered and swayed; mock-horror appearing on the faces of the others" (87). The disaffected Girgis justifies his thieving by citing the callousness of his tourist victims, which is made visible to him by their inability to recognize the inherent danger of his highly physical street performances.

Profane's morning routine likewise demonstrates how the designed chance of slapstick encourages readers (or tourists) to ignore or dismiss the violence on which the humor depends. As his attempts at salad-making or lovemaking attest, much of Profane's day consists of relentless assaults by inanimate objects:

> He made his way to the washroom of Our Home, tripping over two empty mattresses on route. Cut himself shaving, had trouble extracting the blade and gashed a finger. He took a shower to get rid of the blood. The handles wouldn't turn. When he finally found a shower that worked, the water came out hot and cold in random patterns. He danced around, yowling and shivering, slipped on a bar of soap and nearly broke his neck. . . . It wasn't that he was tired or even notably uncoordinated. Only something that, being a schlemihl, he'd known for years: inanimate objects and he could not live in peace. (31–32)

What again seems important is not the specific misfortunes that befall Profane, but their persistence and proliferation.[15] Chance is elevated to the center of the plot, and if readers smile at such a sequence, they do so because of the sheer improbability of all this happening to one poor sad sack. We recognize that Pynchon has designed these accidents for Profane so we are free to feel pleasure in the reminder that a real person is not being injured. If slapstick is about "inanimate objects" assailing the animate, then the animate always triumphs, since there are no real consequences to the dangerous acts that occur. As Ross Hamilton writes: "By allowing the audience to experience simulated accidents, rendering them 'safe,' adding acrobatics to exaggerate the impact, yet at the same time removing the viewer from real risk, the [slapstick] film detaches pleasure from any actual pain."[16] Hamilton's suggestion underscores the notion that slapstick comedy exaggerates pain in order to render it "safe." But when such an aesthetic moment occurs in the context of a novel about chance and violence, it encourages readers to wonder how safe from "actual pain" Profane remains.

In fact, by lingering over Profane's specific accidents, we might see how the novel implies that violence can be a product of the wrong kind of engineering, marked often by moments of narrative chance, which are passed off as absolute chance. In the midst of Profane's slapstick routine, the narrator describes the water as coming out in "random patterns"—it is in this apparently antinomic term that one can begin to understand the logic of the novel as it relates to the tension between absolute chance and design, and how this tension could produce violence. As in a slapstick film, in *V.* there is a paradox with respect to accident and control—the events that befall Profane are remarkable or entertaining only if they are simultaneously examples of absolute chance and ultimately harmless. But they can only be harmless if they are not examples of absolute chance, if they are, as Hamilton puts it, "simulated" by some guiding consciousness. The phrase "random patterns" suggests this paradox and reminds us that since narrative accidents are indeed arranged, we ought to register the violence being done to Profane: he is "cut" and "gashed," left "yowling and shivering," and has come close to a broken neck. Rendered in these terms, Profane's experience is hardly funny, and yet there is a tendency to pass over his injuries because they are products of accumulated chance, and in the context of a fictional narrative, chance seems less threatening as a result of design. Yet what may be ominous, however, is the awareness that Profane's injuries are inflicted upon him by the very "conscious organization" that made sure "the water came out hot and cold in random patterns."

So suggestive are the connections among accident and violence in slapstick that later writers in the postmodern tradition have used it to comment on the place of chance in a fictional narrative. Pynchon's sense that slapstick is an aesthetic form that simultaneously foregrounds and passes over accumulated accident is in fact echoed in David Foster Wallace's *Infinite Jest* (1996), a novel that many readers see as Pynchonian in its encyclopedic scope. In one of the novel's many comic riffs, Wallace extends *V.*'s incorporation of slapstick to imagine what would happen if the aesthetic world of slapstick were to collide with the real world of corporate risk management. In a letter as deadpan as Buster Keaton's expression, a hapless bricklayer applies to his insurance company for worker's compensation due to injuries sustained on the job:

> I am writing in response to your request for additional information. In block #3 of the accident reporting form, I put "trying to do the job alone", as the cause of my accident. You said in your letter that I should explain more fully and I trust that the following details will be sufficient.
>
> I am a bricklayer by trade. On the day of the accident, March 27, I was working alone on the roof of a new six story building. When I completed my work, I discovered that I had about 900 kg. of brick left over. Rather than laboriously carry the bricks down by hand, I decided to lower them in a barrel by using a pulley which fortunately was attached to the side of the building at the sixth floor. Securing the rope at ground level, I went up to the roof, swung the barrel out and loaded the brick into it. Then I went back to the ground and untied the rope, holding it tightly to insure a slow descent of the 900 kg of bricks. You will note in block #11 of the accident reporting form that I weigh 75 kg.

Due to my surprise at being jerked off the ground so suddenly, I lost my presence of mind and forgot to let go of the rope. Needless to say, I proceeded at a rapid rate up the side of the building. In the vicinity of the third floor I met the barrel coming down. This explains the fractured skull and the broken collar bone.[17]

The report continues to detail how the luckless bricklayer, still hanging onto the rope as the barrel smashed into the ground (thus losing the weight of the bricks), then began a "rather rapid descent" from the pulley down to the ground, which "accounts for the two fractured ankles and the laceration of my legs and lower body."[18] Wallace is recycling a well-known urban legend that circulated around construction sites at least as far back as 1915, but, like Pynchon, has a larger point in mind.[19] Presented in this way, the story is amusing, but eventually readers may pause, as they do with Profane's painful morning routine, over the undeniably serious injuries sustained in this undeniably funny manner. The passage in fact points to something unique and significant about fictional narrative when it comes to representing chance: in a film, one might imagine that the accidents are merely being captured by the camera, so even if one is watching a slapstick film rather than, say, *America's Funniest Home Videos*, with its stock of bicycle crashes and bats-to-the-groin, one can believe, as Hamilton puts it, that the subjects are safe from actual pain. In a fictional narrative, by contrast, the physical injuries caused by the accumulated accidents are not merely by-products of the humor, but rather take on a more visible role because they need to be deliberately narrated.[20]

Slapstick routines are thus a way for Pynchon—and Wallace after him—to think about how chance operates differently in the realm of fictional narrative than it does in real life. As examples of narrative chance, Profane's accidental injuries as he fumbles with inanimate objects become metaphors for the potential complicity a novelist has in engineering a world. *V.* demonstrates the high stakes of this complicity by off-setting Profane's story with chapters about a modern world in which states produce the most far-reaching fictions of all. In a novel whose chapters make sense in relation to one another once readers look for echoes and associations (rather than for logical causal links) Profane's nearly broken neck is profitably read as an echo of the institutionalized neck-breaking and preoccupation with an enslaved population's "neck-rings" that dominate a chapter about genocide in colonial Southwest Africa. Although Profane's clumsy pratfalls are a long way from genocide, in *V.*, both phenomena are symptoms of the same problem: an attempt to erase or manipulate chance by specific types of "conscious organization"—whether by the novelist himself or by military officers and state functionaries merely carrying out the "irreversible tide" of history.

Engineering Accidents

As suggested by the passage from *The Taming of Chance* that opened this chapter, the scientific and technological advances of the twentieth century have meant that people have a new relationship to chance. In recent years, Paul Virilio has written provocatively about the changing phenomenon of accident in the past century. For Virilio, the technological advances of the postwar period made possible new varieties of accident, which paradoxically become the most telling phenomena in our experience because they remind us of the systems we live in but of which we are not normally aware. Invoking Aristotle, Virilio notes that in the classical sense, "'the accident reveals the substance.'" "If so," he writes, "then invention of the 'substance' is equally invention of the 'accident.' The shipwreck is consequently the 'futurist' invention of the ship, and the air crash the invention of the supersonic airliner, just as the Chernobyl meltdown is the invention of the nuclear power station."[21] Since shipwrecks and nuclear accidents are not possible without the technological advancements of ships and nuclear fission, Virilio sees scientific progress as ironically tied to what he calls the "invention of accident."

In the twentieth century, as this progress has accelerated at a head-spinning rate, accidents become more common as we become increasingly wired and otherwise systematized: "From the Latin *accidens*, the word 'accident' signifies what arises unexpectedly—in a device, or system or product; the unexpected, the surprise failure or destruction. As though this 'temporary failure' was not itself programmed, in a way, when the product was first put to use."[22] In this conception, there is always a relationship between technological advancement and accident—we pretend that we can insulate ourselves from accident—as, for instance, with "the multiple security systems our vehicles are equipped with"— but we are really creating more opportunities for "artificial accidents" rather than "natural" ones (earthquakes, tsunamis, and the like).[23]

During the Cold War, there was an insistent and recurrent cultural need for Americans to tell themselves that accident was manageable because of the overwhelming psychic weight of a possible accidental nuclear exchange, an idea I explore in depth in chapter 5.[24] In "We Are Safer Than We Think," a 1951 *New York Times* feature, for example, Edmund C. Berkeley, statistician and popular book author, dismisses the possibility of a nuclear exchange as irrational. Of "man-made" disasters, he writes: "Government and private safety agencies and social institutions study and seek to prevent such accidents."[25] With respect to such man-made disasters, Virilio is not so optimistic, and in fact finds the atomic bomb a manifestation of both scientific progress and accident. He writes: "From the arsenal of Venice in the age of Galileo right up to the secret laboratories of the post–Cold War, via the Manhattan Project of Los Alamos, science has become the arsenal of major accidents, the great catastrophe factory toiling away in anticipation of the cataclysms of hyperterrorism."[26] Virilio thus offers a third perspective to Gaddis's sense that science will never explain absolute chance and Hacking's sense that science has made chance more legible by arguing that science is actually an active progenitor of accident, a connection that is, for him, a defining characteristic of the Western world in the twentieth century.

Amidst these theories we might look at the work of a young employee at Boeing's Seattle facility, who published an essay in the trade journal *Aerospace Safety* in 1960. This was a journal whose broad function was to help prevent the sort of accidents Virilio has in mind, and the essay's title, "Togetherness," might have confirmed Berkeley's sense that state-of-the-art safety engineering would render nuclear accidents statistically unlikely. While not quite so rosy as Berkeley's claim that man-made accidents would not lead to major catastrophes, "Togetherness" joins the effort to prevent serious accidents by examining some "near-misses" that occurred when transporting Bomarc supersonic antiaircraft missiles:

> Airlifting the IM-99A missile, like marriage, demands a certain amount of "togetherness" between Air Force and contractor. Two birds per airlift are onloaded by Boeing people and offloaded by Air Force people; in between is an airborne MATS C-124. One loading operation is a mirror-image of the other, and similar accidents can happen at both places. Let's look at a few of the safety hazards that have to be taken into account when Bomarcs are shipped....
>
> In the July 1960 issue of *Aerospace Safety*, mention was made of the second Air Force–Industry conference on missile safety; and of plans to create Air Force–Industry Accident Review Boards. If future emphasis is to be placed on such joint action, much can be gained from a positive, realistic—above all, cooperative—approach to safety problems.[27]

Here is a person working from within the Cold War military–industrial complex who demonstrates his faith in the ability of this complex to prevent or greatly reduce what Virilio calls "major accidents." The enormous risk that attends military buildup is, of course, acknowledged, but there is also the sense that the system will provide the appropriate safety measures. Control, in this view, can effectively manage accident.

"Togetherness," written by Thomas Pynchon himself as he divided his time between his work at Boeing and on *V.*, represents the establishment perspective that, with respect to chance, more control is better. Whereas Pynchon's writing from within the Cold War establishment is a comparatively gentle chiding about safety that assumes the general logic of the industry as a whole (safe missiles are possible), as a literary novelist, he becomes far more critical of the attempts to control or manage chance in the name of scientific (and political) explanation.

Benny Profane, in one of the many odd jobs he experiences over the course of the novel, comes to work for one of those "private safety agencies" that Berkeley finds so comforting (and a writer for *Aerospace Safety* might applaud) but that Virilio would see as a birthplace of new accidents, new potentials for violence. As night watchman at Anthroresearch Associates, which performs research and testing for "the National Safety Council on Automobile Accidents," Profane sees firsthand those technological advancements meant to reduce accident. As Pynchon writes in the trade journal, the ostensible goal of such research is to eliminate injury by insulating people from accidents; but Profane, experienced as he is in the grammar of slapstick, is attuned to the potential carnage wrought by engineering accidents: "At first there'd been a certain interest in visiting the accident research area, which was jokingly referred to as the chamber of horrors. Here weights were dropped on aged automobiles, inside which would be sitting a manikin" (310). Profane feels a kinship with such "manikins," and much is made of how realistic they are: SHOCK is an acronym for the "synthetic human" dummies that so convincingly mimic the behavior of real organs and skeletal systems that they are called "entirely lifelike in every way" (311). As Profane spends long nights guarding the facility, he begins to have imaginary conversations with another manikin, SHROUD, who reflects on the differences and similarities between the animate and inanimate ("Me and SHOCK are what you and everybody will be someday," he says to Profane [311]). SHROUD intimates that Profane and mankind are the walking dead, and the violent potential of chance is again invoked as this "human object" (310) informs Profane that "fallout and road accidents" are the likely ways he and others will die (312).

The research facility is a "chamber of horrors" because it manufactures or engineers accidents that are then made to act on SHOCK and SHROUD. And yet the paradoxical joke is that these designed accidents are not of course products of absolute chance, but are rather part of a larger narrative—the narrative of scientific progress, which means, in part, the technical ability to insulate human beings from accidents. One problem with this narrative, given the logic of the novel already discussed, is that to insulate humans from chance is to insulate them from life—however dangerous accidents have the potential to be, they still mark objective reality. While the narrative of scientific progress may come from a desire to better humanity rather than degrade it, Pynchon, as though again taking a cue from Frankfurt School analyses, draws a parallel between the engineered accidents at Anthroresearch and the totalitarian ideology that resulted in genocide.[28] At one point in their imaginary conversations, for example, SHROUD makes a striking comparison between the smashed cars in a junkyard and "the photographs of Auschwitz[.] Thousands of Jewish corpses, stacked up like those poor car-bodies" (321–322). Of this passage and its connections and continuities with Pynchon's second and third novels, *The Crying of Lot 49* (1966) and *Gravity's Rainbow* (1973), Laurent Milesi has written that it takes "up the theme of the trashable, convertible Jewish schlemihl, and remind[s] us implicitly that the massively technologized Jewish Holocaust bore witness to the 'advance' as much as to the failure of modern civilization."[29] Milesi's point, that Auschwitz marks both the nadir and zenith of "modern civilization," underscores Pynchon's interest in the ways that those most modern of civilizations—Nazi Germany and Soviet Russia—strive to erase accident in order to consolidate political power.

The Fortuitousness That Pervades Reality

As Virilio suggests, the notion that accident is tied to scientific progress is not merely of aesthetic or academic concern but also has serious political ramifications ("[E]ach of us," he writes, "has learned from experience that dictatorships are not 'natural disasters'").[30] The heart of *V.* is the connection between Profane's experience with chance and an exploration of the totalitarian impulse.[31] The structural center of the novel, "Mondaugen's Story," is a lengthy meditation not on the "photographs of Auschwitz" mentioned by SHROUD, but rather on an earlier, less well-known instance of genocide, when in 1904 the German colonial administration in Southwest Africa sought to "exterminate systematically every Herero man, woman and child they could find" (264).[32]

As others have noted, Pynchon's critique of imperialism as containing the roots of totalitarianism owes much to Hannah Arendt's *The Origins of Totalitarianism* (1951), and it is worth parsing some of Arendt's formulations.[33] Arendt's controversial study was influential in arguing, among other things, that however far left or right they are on the political spectrum, Nazism and Stalinism are both varieties of totalitarianism, a modern form of state that has developed from imperialist tendencies.[34] While Arendt's ideas about the relationship between imperialism and totalitarianism certainly clarify the echoes and associations among *V.*'s constituent parts, I want to turn attention to those aspects of her work that explain why Pynchon would be so interested in the potential violence of designing chance.

One of Arendt's more influential arguments in *Origins* is that totalitarianism perverts reality itself, so that it becomes difficult for those living under totalitarian regimes to distinguish fictions of the state from objective reality. This idea was taken up, as we saw in chapter 1, by many thinkers critical of Soviet-style totalitarianism. Arendt frames her discussion specifically in terms of fiction as she argues that the presence of chance can be a way to distinguish objective reality from ideology:

> What the masses refuse to recognize is the fortuitousness that pervades reality. They are predisposed to all ideologies because they explain facts as mere examples of laws and eliminate coincidences by inventing

an all-embracing omnipotence which is supposed to be at the root of every accident. Totalitarian propaganda thrives on this escape from reality into fiction, from coincidence into consistency.

The chief disability of totalitarian propaganda is that it cannot fulfill this longing of the masses for a completely consistent, comprehensible, and predictable world without seriously conflicting with common sense....

In other words, while it is true that the masses are obsessed by a desire to escape from reality because in their essential homelessness they can no longer bear its accidental, incomprehensible aspects, it is also true that their longing for fiction has some connection with those capacities of the human mind whose structural consistency is superior to mere occurrence. The masses' escape from reality is a verdict against the world in which they are forced to live and in which they cannot exist, since coincidence has become its supreme master and human beings need the constant transformation of chaotic and accidental conditions into a man-made pattern of relative consistency.[35]

In this formulation, totalitarianism thrives on eliminating the threat of absolute chance. For reasons evident in *V.*—from the random destruction wrought by bombs to the minor accidents that plague Benny Profane—a reality rooted in the existence of absolute chance is threatening, and it would perhaps be more comforting to live under the aegis of a different kind of reality, one in which there is no chance, but rather an "all-embracing omnipotence which is supposed to be at the root of every accident." Arendt's argument emphasizes the narrative quality of totalitarianism, and her conceptualization is marked by the language of fiction. The totalitarian phenomenon is characterized by an "escape from reality into fiction" precisely because it is "all-embracing," "consistent, comprehensible . . . predictable" and subject to a "man-made pattern." The result is an extermination of absolute chance.

Viewed from a slightly different perspective, Arendt's remarks could describe Herbert Stencil's approach to the world: he denies the operation of absolute chance in favor of a theory that reads ostensible accidents as evidence of a conspiracy so "all-embracing" that it explains "every accident." The parallels between Arendt's analysis and Stencil's worldview in fact suggest the political dimension of the novel's explorations of chance and violence. Arendt's version of totalitarianism functions by closing "the masses" off from reality and replacing this reality with a fiction so vast that it explains even the inexplicable (think Jimmy Concannon's thrown wheel). In *V.*, Pynchon takes this important insight and plays with varieties of design, so it is not only Stencil's conspiracy theories that design chance but also the novel itself, whose "random patterns" betoken the "structural consistency" of all narratives.

Arendt's thoughts about totalitarianism help explain how attention to the differences between absolute chance and narrative chance allows Pynchon to analyze the workings of political regimes undergirded by all-encompassing fictions in *V.*'s chapter about nascent totalitarianism and genocide. This chapter is told from the perspective of Kurt Mondaugen, a young German engineer who travels to Southwest Africa in 1922 to monitor atmospheric radio disturbances, or sferics, in the area. He arrives as the local Bondel population is rising up against the Germans, who still occupy the area and control its wealth by exploiting native labor. To avoid what one character calls the impending "blood bath" (251), Mondaugen heads to the fortresslike villa of the farmer Foppl. Once Mondaugen reports the news of the uprising, Foppl decides to seal off the villa from the outside world and begins a months'-long "Siege Party" rife with all manner of drunken excess and sexual license. Although Mondaugen attempts to remain detached from the debauchery around him by attending his equipment, he eventually finds himself drawn into the decadent, hallucinatory world of Vera Meroving, an instantiation of Lady V, and her protégée, the young Hedwig Vogelsang. During his time sealed in Foppl's compound, as Mondaugen's days and nights become increasingly dreamlike, he is told stories of what happened in 1904, when General Lothar von Trotha issued the order to exterminate the local population.

Although he claims to have no hand in political matters, the novel implicates Mondaugen in the ways the genocide was enacted, an idea made visible by amplifying the issues of chance versus design found in the Profane sections. As is the case in much of *V.*, the facts in "Mondaugen's Story" are unstable because they are products of a story—or, in the parlance of the novel, a series of "yarns" far removed from any present event. Like the tale of his fictional predecessor Mr. Kurtz, Kurt Mondaugen's story about venturing into Africa is highly mediated by the time it reaches the novel's readers.[36] After experiencing two-and-a-half months at Foppl's in an alcohol-clouded, scurvy-wracked haze, Mondaugen tells his tale to Stencil—thirty-four years later—and Stencil then retells the story to Eigenvalue, so the version we read has become "Stencilized." In this way, Pynchon adds another level of uncertainty to the framed narrative of a book like *Heart of Darkness* (a haunting presence throughout the chapter) by having the whole story viewed through Stencil's peculiar interests and preoccupations. Moments of chance in "Mondaugen's Story" are therefore presented as evidence of a mystery or conspiracy that Stencil cannot quite put his finger on. When, for example, Mondaugen first encounters Hedwig Vogelsang, readers learn that "Mondaugen, overcome by the sudden scent of musk, brought in a puff to his nostrils by interior winds which could not have arisen by accident" (258). These winds could not be products of chance because for Stencil, Hedwig is connected to the Lady V and therefore to the V conspiracy, so there can be no such thing as accident, even an accidental breeze. When Mondaugen encounters

Vera Meroving herself, readers sense the Stencilization of statements such as: "Voilà: conspiracy already, without a dozen words having passed between them" (255) or "despite all efforts to hold it in check, their conspiracy grew" (261). Thus the form of the chapter itself—like all of the chapters that convert "random caries into cabals"—enacts the tension between chance and design that implies a similarity between Stencil's actions and incipient totalitarianism.

By making "Mondaugen's Story" thoroughly Stencilized, Pynchon emphasizes that, while not totalitarian in the later sense of Stalinism or Nazism that Arendt discusses, Southwest Africa under German rule is nevertheless a world in which absolute chance is given little room to maneuver. The sense that total design can make for more efficient genocide is suggested early in the chapter, when Mondaugen is "cornered" in the billiard room by Lieutenant Weissmann, the masochistic German official who will attain full-flowering as a Nazi in *Gravity's Rainbow*. In *V.*, Weissmann is Vera Meroving's lover, an attachment consistent with the novel's internal logic, which links Lady V to violence and states of siege. As he traps Mondaugen in the billiard room, site of random trajectories and an echo of Profane's misfortunes with his lover Fina, Weissmann proves himself a proto-Nazi by asking Mondaugen whether he has heard of "Mussolini? Fiume? Italia irredenta? Fascisti? National Socialist German Workers' Party? Adolf Hitler?" (261). As Weissmann is connected to the genocidal violence done to the Hereros in the name of imperialism, his barrage of questions reflects Arendt's idea that the seeds of totalitarianism are found in imperialist sensibilities.[37] But beyond identifying the continuities among capitalism, Western imperialism, and totalitarianism, Weissmann's interaction with Mondaugen also emphasizes the centrality of a particular kind of design to an imperialist—and later totalitarian—genocidal project.

When Weissmann dismisses Mondaugen by saying "From Munich, and never heard of Hitler" (Ibid.), Mondaugen responds by claiming exemption from political matters:

> "I'm an engineer, you see. Politics isn't my line."
> "Someday we'll need you," Weissmann told him, "for something or other, I'm sure. Specialized and limited as you are, you fellows will be valuable...."
> "Politics is a kind of engineering, isn't it. With people as your raw material."
> "I don't know," Weissmann said. (262)

As an engineer who takes refuge in "the comforts of Science" (271), Mondaugen thinks he can remain apolitical and roam the countryside avoiding the violence around him. But Weissmann makes it clear that it is precisely his specialization, his engineering ability, that will make him valuable "someday"—a someday marked, readers know, by the ascension of German fascism. As an emblem of a particular kind of science, Mondaugen represents the incipient totalitarian's claims to "scientificality," which Arendt calls a "surrogate for power."[38] The specific dangers of such scientificality are apparent in Mondaugen's comparison of politics to engineering: his notion that "people [function] as your raw material," recalls the eerie "chamber of horrors" in which SHROUD and SHOCK are subjected to meticulously engineered torture.[39]

If SHROUD and SHOCK are the clearest examples of things "entirely lifelike in every way" crushed by the violence of engineered accident, then their bizarre presence in the novel helps us see that far from being exempt from genocidal policies, Mondaugen and his colleagues can in the wrong context actually make them more efficient (311). The control of chance is "valuable" to both the creation of the current imperialist project, and to what was depicted in those "photographs of Auschwitz," because both depend on design, coordination, and engineering that attempts to leave nothing to chance. In *Gravity's Rainbow*, Mondaugen himself works on the cooling systems of Nazi rocketry; in *V.*, the benefits of an "engineer's way" is intimated as Foppl tells stories about 1904, when he participated in the extermination of the Hereros: "Logistics at the time were sluggish. Procedure was simple: one led the fellow or woman to the nearest tree, stood him on an ammunition box, fashioned a noose of rope (failing that, telegraph or fencing wire), slipped it round his neck, ran the rope through a fork in the tree and secured it to the trunk, kicked the box away" (265).[40] This passage could serve as an illustration for what Arendt called the "peculiar 'shapelessness' of the totalitarian government"; she suggested that the state's fantasy of total control—of escaping reality into fiction—was undermined by the relative inefficiency of the bureaucracy.[41] As an engineer with little concern for people, Mondaugen responds to this talk of "logistics" and "procedure" in "his nit-picking engineer's way, 'but with so much telegraph wire and so many ammunition boxes lying around, logistics couldn't have been all that sluggish'" (265).[42] His reflexive interest in "logistics" rather than the people being hung in trees demonstrates Mondaugen's potential value: he can streamline the killing process by attending to minute details. It is Mondaugen who views people as "raw material": he hardly blanches at the ethicality of what Foppl describes, but instead focuses on the logistics of the problem as presented him. In viewing the situation as a design problem to be solved, he ignores the human element of the situation in favor of a fiction of total control.

A more pointed critique than even Mondaugen's inability to see human suffering for the engineering problem (whose solution would create more suffering) is found in another chapter, which includes poetry by a Maltese "engineer-poet" named Dnubietna. That chapter takes place on Malta as German planes are bombing the island. The guiding metaphor of the poem is the catenary, the mathematical expression of how a chain hangs when acted on by gravity:

> If I told the truth
> You would not believe me.
> If I said: no fellow soul
> Drops death from the air, no conscious plot
> Drove us underground, you would laugh
> As if I had twitched the wax mouth
> Of my tragic mask into a smile—
> A smile to you; to me the truth behind
> The catenary: locus of the transcendental:
> $y = a/2\ (e^{x/a} + e^{-x/a})$. (360–361)

The first thing one may notice is the echo of Eigenvalue's critique of Stencil's method: Dnubietna sees no "conscious plot" to the world, just as Eigenvalue chides Stencil's efforts to see "conscious organization" everywhere. For Dnubietna, the universe is unplanned: physics and mathematics may explain its rules, but these rules themselves do not imply conscious engineering. And yet subjected as he is to constant bombardment by Nazi war planes, Dnubietna's compatriot, Fausto Maijstral, considers the poem a "lie" since there is indeed an obvious and inescapable "conscious plot" to lay siege to Malta. While it is doubtless the case that the exact locations of discrete bomb hits are matters of chance, what is relevant to Fausto (and Pynchon) is that a "fellow soul" certainly does drop "death from the air." By privileging mathematical proofs like the catenary, which are just "out there," Dnubietna ignores the uses to which such proofs may be put. Humans can exploit the laws of the universe so that things that appear matters of chance are actually the products of design.

Thomas Schaub has written that Dnubietna's poem, "denuded of human experience and value, is an early example of the threat which the engineering mind poses."[43] In conceptualizing the world with an "engineering mind," Dnubietna sees the bombings not as "the result of conscious design but merely the way things 'hang.' Such a view takes the consciousness out of history and divorces events and values. It is an engineer's poetic: things happen because it is in their nature to do so; an apple falls not because someone wills it but because in this world that is what ripe apples do." It certainly seems accurate to suggest that Dnubietna's aesthetic "divorces events and values"; after all, noticing the randomness of the universe does not necessarily legitimate treating people like the "raw material" necessary to sustain a V conspiracy or a genocidal campaign. When Schaub identifies the "threat which the engineering mind poses," he implies that this mind leads to overdetermination and overdesign without regard to human value. Dnubietna's poem is one way the novel demonstrates the ethical implications of designing chance—things that appear to merely "hang," as Schaub puts it, are in fact dangerous precisely because real human beings are being made to hang at the hands of other human beings. An engineering mind like Mondaugen's or Dnubietna's will fret about how such phenomena may be accounted for statistically or mathematically, rather than whether or why they should occur at all—hence Mondaugen's blinking response to Foppl's tales of hanging Hereros from trees.

Put differently, the problem in *V.* occurs when things are *purported* to be chance—or simply "out there"—which are not. An example from "Mondaugen's Story" illustrates the ways that *V.*'s own design differs from the design implied by Dnubietna and Mondaugen, and enacted by Stencil. Earlier in the chapter, before he is cornered by Weissmann, Mondaugen comes upon Foppl in the process of whipping a Bondel, Andreas, to death: "As if the entire day had come into being only to prepare him for this, he discovered a Bondel male, face-down and naked, the back and buttocks showing scar tissue from old sjambokings as well as more recent wounds, laid open across the flesh like so many toothless smiles" (259). The odd simile recalls the "smile" of the catenary in Dnubietna's poem, something that merely happens in the universe and so ought to be accepted without value judgment. But the open wounds on the Bondel's back are, of course, not simply phenomena that appeared in the universe by chance or natural law—unlike the catenary, this smile is evidence of a perversion of nature. To Foppl, it seems natural to exercise his superiority through violence; just as physical laws dictate a chain hang in uniform ways, the subjugation of the local population by the Germans, bound up as it is in millennial Christian rhetoric, seems inevitable to him. As he says to Andreas: "Your people have defied the Government . . . they've rebelled, they have sinned. . . . Like Jesus returning to Earth, von Trotha is coming to deliver you. . . . And until then love me as your parent, because I am von Trotha's arm, and the agent of his will" (Ibid.).

But Foppl's argument is undercut by the structure of the novel as a whole. By drawing a metaphorical connection between the catenary (which is simply "out there") and the wounds on Andreas's back (which represent a perversion of nature), Pynchon demonstrates that although someone like Mondaugen or Dnubietna may emphasize the continuities between them, there is a crucial value difference to be recognized. It is not that Pynchon is making the banal point that torture is bad, but rather that confusing ideology with objective reality legitimates atrocity because atrocity is seen as part of the "natural" order of the ideology-as-reality, and thus not atrocity at all.

The larger structure of *V.*, in fact, contextualizes the claustrophobic impulse to total design in "Mondaugen's Story" as evidence of imperialist, proto-totalitarian ideology. Another perversion of reality that turns on the catenary occurs in a later scene, set back in 1904 during the days of von Trotha, when the captured Hereros were chained together by the neck and force-marched: "From the side it always looked medieval, the way the chain hung down in bights between their neck-rings, the way the weight pulled them constantly toward earth, the force only just overcome as long as they managed to keep their legs moving" (284). As a striking, real-life example of the catenary described in Dnubietna's poem, the hanging chains used to subjugate a population might be read by an engineer like Mondaugen as only an "out there" law of the universe. Were Mondaugen thus to observe this scene (and it may indeed be he who is imaginatively reconstructing it in a dream), he would pause on the evidence of gravitational force ("the weight pulled them constantly toward earth") and the counteracting physical "force"—he would, in other words, note the interaction of physical forces rather than the human suffering caused by such forces.

When Pynchon incorporates an awareness of the physical laws of the universe, however, he does so to remind readers that even though such laws are indeed acting on the chain linking the neck-rings (and that this force is itself not, as Dnubietna points out, a product of a "conscious plot"), the fact of the neck-rings and chains themselves are nevertheless evidence of atrocity and terror. The problem with Mondaugen's point of view is that it focuses on the physical laws of the universe to the exclusion of all other considerations—hence his interest in the logistics of hanging rather than in, say, the people being murdered. In V., genocide depends on absorbing chance insofar as it incorporates physical laws like the catenary—something merely "out there"—as part of its larger project, a project that cannot exist without exploiting such physical laws. This relationship is made visible by the catenary itself, the physical chains linking the Hereros and converting them to what Mondaugen calls "raw material."

Sparks, Nose Jobs, and Mid-Century America

Given all this discussion of atrocious acts committed sixty years before the novel's publication and in a place most Americans could probably not identify on a map, it is worth asking why Pynchon weaves this material in with descriptions of Benny Profane bouncing around New York City in 1956. Part of the reason is that these acts are analogues to acts committed in the name of a Cold War cultural logic that dictated the norms not only of orthodox Marxists like the huge and homicidal Russian but also of another modern scientific nation—triumphant postwar America. As Profane discovers with SHOCK and SHROUD, a faith in scientific progress leads many Americans to confuse or substitute ideologies for objective reality; for Pynchon, science is its own ideology, but for many of his characters, science is a way to control or master objective reality. If Profane's "Whole Sick Crew" is an echo of the "curious crew . . . thrown together" at Foppl's compound, then the goings-on of Profane and his acquaintances are the inheritance of the imperial histories depicted in the other chapters (253).

One chapter, for example, is a highly detailed description of Esther Harvitz's nose job. Despite the numerous instances of genocidal atrocity in V., Ronald Cooley finds in this short chapter "[p]erhaps the most unpleasant passage in the entire novel," partly because it brings together the clinical and the pornographic in an act of aesthetic murder.[44] Esther, who wants "a Jew nose in reverse," trusts her lover and plastic surgeon, Dr. Schoenmaker, to give her a nose "[i]dentical with an ideal of nasal beauty established by movies, advertisements, magazine illustrations. Cultural harmony, Schoenmaker called it" (106). As Schoenmaker operates on Esther, he seems to turn her into a lifelike object on the order of SHOCK or SHROUD; Mondaugen might approve of his treating her as the "raw material" that could achieve an abstract "ideal," a connection emphasized as Schoenmaker slips occasionally into a cartoon German accent: "Now ve shorten das septum, ja" (111). The implication, of course, is that contemporary American attitudes, though by-products of capitalism and democratic freedom, nevertheless echo the fictions of totalitarian ideology—even to the extent that Esther would sacrifice her own body to conform to the aesthetics of magazine illustrations.[45] Another such echo occurs later in the novel when, during a debate about the morality of abortion, Esther compares that sacrifice to the Holocaust. To another character, who has just referred to a fetus as "[a] complex protein molecule, is all," Esther replies, "I guess on the rare occasions you bathe you wouldn't mind using Nazi soap made from one of those six million Jews" (393).[46] There is not necessarily a logical or causal connection between "Mondaugen's Story" and Esther's story, but this is part of the novel's structural point: there are nevertheless aesthetic correspondences and ineffable thematic echoes that cannot be rationally accounted for, but that are crucial to understanding the novel's view of reality and history, which is that sometimes things just happen.

Indeed, for all of Stencil's impulses to draw connections and impute motives to "the surface accidents of history" (164), the novel still suggests that, like the caries that occur in teeth, history is subject to accident—no matter the fantasies of political systems that would insist otherwise. In the epilogue, which depicts the buildup to the 1919 June Disturbances on Malta (another result of colonialism, this time British rather than German), Stencil's father, Sidney, muses about a "few Mizzists and Bolshevists [who] were doing their best to drum up enthusiasm for a riot among the Dockyard workers . . . But for some reason a spark was missing" (530), a passage that recalls Lenin's famous assertion that "Revolution is Communism plus spark."[47]

Ultimately, V stands for absolute chance, for that "spark" that can never quite be explained. "Why do wars start," Stencil asks, "if one knew why there would be eternal peace. So in this search the motive is part of the quarry" (428). *V.* is in part an attempt to understand the spark, that which cannot be narrated, which is coded in the novel as absolute chance. This is the spark, the "V-ness" that will always elude Stencil the younger: in order to have a total comprehension of any event, however major or minor, in order to characterize it as an example of design, one must find "that missing catalyst. Any minor accident: a break in the clouds, a catastrophic shivering at the first tentative blow to a shop window, the topology of an object of destruction . . . anything might swell a merely mischievous humor to suddenly apocalyptic rage" (531). The irony is that a "minor accident" cannot be explained as evidence of a larger design, and those who try are left, like Stencil is at the end of the novel, endlessly chasing another glimmer of Lady V, this one even farther removed from reality, "Mme. Viola, oneiromancer and hypnotist" (502).

Narrative Chance After *V.*

As one of the first in a growing line of big postmodern novels, *V.* is significant for the ways that it represents the complexities of the twentieth-century political and cultural landscape; as a Cold War novel, it is significant for the ways it reflects cultural preoccupations with the control or manipulation of chance. In his analysis of the violent potential of narrative chance, Pynchon is a precursor to a body of later twentieth-century American fiction that attempts to navigate an individual's place in a historical epoch increasingly characterized by political rhetoric. The foregoing reading of *V.*—which emphasizes Pynchon's interest in representing chance in narrative that does not amount to the sort of totalitarian fiction making described by Hannah Arendt—suggests one entry point for exploring numerous other American novels that both register the Cold War and exhibit an interest in chance and accident.

One way to read Pynchon's own career, in fact, is as a series of experiments with the ways chance functions in the world and in fictional narrative; as Michiko Kakutani noted in a review of *Mason & Dixon* (1997), "The Great Big Question in Thomas Pynchon's novels, from 'V.' (1963) through 'Gravity's Rainbow' (1973) and 'Vineland' (1990) has been: Is the world dominated by conspiracies or chaos? Are there patterns, secret agendas, mysterious codes—in short, hidden design—to the burble and turmoil of human existence, or is it all a product of chance?"[48] As I have suggested throughout this chapter, this great big question cannot be answered without remarking the presence of Cold War cultural logic, a connection that has potential to illuminate much of Pynchon's work. His next novel, for example, the intricately plotted *The Crying of Lot 49* (1966), is aware of this cultural logic to the point of inducing "the orbiting ecstasy of a true paranoia"—the drive to create meaning from what are perhaps random signs— in both its protagonist and its reader.[49] Early on, the narrator describes an invented naval encounter off the coast of Carmel in 1863 as "the very first military confrontation between Russia and America. Attack, retaliation, both projectiles deep-sixed forever and the Pacific rolls on. But the ripples from those two splashes spread, and grew, and today engulf us all."[50] As the heroine Oedipa Maas moves through a world engulfed by the logic of the Cold War, she embarks on a special kind of hermeneutic enterprise as she tries to determine whether the strange signs she encounters are evidence of a conspiracy and thus a hidden explanation of Western history, or whether they are rather chance products of her own interpretations. As Oedipa wonders "how accidental" her brushes with this possible conspiracy are, the novel reminds us that these encounters occur in a specific cultural and political moment, one which is informed by those consequential ripples mentioned above.[51] Even Pynchon's more recent *Against the Day* (2006), his lengthiest novel to date, exhibits the vestiges of the relationship between chance and the Cold War. Set at the end of the nineteenth century, *Against the Day* explores the roots of modern American capitalist democracy and has as one unifying thread (among many) the antics of a group of dime-novel-inspired adventurers, The Chums of Chance, who float just above history in their airship, entangling themselves in swashbuckling of various sorts, including—in an early nod to Cold War rivalry that echoes the naval skirmish in *Lot 49*—encounters with their Russian counterparts in the airship *Bol'shaia Igra*, the Great Game.[52] While these brief examples are only suggestive, I hope that they are also somewhat provocative and indicate that attention to Pynchon's interest in chance within the context of the Cold War cultural frame has potential to explain some of his more puzzling formulations.

Once one looks for fiction that combines an interest in chance with an attempt to theorize the impact of the Cold War on individuals specifically and the notion of history more broadly, they seem to be everywhere. In naming just three novels, one from each successive decade after *V.*'s publication, one has the makings of a formidable list of American fiction with a postmodern bent: Robert Coover's *The Public Burning* (1977), Don DeLillo's *Libra* (1988), and Richard Powers's *The Gold Bug Variations* (1991) have all been thought of as enacting, challenging, or otherwise engaging a postmodern sensibility, and all in turn thematize Cold War history and ask questions about absolute chance and its relationship to various kinds of design.[53]

Coover's *The Public Burning* is a hallucinatory account of that emblem of Cold War logic, the trial and execution of Julius and Ethel Rosenberg in June 1953. The role of chance in history is a pervasive question throughout the novel, as when Richard Nixon himself seizes the idea that American freedom is somehow connected to absolute chance because it is opposed to Soviet design: "I'd realized what it was that had been bothering me: that sense that everything happening was somehow inevitable, as though it had all been scripted out in advance. But bullshit! There were no scripts, no necessary patterns, no final scenes, there was just *action*, and then *more action*! Maybe in Russia History had a plot because one was being laid on, but not here—*that was what freedom was all about!*"[54] Coover's ironic take on the American association of chance with democratic freedom suggests that those in power—in this case, Richard Nixon—actually conscript this freedom into unilateral action that winds up being as despotic as the Communist practice such action is purported to combat. As in *V.*, identifying the place of chance in history allows *The Public Burning* to draw an analogy between authoritarian states and the American political theater that had the Rosenbergs at its center.

As Coover uses the Rosenberg case as a focal point for his account of the high Cold War, Don DeLillo imagines another watershed moment little over a decade later, the assassination of President Kennedy. *Libra* is structured around the possibility that the event was a result of an elaborate conspiracy that could have ironically succeeded "in the short term due mainly to chance."[55] In an echo of the totalitarian fiction makers described in the preceding pages, DeLillo's conspirators (mainly ex-CIA men who plan to engineer an attempt on the president's life in order to justify a war with Castro's Cuba), want to "extend their fiction into the world" so that people become "characters in plots."[56] As is the case with numerous other works already discussed in this book, in *Libra*, there is the sense that, within the context of the Cold War rhetorical game, what is chance-based represents what is real so that, conversely, "conspiracy is everything that ordinary life is not."[57] Given this opposition, the conspirators of course want the conspiracy to *look* as though it was merely the unlikely success of a lone actor, and thus attempt to write Lee Harvey Oswald into history by creating a string of (seemingly) chance events that would confirm for the world that he acted alone—as one of them remarks, they endeavored to "Create coincidence so bizarre they [the public] have to believe it."[58] If a mark of "Soviet reality" is the denial of the accident, in DeLillo's paranoid novel, those behind the façade of American democratic freedom marshal chance in like ways to create a plot that does not seem like a plot in order to advance their Cold War agenda.

While Coover and DeLillo are explicitly interested in reviewing American political history, Richard Powers uses the Cold War as a backdrop for his big novel about chance and design, *The Gold Bug Variations* (the twinned plots take place in 1957 and in the early 1980s). The persistence of the Cold War, in other words, offers Powers a fertile rhetorical field in which to explore even larger questions about the chance nature of the universe. The 1950s plot concerns a team of American scientists exploring the newly discovered genetic code and trying to conjecture a coherent design to human life, which is the product of chance mutations on a evolutionary scale. The 1980s plot concerns a librarian, Jan O'Deigh, trying to piece together what happened to one of these scientists, Stuart Ressler, who fell off the map after the start of a promising career. As Jan becomes entangled in a love triangle, she discovers both Ressler's own love triangle and the notion that the universe is subject to absolute chance; there is, "[a]t bottom, no cause: only the life molecule, copying or failing to copy. . . . Life consists of propositions about chance by chance."[59] Such a revelation returns us both to the explorations of chance by Jacques Monod touched on in chapter 1 (Jan reads the same passage from *Chance and Necessity* about "our number" having come up in the cosmic "Monte Carlo game" discussed earlier) and also to the passage from *The Recognitions*, which opened this chapter.[60] This is not surprising as Powers has remarked that *The Recognitions* and *V.* have been particular influences on his own writing career, and, like Gaddis and Pynchon before him, he suggests that although science purports to solve the mysteries of existence, there are still innumerable moments, often coded as absolute chance, which simply are and which cannot accordingly be accounted for.[61] The project of *The Gold Bug Variations* is thus to recognize the power of chance, but to do so while also acknowledging the complex designs—prominent ones in the novel are genetic, musical, and aesthetic—that give coherence and meaning to human life.

I mention these novels to suggest, if only briefly, that the intersections among chance and Cold War rhetoric found in *V.* are hardly anomalous, and that for those writing in the postmodern tradition—the books mentioned in this chapter are dense, often difficult novels with an unusual range—chance was a consistent source of interest because of its circulation in Cold War culture. Pynchon's first novel is merely an early example of an interest that would in other hands encourage an even more radical innovation in the ways that fictional telling could embody political engagement.

3

The Zemblan Who Came in from the Cold

Nabokov's Cold War

In his revised autobiography, *Speak, Memory* (1966), Vladimir Nabokov recounts two chance events that had come to haunt his later life and fiction: the moment when his father was murdered by an assassin's bullet meant for another and the moment when as a boy Nabokov happened upon his brother Sergey's diary. That the accidental death of Nabokov's father (born July 20) was personally significant—and a plausible germ for the accidental shooting of John Shade in *Pale Fire* (1962) on July 21, 1959—seems obvious; what is less clear is why his youthful snooping should be so poignant to him as a man in his sixties. Part of the answer comes toward the end of *Speak, Memory*, when the usually eloquent Nabokov admits that for "various reasons I find it inordinately hard to speak about my other brother [Sergey]."[1] What he does remember with characteristic vividness, however, is the moment he transgressed his brother's personal privacy: "[A] page from his diary that I found on his desk and read, and in stupid wonder showed to my tutor, who promptly showed it to my father, abruptly provided a retroactive clarification of certain oddities of behavior on his part."[2] These "oddities" pertained, no doubt, to Sergey's homosexuality, about which the grown Nabokov had long felt uncomfortable, and which is referred to so obliquely in the autobiography that it remains—like Sergey himself—virtually absent. By couching his brother's homosexuality as an unspoken secret that would have been better left undiscovered, Nabokov in *Speak, Memory* confines the treatment of homosexuality to elliptical code words: Sergey is accorded a scant few sentences and thus barely exists for the reader. In the novel *Pale Fire*, on the other hand, the voluble Charles Kinbote gives over hundreds of pages of his "Commentary" to the tale of mythical Zembla, a narrative that functions, in part, to manage the open secret of Kinbote's own homosexuality. This secret makes him the object of persecution by a Cold War community that displaces a patriotism based on anti-Communism with a patriotism based on something equally destructive—homophobia. If the previous chapter showed that Pynchon used chance to ask questions about narrative representation, this chapter turns attention to chance to change how we understand one of the most important and written about novels of the later twentieth century. Indeed, to read *Pale Fire* as reproducing the homophobia Kinbote encounters is to misread it, to fall for one of the critical traps Nabokov was so fond of laying for his readers. This chapter thus reads the numerous and varied chance moments in *Pale Fire* as central to the design of the novel and suggests that these moments make visible the ways the work intervenes in mid-century controversies about Communism and sexuality.

Aesthetics as Politics

Although *Pale Fire* has long been read as only an old-world aesthete's novel of wordplay and allusion that is blissfully disengaged from real-world Cold War politics, it is in fact this very wordplay that allows Nabokov to engage cultural narratives that prescribed the limits of mid-century reality—a word that Nabokov tended to use gingerly, with quotation marks.[3] In *Pale Fire*, the politics of late 1950s America look enough like the containment narrative touched on in chapter 1 (and Kinbote's invented Zembla looks enough like a Soviet satellite state) that we ought to ask to what end Nabokov is refracting real-world politics through the prism of his aesthetics. The aspect of Cold War political culture of particular importance to *Pale Fire* is the pervasive practice of eliding differences among the so-called enemies of democratic freedom to read homosexual people as political threats on par with Communists. For Nabokov, the logic of what I will refer to as the homophobic narrative was as tragically absurd as the logic of Kinbote's tale of Zembla, a parallel made visible by noticing how both phenomena attempt to control or manage chance.[4] Nabokov challenges the cultural logic of the homophobic narrative by allowing chance to infiltrate his novel on the local linguistic level, as well as on the broader level of plot. The novel's form frustrates linear reading not only because we are asked to hop from footnote to footnote—in a manner familiar to those who read hypertext—but also because the text itself is dense with allusions, puns, and other wordplay. Such moments are more than just examples of Nabokov's multilingual virtuosity, however, for they can be read as instances of political intervention. As Jonathan Culler reminds us, puns foreground "an opposition that we find difficult to evade or overcome: between accident or meaningless convergence and substance or meaningful relation. We treat this opposition as a given, presuming that any instance must be one or the other. But puns, or punning, may help us to displace the opposition by experiencing something like 'meaningful coincidence' or 'convergence that affects meaning,' convergence that adumbrates an order *to be* comprehended or explored."[5] Culler's proposition is helpful for understanding *Pale

Fire in the Cold War rhetorical context I have sketched in the previous chapters because it suggests that puns negotiate the difference between chance and design. As sites of "meaningful coincidence," of two perhaps-chance vectors meeting to form meaning, puns are also examples of how chance can expose the explanatory poverty of narratives that shun absolute chance in the hope of diminishing or closing off meaning—not only those totalitarian narratives described in previous chapters but also the American homophobic narrative, which equates homosexuality with everything from minor forms of subversion to outright treason.

The play among various types of designed coincidence and the sort of chance "meaningless convergence" that, Culler suggests, puns make possible characterizes much of *Pale Fire*. Not only do puns, slips of the pen, life-changing accidents, and uncanny coincidences abound in Shade's poem "Pale Fire" and in Kinbote's "Commentary" on this poem, but as virtually every *Pale Fire* critic has noticed, the novel also crackles with coincidences and correspondences among its parts. That is, the distinct sections of *Pale Fire*, ostensibly written by two separate characters, exhibit coincidental similarities and echoes that demand attention; I suggest that we ought to take such coincidences as thematic.[6] Nabokov associates the profuse meanings of his text with the complexity of the real world, neither of which can be accounted for by cultural narratives that close down varieties of meaning.[7]

Kinbote's scholarly work in *Pale Fire* makes meaning from coincidences—he perceives a meaning in Shade's text that is unrelated to the meaning we presume is intended by the poet, a perception based on chance textual or linguistic associations. This misreading does to Shade's text what Culler's puns do for readers: it exposes the uncomfortably short distance between "meaningless convergence" and "meaningful relation." Some plot exposition will clarify how this relationship works in *Pale Fire*: Charles Kinbote, an annoying and mentally unstable scholar, has rented the house next door to the famed and beloved poet John Shade, who is working on a longish poem in heroic couplets called "Pale Fire." When Shade is accidentally shot by an insane-asylum escapee (who mistakes him for Judge Goldsworth, the owner of the home Kinbote is renting), Kinbote absconds with the manuscript of "Pale Fire" and begins to compose the annotations that make up the bulk of *Pale Fire*-the-novel. Although Shade's poem is about his marriage, the suicide of his daughter, and his own mortality, Kinbote's exegesis centers on an imagined version of himself: his notes have little to do with Shade's subject but instead tell the tale of the deposed King Charles II of Zembla, a political refugee who turns out to be Kinbote himself. We also learn that in Kinbote's fantasy, he is posing as a college professor in order to evade Jakob Gradus, a Communist-like "Extremist" assassin who is hunting Kinbote across the globe. When Gradus finally arrives in New Wye, home of Shade and quiet Wordsmith College (sometimes referred to as Wordsmith University), he aims for Kinbote but "quite accidentally" hits Shade, which for Kinbote neatly explains the poet's meaningless death at the hand of a mental patient actually seeking revenge on the judge who put him away.[8] While the genesis of the Zembla narrative is Kinbote's pariah status as a homosexual in the New Wye (New York) community of 1958 to 1959, the engine driving much of the tale—the assassination plot—exists to convert Shade's accidental death from a freak chance event to an effect explicable by clear causal progression.[9] In short, through Kinbote's narrativization, Shade's death paradoxically becomes both cause and effect of the Zembla story.[10]

Chance and the Homophobic Narrative

As Kinbote relates the gripping tale of his escape from Revolutionary Zembla, he also insists that before the Extremists staged their coup Zembla was a land where sexuality could be practiced in all its forms, and King Charles himself was openly homosexual, but is now compelled to keep a lower profile—both politically and sexually—in the States. The novel's emphasis on Kinbote's sexuality parodies the contemporary homophobia of Cold War psychiatrists and social critics, and, as I have said, ultimately suggests that homophobic narratives are as far-fetched as Kinbote's Zembla narrative. This idea can be made visible by looking at the ways Nabokov is writing in and against very specific cultural narratives; and the ways the novel exploits chance, linguistic and otherwise, as a strategy for destabilizing the staid homophobic narrative of the 1950s and early 1960s. In the end, I hope this argument will not only suggest that greater attention be paid to the ways that Nabokov's ethics are enfolded into his aesthetics in this and all his mature works but also the ways in which *Pale Fire* in particular makes chance legible as political critique.[11]

Nabokov links the chance inherent in language with homosexual political treason by having Kinbote conflate or confuse his sexuality with his insistence that he is King Charles, a claim made visible to readers by his coincidental analysis of "Pale Fire." In the "Foreword," for example, the chairman of his department at Wordsmith College takes Kinbote aside to urge that he "be more careful" because a "boy had complained to his adviser" (25). After explaining that he merely criticized the literature course of a fellow professor, Kinbote laughs in "sheer relief" and muses to himself: "[The chairman] always behaved with such exquisite courtesy toward me that I sometimes wondered if he did not suspect what Shade suspected, and what only three people (two trustees and the president of the college) definitely knew" (25). Kinbote figures himself as suspect, yet the thing that few people "definitely knew" would differ depending on who was asked—the chairman is warning Kinbote about monitoring his sexuality, whereas Kinbote assumes the warning is about maintaining his incognito as mild-mannered college professor.[12]

An iteration of this early conflation bookends the final movement of the novel: when Kinbote and Shade are walking across the lawn where Shade will soon be shot. Knowing that "Pale Fire" is complete, or nearly so, Kinbote makes Shade an offer:

"And if you agree to show me your 'finished product,' there will be another treat: I promise to divulge to you *why* I gave you, or rather *who* gave you, your theme."
"What theme?" said Shade absently...
"Our blue inenubilable Zembla..."
"Ah," said Shade, "I think I guessed your secret quite some time ago."
(288)

Despite his best efforts, Kinbote-the-suspect is unable to stabilize the meaning of certain words—in this case "secret." Although Shade has been privy to the fevers of Kinbote's mind (unlike the chairman), the guessed secret here refers to Kinbote's mental instability, a state of mind at least partly induced by the fact that the homophobic narrative figures Kinbote's homosexuality as pathological, the results of which, as Shade has also guessed, trigger the Zembla narrative.[13] By this late in the novel, moreover, most readers also realize that for Kinbote the "extraordinary secret" (215) of his homosexuality and that of Zembla are virtually indistinguishable.

But this collapse invites certain questions about why Nabokov makes Kinbote a homosexual in the first place; why Kinbote's sexuality makes him the object of ridicule and distrust by the campus community; and why he covers his homosexuality with a narrative about a king deposed with the aid of the "ruddy Russia of the Soviet era" (77). Appending homosexuality to evil or subversive characters was standard practice for many American writers during the Cold War, so one might first assume that Nabokov's work merely exemplifies rather than criticizes such practice. In Norman Mailer's 1954 essay "The Homosexual Villain," for example, he writes: "At the time I wrote those novels [*The Naked and the Dead* (1948) and *Barbary Shore* (1951)] ... I did believe—as so many heterosexuals believe—that there was an intrinsic relation between homosexuality and 'evil,' and it seemed perfectly natural to me, as well as *symbolically* just, to treat the subject in such a way.... What I have come to realize is that much of my homosexual prejudice was a servant to my aesthetic needs."[14] Whereas Mailer suggests a relatively straightforward connection between a character's sexuality and his moral status, for Nabokov, such connections are far more subtle and complex, a complexity made visible by the novel's treatment of chance. As I explain below, Kinbote constructs a narrative so distrustful of chance that it offers the illusion of linguistic control—the very illusion of control that homosexuality was seen to threaten during the 1950s.[15]

Given Nabokov's well-known disdain for Sigmund Freud and his more savage applicators, it may seem strange indeed that he should endow Kinbote with the battery of negative psychological traits suggested by a homophobic narrative descended from Freud.[16] Kinbote is paranoid, megalomaniacal, disagreeable, jealous, petty, voyeuristic, and predisposed to seducing boys and young men, all of which were understood by 1950s psychiatrists and psychologists as characteristic psychological traits of homosexual people. Edmund Bergler's *Homosexuality: Disease or Way of Life?* (1956) is a representative example of mid-century thinking about homosexuality that identifies a short list of traits homosexual people are "imbued" with:

1. Masochistic provocation and injustice-collecting;
2. Defensive malice;
3. Flippancy covering depression and guilt;
4. Hypernarcissism and hypersuperciliousness;
5. Refusal to acknowledge accepted standards in nonsexual matters, on the assumption that the right to cut moral corners is due homosexuals as compensation for their "suffering";
6. General unreliability, also of a more or less psychopathic nature.[17]

Interested readers can find abundant examples of such traits in *Pale Fire*: Kinbote undoubtedly has general "defensive malice" toward people he thinks have injured him, from Shade's protective wife Sybil Shade to Gerald Emerald, the instructor who spurned his advances. His "hypernarcissism," "hypersuperciliousness," and "general unreliability" could be said to characterize the "Foreword," "Commentary," and "Index," and his remark on the penultimate page of the "Commentary" that "I have suffered very much, and more than any of you can imagine" (300) implies an explanation for his moral corner-cutting. In *Society and the Homosexual* (1953), Gordon Westwood asserted the Freudian notion that "[n]ot all homosexuals become even mild paranoids, but nearly all paranoids have repressed homosexual tendencies."[18] Kinbote is nothing if not paranoid, for even by the "Index" he is not "able, owing to some psychological block or the fear of a second G[radus], [to travel] to a city only sixty or seventy miles distant, where he would certainly have found a good library" (309). Jess Stearn begins his best-selling *The Sixth Man* (1961) with a lengthy catalogue of similar ills that accompany homosexuality, from jealousy-motivated murder to the indoctrination of boys, all of which culminates in the warning: "*Homosexuals can be anybody.*"[19]

I am suggesting, then, that *Pale Fire* criticizes the sociopolitical implications of a pop-Freudian understanding of homosexuality. This critique is evident not simply because Nabokov makes the paranoid Kinbote homosexual but because he has Kinbote displace homophobic logic with a political tale that reflects the norms of classic containment thinking (minus the homophobia). In his capacity as both sexual subversive and Cold Warrior, Kinbote challenges what the homophobic narrative claimed a homosexual person could be or do. Such claims are by now a familiar story: throughout the 1950s and into the 1960s, homosexuals were dangerous because they could convert heterosexuals and because they were yoked in specific ways to Communist subversion.[20] One finds a remarkable example of such linking in the 1951 Senate subcommittee report "Employment of Homosexuals and Other Sex Perverts in Government":

> The conclusion of the subcommittee that a homosexual or other sex pervert is a security risk is not based upon mere conjecture.... The lack of emotional stability which is found in most sex perverts and the weakness of their moral fiber, makes them susceptible to the blandishments of the foreign espionage agent. It is the experience of intelligence experts that perverts are vulnerable to interrogation by a skilled questioner and they seldom refuse to talk about themselves.... It is an accepted fact among intelligence agencies that espionage organizations the world over consider sex perverts who are in possession of or have access to confidential material to be prime targets where pressure can be exerted.[21]

According to the Senate subcommittee, homosexual people are dangerous for the opposite reason that spies are dangerous: whereas spies craftily manipulate people and situations to glean information, homosexuals are weak-minded and emotionally fragile and are thus susceptible to the machinations of the subversively strong-willed. Put in terms described earlier in this book, homosexual people are unsuitable for government employment because they embody the power of chance to disrupt design and control. The presence of homosexuals who "seldom refuse to talk about themselves" (is a better description of Kinbote possible?) heightens the chance of subversion, which in turn threatens the fantasy of governmental control. To remove homosexuals from government office based on the vulgar Freudian theories of Bergler and others is thus to remove another possibility that the democratic status quo would be subverted. *Pale Fire*, on the other hand, presents heterodox sexualities freed from the insistent conflations with treason.[22]

Nabokov uses chance to question the logic of such homophobic constructions of sexuality descended from Freud; by focusing attention on how coincidence operates in *Pale Fire*, we see that the chance present in the novel's shifting registers is controlled by both the driving narrative of Kinbote's Zembla tale and by those containment norms it apparently reflects. There is a moment in *Pnin* (1957)—the *New Yorker* sketches-turned-novel about another professor who appears at Wordsmith College—when the narrator remarks that a gas station attendant looks markedly like one of Pnin's colleagues, "one of those random likenesses as pointless as a bad pun."[23] This pronouncement bears special significance to *Pale Fire* because it links the potential for real-life coincidences to textual or linguistic coincidences. For Nabokov, in fact, it seems that part of a pun's work is to suggest, even on the minute phonemic level, that in a fictional world all ostensibly chance moments are actually examples of what I have called narrative chance. In 1967, Alfred Appel questioned Nabokov about coincidence by noting that "[s]ome critics may find the use of coincidence in a novel arch or contrived." Nabokov answered:

> But in "real" life they do happen. . . . Very often you meet with some person or some event in "real" life that would sound pat in a story. It is not the coincidence in the story that bothers us so much as the coincidence of coincidences in several stories by different writers, as, for instance, the recurrent eavesdropping device in nineteenth-century Russian fiction.[24]

The response reminds us once again that absolute chance must become narrative chance when it is interpreted as meaningful. One might say that for Nabokov, "coincidence" names a way of constituting meaning from chance depending on one's point of view. By the end of his response to Appel's question, in fact, Nabokov shifts from what he calls "'real' life" to the textual; what concerns him is "the coincidence of coincidences in several stories by different writers." It is not the mediocre novelist's acknowledgment that both absolute chance and meaningful coincidence occur in real life that annoys Nabokov but rather that popular nineteenth-century literary forms do not allow chance to exist in a fictional world. To exploit stock characters and other familiar devices is to create a world that is meant to be read in a single way, rather like the homophobic narrative that demanded homosexuality be read in the subversive way outlined above.

Returning once again to Culler's ideas about puns, it is doubly important that the arc of the Zembla narrative is described by Kinbote's invention of allusions and puns, an invention that seems to him proof of real-life coincidences. Kinbote writes over the homophobic narrative—which figures him as a political threat—with the Zembla narrative—which figures him as central to a stable government vulnerable to Communist-like Extremists. Despite its outward appearance of baggy monstrosity, Kinbote's "monstrous semblance of a novel" betrays an avid desire for control reminiscent of those totalitarian narratives of reality described in the previous chapters: in Kinbote's necessarily delimited universe, accidents and chance encounters abound, as do linguistic and textual uncertainties, all of which form causal chains to Gradus's accidental murder of Shade (86). What these numerous moments of circumstantial and linguistic chance amount to is not an imaginary world spun out of control, however, but rather one in which chance is introduced precisely so that Kinbote may control and fit it into his narrative explanation of Shade's death. But by narrativizing chance, Kinbote offers only the illusion of control—he attempts to order the inexplicability of Shade's death just as the homophobic narrative attempts to order the apparent inexplicability of homosexuality. In the end, Kinbote's control, like the control offered by the homophobic narrative, is illusory—it is a textual control that Nabokov suggests has little relevance to what Shade would call the "texture" of real life—Shade's poem "Pale Fire" is in fact partly a meditation on the existence and fertility of absolute chance (63).

The line from *Pnin* about "one of those random likenesses as pointless as a bad pun" reminds one of Brian Boyd's counsel to aspiring Nabokovians: "Whenever we hear something called 'pointless' in Nabokov, we should look for the hidden point."[25] With this advice in mind, recall that, although Shade is an Alexander Pope scholar, unlike his subject he will deign to pun, and his poem "Pale Fire" demonstrates that contrary to what *Pnin*'s narrator has to say, Nabokov's puns are hardly pointless. Written, as Kinbote informs us in his "Foreword," on index cards from July 2 to July 21, 1959 in New Wye, Appalachia, an imaginary locale that resembles upstate New York, "Pale Fire" is a collection of meditations on the suicide of Shade's daughter, Hazel, and on the poet's own ripening age. The poem centers around both Hazel's suicide and Shade's description of the events surrounding his short lecture position at the "Institute of Preparation for the Hereafter," an organization whose business it is to manage the ultimate unknown, death. For Shade, the Institute represents man's attempt to grasp fully the wonders of the universe, a notion that seems to Shade preposterous after a later epiphanic moment. He parodies this notion with a bilingual pun in the opening lines of canto three:

> *L'if*, lifeless tree! Your great Maybe, Rabelais:
> The grand potato.
> I.P.H., a lay
> Institute (I) of Preparation (P)
> For the Hereafter (H), or If, as we
> Called it—big if!—engaged me for one term
> To speak on death.
> (52)

Shade's phonetic dexterity here works on several registers: not only does I.P.H. sound like "if," but it also recalls the French *L'if*—yew tree, often associated with death; so thus "you, lifeless tree"; or "life, lifeless tree"—a cross-linguistic pun that points to a play on Rabelais: in "the grand potato" we are meant to hear the *"le grand peut-être"*—the great Maybe. For Shade, this pun, bad or not, is certainly not pointless and in fact allows him to lampoon the idea that the uncertainties of death can be accounted for institutionally. In his gloss on the passage, Kinbote groans over the slickness of the wordplay: "An execrable pun, deliberately placed in this epigraphic position to stress lack of respect for Death. I remember from my schoolroom days Rabelais' *soi-disant* 'last words' among other bright bits in some French manual: *Je m'en vais chercher le grand peut-être*" (222). Kinbote here perceives the explanatory power of puns that Culler articulates: although the narrator of *Pnin* associates puns with randomness, Kinbote worries that Shade has "deliberately placed" the pun to serve epigraphically for the whole of canto three—in other words, Kinbote is put off by the pointedness of Shade's pun. The "grand potato" / "*grand peut-être*" pun does not seem to "stress lack of respect for Death," as Kinbote insists, but rather stresses lack of respect for institutions—and, by extension, other man-made endeavors—that are designed to explain away the mysteries of the universe.[26] A pun is a perfect rhetorical strategy in this case, for its very unknowability makes it a metonym for the unknowability of life itself, a semantic instability that any I.P.H. should have a hard time categorizing, much less explaining.

Nova Zembla in the Cold War

Shade registers death's unknowability with a moment of pointed semantic instability, a significant move within the context of *Pale Fire* because Nabokov is interested in proliferating a meaning that cannot be easily accounted for. But Shade's pairing also bears reading in light of the Cold War rhetorical field; recall, for example, Tony Jackson's thoughts on the psychic weight of death in the Atomic Age: "[B]ecause the nuclear ending will be absolute . . . the idea of chance mushrooms into the Cold War mindset in general."[27] It is fitting that Shade, participant in an "antiatomic chat," should reflect not only on the chances of death but also on the possibility of overcoming the "absolute" nature of death-as-ending (49). Although Kinbote's more radical excursions into fantasy eclipse the semblance of real life manifest in Shade's New Wye existence, Nabokov is meticulous with his dates and cultural references, which reminds readers of a "nuclear ending" that is ever urgent. While New Wye is not a real place name, and Wordsmith College only resembles Cornell, the overt social issues and daily rhythms evident in "Pale Fire" and the glimpses of campus life Kinbote allows are very much of a specific time and place: Shade is a Frostian poet and family man who watches 1950s television with "Professor Pink," an atomic bomb-denouncing campus Communist (49); who mentions Russian spies (58); and who does his best to soften the ostracism of Kinbote-the-homosexual by the campus community (266). Within this context Shade composes his verse on death inspired both by the suicide of his daughter and by the urgency of his own mortality. Once we notice the resemblance of New Wye to the actual cultural landscape of America in the 1950s, then we might say that another reason for Shade's probing the finality of death could be the acute cultural fear of global destruction made possible by the atomic bomb, a fear that contributed to the promotion of cultural narratives such as the homophobic already described.

As the careful flickers of Ithaca in New Wye begin to attest, then, the universe of *Pale Fire* is a culturally specific one, and Nabokov allows flashes of Cold War cultural context to shape the unreal world of Zembla. If the tale of Zembla obscures the politically motivated homophobic narrative, then it explains why Kinbote should invent a tale about a revolution-plagued northern land bordering Russia.[28] Kinbote appropriates the logic of containment by transforming the idea of foreign threat from Communists to Extremists (Gradus and his cohorts) and figures Shade and himself as the domestic front in need of protection. In this way he converts himself, nominally confined to the role of political threat by the homophobic narrative, into an anti-subversive, into a Cold Warrior.

The tantalizing and tenuous connection between Russia and the fantasyland that renders causally explicable Shade's death is apparent in the very name of Kinbote's obsession. As Mary McCarthy was the first to note, Zembla can indeed be found on a map: "[T]here is an actual Nova Zembla, a group of islands in the Arctic Ocean, north of Archangel. The name is derived from the Russian *Novaya Zemlya*, which means 'new land.'"[29] McCarthy does not mention that during the late 1950s, Novaya Zemlya did not merely correlate to the icy land evoked by Swift and Pope, it was also a far-off place with a very particular political importance: the site where the Soviets tested their atomic bombs.[30] In the spring of 1958, something like Kinbote's homeland populated newspapers in both New Wye and New York: "Japanese scientist said today that Soviet nuclear tests last month had been carried out at Novaya Zemlya Island in the Arctic Ocean."[31] By November, a front-page article, "New Soviet Tests of Atom Weapons Disclosed by U.S.," pegged Novaya Zemlya as the testing ground.[32] And in a 1961 article, Hanson W. Baldwin, the well-known military editor for the *New York Times*, included a large map of the world showing that Novaya Zemlya was where the Soviets were conducting the majority of their nuclear testing (see figure 2).

It is fair to say, then, that Nabokov had the real Novaya Zemlya in mind as he set *Pale Fire* in a Cold War world, and that his readership in the early 1960s could have associated the name Zembla with the threat of nuclear war with its mother country, Russia.[33] With the palpable threat of the real Novaya Zemlya in mind, it is clear that the Revolution in Kinbote's Onhava, however romantic and improbable, can stand in its texture as Communism's threat to the status quo in America, as well as Zembla. Nabokov in fact insists on the resemblance between Zembla and a Russian satellite state when he has Kinbote return again and again to such a comparison.

Although Kinbote notes that Zemblans are "given to regicide" (95), he also insists that he (as King Charles) had brought unprecedented order to the land:

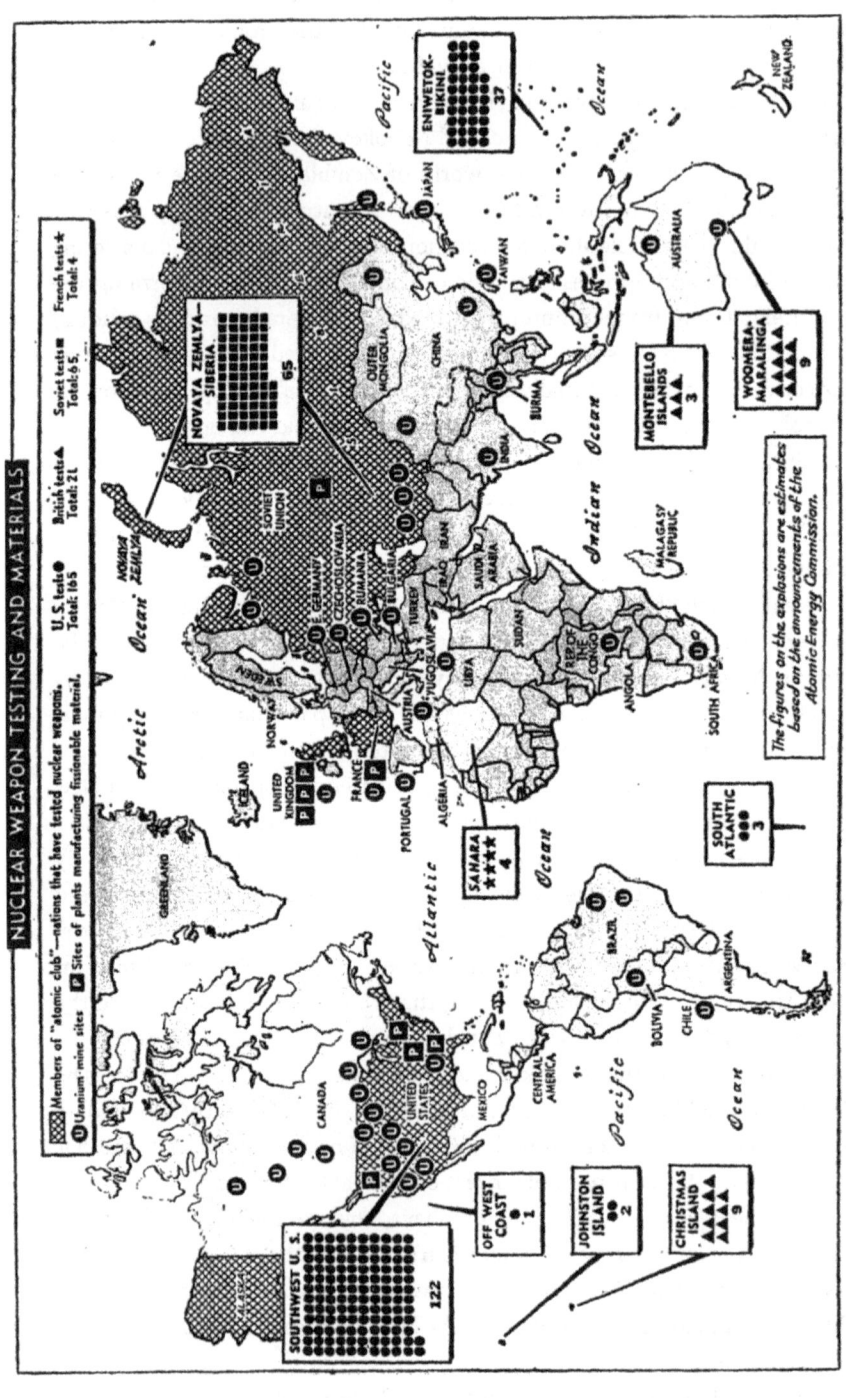

Figure 2. Map of global nuclear testing, circa 1961. Note that the Soviet Union carried out the greatest number of tests at the "Novaya Zemlya—Siberia" locations. From Hanson W. Baldwin, "Decision in Moscow: Khrushchev Is Seen Starting a New Phase of Power Politics," *New York Times* (September 3, 1961): E3.

"Harmony, indeed, was the reign's password" (75). Kinbote goes on to explain how under his reign everything from the "polite arts" to medical care flourished—until, that is, its "gigantic neighbor" began inciting revolutionary ideals (75). In this passage, Kinbote names the neighbor as "Sosed" (Russian for "neighbor" and, according to Brian Boyd, "an echo of *Sovietsky Soyuz*, the Soviet Union"), but at other points in the "Commentary" it is clear that the neighbor *is* Russia.[34] Kinbote mentions the influence of Russia on Zembla numerous times: "When I was a child, Russia enjoyed quite a vogue at the court of Zembla but that was a different Russia—a Russia that hated tyrants and Philistines, injustice and cruelty, the Russia of ladies and gentlemen and liberal aspirations" (245). By the time the hard-won harmony he had brought is challenged, Kinbote associates the chaos of the Zemblan Revolution with the Soviet Union: "The Royalists, or at least the Modems (Moderate Democrats), might have still prevented the state from turning into a commonplace modern tyranny, had they been able to cope with the tainted gold and the robot troops that a powerful police state ["which," Kinbote elsewhere reports, "some say is Russia" (138)] from its vantage ground a few sea miles away was pouring into the Zemblan Revolution" (119). Not only does the Zemblan Revolution take place on May 1, 1958 (Communist May Day), but when two Russians descend on the Royal Palace to find Kinbote's crown jewels, he remarks that "[s]omewhere an iron curtain had gone up," locating Zembla within the Soviet sphere of influence (131). With the Zemblan Revolution, the power Kinbote has over Zembla is shattered by Communist infiltration and fruit of this Revolution, as might be expected, is "gloom." In the gloss for Shade's phrase "gloomy Russians spied," Kinbote again draws a parallel between Zembla and Russia as gloom "is merely the outward sign of congested nationalism and a provincial's sense of inferiority—that dreadful blend so typical of Zemblans under the Extremist rule and of Russia under the Soviet regime" (243). If the real-life strategic importance of Novaya Zemlya as the Soviet Union's nuclear testing site is meant to be evoked in Kinbote's homeland, then it explains why Nabokov has Kinbote catalogue the news items in *The New York Times* Gradus is reading, the first of which is Khrushchev's visit to Zembla (274).[35] In real life, the front page of *The New York Times* on July 21, 1959 (the day Shade is shot), announced that Khrushchev's visit to "the north" had been postponed due to anti-Soviet sentiments.[36]

Kinbote Controls Chance

With the story of Zembla and its Revolution, Kinbote is not only inverting the homophobia of Cold War American culture, he is also reproducing a narrative that legitimates anti-Communist fears of subversion. Assuming Kinbote's Zembla narrative has little basis in the real world of *Pale Fire*, and that its textual existence in "Pale Fire" is a product of his own coincidental interpretations, it is striking that he channels his madness into a version of the classic Cold War contest between Soviet-style Communism and American democratic freedom. Even more striking, perhaps, is that Kinbote replaces democracy with a monarchy that centers on him, a governmental model that, for whatever else it does, offers Kinbote freedoms unavailable to him in the United States. As I have said, Kinbote often confuses or conflates these two narratives so the open "secret" of his homosexuality (for everyone else) is masked by the "extraordinary secret" of the Zemblan Revolution (for Kinbote). By reading the politically motivated homophobic narrative against the obviously political Revolution narrative, it becomes apparent that Kinbote links the American homophobic narrative with Communist-like repression. In other words, Kinbote's fevered narrative exposes a contradiction in a cultural logic that both assigns pathological status to sexual practices outside the mainstream and that attempts to assert freedom from Communism by denying freedom of sexuality. Ironically, however, though Kinbote's conflation amounts to a critique—by Nabokov—of both Communism and the homophobic narrative, Kinbote desires to integrate himself back into mainstream America by mimicking the function of an institution like I.P.H. and attempting to control the uncontrollable—Shade's accidental murder.

Kinbote attempts to control absolute chance by replacing texture with text: the complexity of life that Shade appreciates in "Pale Fire" is converted in the "Commentary" into a causal narrative designed to account for Shade's death. Kinbote's apparent textual control, however, is ineffective precisely because he fails to recognize the importance of wordplay or misprints or other chance moments. One goal of literary scholarship is to parse texts for connections, and Kinbote takes this to extremes—in his notes, Kinbote, like Stencil in Pynchon's *V.*, draws impossible connection after impossible connection so that in the Zembla narrative even accidents are explained and fitted into causal chains. This is similar to the civic logic invited by a government intent on exposing the connections between homosexuality and political subversion in order to reduce the chances of Communist infiltration and nuclear war. It thus makes sense that Kinbote resists anything not explicable by his scholarship/fantasy; in one of the mini-dramas that Kinbote relates, for example, the differences between the poet and his commentator become evident:

> SHADE: Life is a great surprise. I do not see why death should not be an even greater one.
> KINBOTE: Now I have caught you, John: once we deny a Higher Intelligence that plans and administers our individual hereafters we are bound to accept the unspeakably dreadful notion of Chance reaching into eternity.... The demons in their prismatic malice betray the agreement

between us and them, and we are again in the chaos of chance. Even if we temper Chance with Necessity and allow godless determinism, the mechanism of cause and effect, to provide our souls after death with the dubious solace of metastatistics, we still have to reckon with the individual mishap, the thousand and second highway accident of those scheduled for Independence Day in Hades. (225–226)

The first thing one might notice here is that chance is textually linked to the potential for political repression, for the "dreadful notion of Chance" recalls the "dreadful blend [of nationalism and inferiority] so typical of Zemblans under the Extremist rule and of Russia under the Soviet regime" (243) and the "dreadful days" immediately following the Zemblan Revolution (119). Beyond this correspondence, though, the exchange gets to the heart of Kinbote's interactions with the world: having already confessed to losing himself in an "orgy of spying" (87), here Kinbote-the-suspect has "caught" Shade as any Communist hunter might catch a denier of Higher Intelligence. The "chaos of chance" is akin to the chaos introduced into Zembla by the Soviets and the potential chaos introduced into American society by homosexual people. In order to avoid this chaos of chance, which is "unspeakabl[e]" and therefore textually uncontrollable, Kinbote takes on the mantle of an I.P.H. or God or Author so as not to appreciate life's "topsy-turvical coincidence" as Shade does but rather to manufacture those coincidences (63). In other words, Kinbote's suspicion of chance helps him transform from hunted to hunter.

Once we attune ourselves to the presence of chance in the Zembla narrative, it becomes clear that Kinbote includes accidents with the purpose of ordering them in his fantasy world, and that he assigns accidents causal functions. The accidents contained within the Zembla narrative range from the offhand and trivial to the momentous. In the former category are events associated with mortality and the "chaos of chance" such as the deaths of Oleg, Kinbote's young lover, "in a toboggan accident" (128) and his father, King Alfin, in a flying accident (103–104). In addition to such concrete accidents, the language of chance also pervades Kinbote's narrative, as for example when the fleeing King is offered hospitality by a farmer (who he has met accidentally) and he implores the man "to accept an old gold piece he chanced to have in his pocket" (141); of his wife Disa, he writes that she "had to listen to the prattle of a chance visitor" (211); when climbing the mountains to "freedom," he repeats to himself lines from a Goethe poem, "a chance accompaniment" (239). More importantly, however, Gradus himself is chance manifest, not only in the passing details of the "chance leaflets" that fall his way (232) but also in the textual association, at the end of the novel, with him as a "caller" (293) to the Goldsworth house that echoes Kinbote's remark at the beginning about how the house was architecturally inviting to a "chance caller" (19).

Nabokov implies that the presence of this chance is precisely what thwarts Kinbote's attempts for godlike order, even when he tries to put his fantasies on paper: "[An invented 'Pale Fire' variant] describes rather well the 'chance inn,' a log cabin, with a tiled bathroom, where I am trying to coordinate these notes. At first I was greatly bothered by the blare of diabolical radio music from what I thought was some kind of amusement park across the road—it turned out to be camping tourists—and I was thinking of moving to another place, when they forestalled me" (235). Here the "diabolical radio" of the "chance inn" echoes Kinbote's statement a few pages earlier that "demons in their prismatic malice betray the agreement between us and them, and we are again in the chaos of chance" (226). Since Kinbote cannot control everything (or anything) that happens outside of Zembla, the chance demon of an irritating radio reminds him, and maddeningly so, that despite all his best efforts, he is failing to control completely absolute chance.[37]

The question, though, is why Kinbote goes to these lengths to insist on the ostensibly accidental nature of Zembla—and especially of Gradus's progress—when he is in fact attempting to manage the chance components of the narrative. The short answer relates to the issue of point of view mentioned earlier: neither Gradus nor his fellow conspirators think their coded language or discoveries of clues to Kinbote's whereabouts are subject to chance, since each side assumes the other's competence (215–216); from Kinbote's point of view, however, "Chance, in one of its anti-Karlist moods," is propelling Gradus along, not the conspirators' elaborate plan (175). The only character in Zembla for whom absolute chance can have meaning as something else—that is, as evidence of conspiracy—is Kinbote, because he arranges chance events into a causal chain that brings Gradus to New Wye. Retrospectively, then, Kinbote converts the multiple chance events connected to Zembla and Gradus into a series of coincidences that lead to Shade's death—if we keep in mind, however, that Kinbote is not a historian narrating actual accidents, then it becomes clear he is crafting a universe governed by chance from its creator's point of view. But because he is the creator of this universe, it is Kinbote who "plans and administers" (to borrow his own description of a Higher Intelligence) chance, forcing random acts and chance sightings to conform to a teleological picture. Kinbote, in trying to bridge his godlike stance in Zembla to New Wye, uses the numerous "chance" events concerning Gradus to explain the "chance" event of Shade's murder, thereby becoming not only master of Zembla but of Shade's real world as well.

In addition to these relatively trivial chance moments in the Zembla and real-life narratives, Kinbote also includes major accidents that inform his whole story. As I have said, Gradus himself could be read as chance incarnate, an idea which becomes apparent when we learn that after Gradus was caught "[h]e insisted . . . that when he found himself designated to track down and murder the King, the choice was decided by a show of cards" (150). The blind turn of a card makes Gradus an agent of chance. But just as Kinbote orchestrates the accidents in Zembla, so too does he admit the possibility that Gradus's card-draw was arranged, for he urges us not to forget "that it was Nodo ["who cheated at cards"] who shuffled and dealt them out" (150). Like many other things in *Pale Fire*, in Gradus's beginning is his end: his participation in the assassination plot hinges on drawing the "ace of spades" (150); after Gradus shoots Shade, "[Kinbote's] gardener's spade dealt [Gradus] . . . a tremendous blow on the pate" (294). Gradus, having been dealt the ace of spades, is now dealt for his luck the business end of a real spade, a correspondence which again suggests Nabokov's intelligence remains higher than Kinbote's.

Chance in Shade's "Pale Fire"

The counterpoint to Kinbote's willful control over chance in his "Commentary" is, as the passage about I.P.H. suggested, Shade's "Pale Fire," in which accidents are allowed to stand as "ornaments" (63) that point to a metaphysical design that cannot be known. True to the association of chance with objective reality described in chapter 1, in the climax of "Pale Fire," a chance misprint seems to make "Life Everlasting" (62) available for Shade, only to then be foreclosed when the mistake is revealed. Shade's epiphany is occasioned by a near-death experience in which he saw a white fountain; some time after he reads a magazine article about a woman who says she saw the same fountain in her own near-death experience. After Shade investigates the matter, he discovers from the author of the article that "[t]here's one misprint—not that it matters much: / *Mountain*, not *fountain*. The majestic touch" (62). Rather than wring his hands over death's uncontrollability as Kinbote does, Shade uses the opportunity to recognize that the "texture" of life includes such mistakes—examples of absolute chance—that could nevertheless point to an ineffable "web of sense." This matrix of meaning seems to destabilize the authority of institutional narratives such as the I.P.H.'s line on death:

> Life Everlasting—based on a misprint!
> I mused as I drove homeward: take the hint,
> And stop investigating my abyss?
> But all at once it dawned on me that *this*
> Was the real point, the contrapuntal theme;
> Just this: not text, but texture; not the dream
> But topsy-turvical coincidence,
> Not flimsy nonsense, but a web of sense.
> Yes! It sufficed that I in life could find
> Some kind of link-and-bobolink, some kind

> Of correlated pattern in the game,
> Plexed artistry, and something of the same
> Pleasure in it as they who played it found.
> (62–63)

It is indeed not accidental that Nabokov has Shade make the following contrapuntal declarative: "Life Everlasting—based on a misprint!" For as the aging poet of the Atomic Age discovers, it is foolhardy to rely on "text" to explain the mysteries of a universe built on "plexed artistry" and "topsy-turvical coincidence." The monumental misprint that momentarily convinces Shade that he has the keys to the afterlife functions similarly to puns; recall that according to Culler puns "may help us to displace the opposition [between accident and substance] by experiencing something like 'meaningful coincidence' or 'convergence that affects meaning,' convergence that adumbrates an order *to be* comprehended or explored." For Shade, the misprint has meaning precisely because it is an accident with substance—the misprint creates a "meaningful coincidence" for Shade not because he has had the same experience as another person but because he has had a unique experience that is nonetheless connected in the universe's "web of sense"—an experience made visible by chance.[38] Because a misprint demands we attend to the volatility of text, it invites us to recognize what the text is pointing to, the real, irreducible world of "texture."

What this reading of *Pale Fire* ultimately suggests, then, is that there is more room for political work in Nabokov's linguistic wordplay than has been supposed; indeed it tells us that we should read Nabokov's aesthetics as enfolding rather than shunning political and social critique—not simply in *Pale Fire* but in all his mature novels. Just as *Lolita*'s "aesthetic bliss" contains a sober denunciation of Humbert's thoroughly unethical behavior toward his fellow human beings, so too does *Pale Fire* contain a denunciation of Kinbote's behavior in the New Wye community.[39] And yet beyond this critique of a man who annoys his community and engages in what Nabokov would probably characterize as unsavory sexual behavior, the whole of *Pale Fire* amounts to a denunciation of the cultural circumstances that made Kinbote's Zembla narrative not only possible but a necessary strategy for survival. For all of Kinbote's infelicities, it is the homophobic narrative that has assigned him pathological status in the first place, that has equated his sexual behavior with political treason, and against which he must position himself if he hopes to participate in a Cold War American community. Nabokov's answer to such apparently pandemic cultural narratives is the incorporation and exploitation of chance in its various forms, from linguistic chance (puns and misprints) to circumstantial chance (accidents and effects with unplanned causes), so that for all his elaborate narrative machinations, Kinbote is in the novel's final moments plucked from the perch of godlike coordinator and relegated by the New Wye community to a mere "chance witness" (299). Thus the revelatory "retroactive clarification" once demanded by Sergey's diary entry is unavailable in *Pale Fire*; the chance moments in the novel, however aesthetically just and involutedly mimetic, are ultimately Nabokovian plants that function to expose cultural narratives as at best crude proxies for reality and at worst instruments of willful authoritarianism.

4

Accidents Going Somewhere to Happen

African-American Self-Definition at Mid-Century

Colson Whitehead may be the first person in history to have asked what elevator inspection has to do with race relations. In his 1999 novel, *The Intuitionist*, Whitehead explores this question through the story of Lila Mae Watson, the first black female elevator inspector in a city that looks a lot like New York—in a time that feels a lot like the 1950s.[1] In Whitehead's noir Gotham, there are two rival factions, the Empiricists and the Intuitionists, struggling for dominance in the elevator-inspecting field. The Empiricists, as their name implies, rely on visual inspections, physical measurements, and rational methodologies. Lila Mae, on the other hand, has been trained in the art of Intuitionism, which proceeds from unspoken feelings and intuitive, emotional connections with the elevator's metaphysical presence. "No one can quite explain," writes Whitehead, "why the Intuitionists have a 10 percent higher accuracy rate than the Empiricists."[2]

So far the winking allegorical resonances of Whitehead's world may seem clear enough: the Empiricists are associated with Western (white) rationality (as Lila Mae puts it late in the novel: "White people's reality is built on what things appear to be—that's the business of Empiricism" [239]); whereas the Intuitionists represent alternative ways of knowing that seem of a piece with Lila's status as a racial outsider (which is why "No one can quite [rationally] explain" Intuitionism's effectiveness). In keeping with this dichotomy, one of the novel's key revelations is that James Fulton, the author of Intuitionism's foundational texts, was a black man passing for white his whole life, a fact that would be as shocking to the Intuitionists as to the Empiricists, who disparage their "renegade colleagues" with racially charged nicknames: "swamis, voodoo men, juju heads, witch doctors, Harry Houdinis. All terms belonging to the nomenclature of dark exotica, the sinister foreign. Except for Houdini, who nonetheless had something swarthy about him" (57–58). Into this opposition between a kind of rationality based on appearances and one based on intuition—Fulton is described as having "No kind of sense at all in his head except his own kind of sense" (236)—Whitehead introduces a third category for which neither approach can completely account: accident.

The novel's plot is motivated by an elevator accident at the Fanny Briggs Memorial Building, a city-owned structure named for a former slave who taught herself to read. Much is made of the extraordinary nature of this accident: "This elevator went into total freefall, which hasn't happened in five years, and that was in the Ukraine and who knows what kind of backward standards they got there" (110); "this isn't a standard accident" (36); "The accident is impossible. It wasn't an accident" (42); "An elevator doesn't go into freefall. Not without help" (63). The accident seems "impossible" because total freefall would mean that the elevator's multiple modern safety systems all failed simultaneously. Given the growing tension between the Empiricists and the Intuitionists because of a coming election in the Department of Elevator Inspectors, the factions accuse each other of sabotage, and Lila Mae, who gave the Fanny Briggs elevator a seal of approval, finds herself caught in a political battle.

On first coming to the novel, readers may wonder, as I did, why it would make sense to Whitehead to put so much weight on accident when writing a novel about American race relations. Part of the answer comes from the temporal setting. Lila Mae lives in a land of rotary dial telephones, calendars with "picture-show starlets in erotic repose" (205), Chinese laundries, Tiki bars, and Bickford's. Men wear fedoras and drive cars with prominent fins. And at the annual Funicular Follies, elevator inspectors are entertained by Rick Raymond and the Moon-Rays, who sing of "Peggy Sue and her love so true" (147). It is a land, in other words, which touches on the pop-nostalgic aspects of the 1950s while only glancing at Cold War politics—not only the oblique dig at Soviet-sphere technology behind the quip about a shoddy Ukrainian elevator but also when Lila Mae's cultural geography is contextualized by a lone mention of someone who sounds like Martin Luther King, Jr., "the famous reverend. The man who is so loud down South," which anchors the allegory in the growing Civil Rights movement (248).

Whitehead's choice to set the action in a past characterized by a sort of collective nostalgia is in fact key to understanding why a novel about race is also so preoccupied with chance. As I will argue in this chapter, in the postwar era, Cold War politics meant that chance and accident became attached to ideas of African-American agency, and, subsequently, self-definition.[3] The structural logic of *The Intuitionist* illustrates why this was so—an intractable conflict between two categorically opposed philosophical schools, with an African American caught in the middle, echoes the situation that many African Americans found themselves in during the Cold War. One way African-American writers responded to the rhetorical conflict between the United States and the Soviet Union—both of which demanded conformity to differing notions of identity— was to exploit chance as a marker of identity that could not be absorbed or otherwise defined by either system.

In *The Intuitionist*, after detailed investigations, Lila Mae ultimately discovers that the elevator's total freefall was not the product of any political conspiracy, but was simply a "catastrophic accident"—functionally, an example of what I have been calling absolute chance. The "catastrophic accident" is so unimaginable to the power players in either faction because it lies beyond their ability to either control or describe; in revisiting the elevator, Lila Mae discovers "[n]othing at all. . . . Something gave in the elevator for no reason and its brother components gave in, too. A catastrophic accident. The things that emerge from the black, nether reaches of space and collide here, comets that connect with this frail world after countless unavailing ellipses. Emissaries from the unknowable. . . . What her discipline and Empiricism have in common: they cannot account for the catastrophic accident" (227). Although a catastrophic accident is "unknowable" both to the Empiricists and to the Intuitionists (even Fulton, "in explicating the unbelievable . . . never dared broach the unknowable" [229]), Lila Mae comes to accept accident as such, and in so doing grows into her own autonomy. Despite the ending's Pynchonian ambiguity, which leaves it unclear whether Lila Mae is meant to be Fulton's inheritor, or whether her presence in his notebooks is merely an accidental scribble, by the book's close, she feels she is no longer an actor in someone else's plot, but rather has more control over her own destiny.[4]

The Black Experience in the Cold War

A look through mid-century African-American writing shows that Whitehead's impulse to set his novel during that time is a vestige of the changing relationship between the African-American individual and the state. The sense that chance was potentially generative because it is beyond the knowledge of either the American or Soviet systems made it of special interest to numerous African Americans writing during the Cold War. Although the connections of African Americans to Communism is too complex to adequately discuss in this book, a brief sketch of the relationship helps explain why chance came to be viewed in this way. Like their white counterparts, prior to WWII, left-leaning African-American writers and intellectuals were caught between the promises of American democracy, on the one hand, and the programs for social equality proposed by Communism, on the other.[5] But during the Cold War, when achieving integration into the mainstream required a visible if not strident anti-Communism, many African Americans once sympathetic to the Communist Party of the United States (CPUSA) became some of its most vocal critics. The conventional wisdom—perhaps articulated most memorably by Richard Wright's essay "I Tried to Be a Communist" (1944)—was that the CPUSA claimed to be for racial equality, but in actuality just used African Americans to further its own power-hungry agenda set by Moscow.[6] As William Nolan wrote in 1951, the CPUSA's professed concerns for racial equality were merely propagandistic lies, since "every one of its activities must be subordinated to the aggressive ambition of a foreign power, whose interests frequently conflict with those of *American* Negroes."[7]

Although since the end of the Cold War such rabid anti-Communism has largely subsided, certain ideological legacies are nevertheless still potent enough in the United States, and many readers have assumed that Stalinists in Moscow did as a rule control the CPUSA, which in turn manipulated African Americans by using them as tokens of racial tolerance. William Maxwell has observed, for example, that Ralph Ellison's *Invisible Man* (1952), with its damning characterization of the Communist-inspired Brotherhood, "remains one of a diminishing few must-read inscriptions of U.S. anti-Communism, an ideology that English majors may now know most vividly as a black intellectual response to false 'Brotherhood.'"[8] As a corrective to this situation, Maxwell's *New Negro, Old Left* "reviews the bonds between black writing and Communism with eyes open for African-American agency, understood in this case as a fully historical ability to affect Old Left history, not an ever-ready, subjective power to decree it."[9] This chapter shares Maxwell's interest in African-American agency with respect to both Communism and American democracy, but does so by looking at how writers theorized new kinds of agencies by linking the African-American experience to chance, which in turn created a sense of identity defined by neither ideological system, but rather idiosyncratically, by the writers themselves.

In 1957, sociologist E. Franklin Frazier wrote that the black middle class "have often become the worshippers of the God of Chance," a suggestive observation because attention to chance was a way to negotiate and evade the norms of American democracy and the CPUSA, both of which could look quite authoritarian from a black perspective.[10] Some of the most influential African-American fiction of this era not only shares Frazier's observation but in fact relies on various instantiations of chance to express senses of self independent of both American democracy and Communism as practiced. This chapter brings together a range of African-American writing, from the most canonical novels of mid-century to lesser known work that extends or modifies the question of chance's relationship to self-definition. In work by Wright, Ellison, and John A. Williams, one finds explicit explorations of how race inflects the binaries Cold War cultural narratives sought to maintain. For these and other writers, chance is a fecund concept useful not only for describing the sometimes uncomfortable similarities between democracy and Communism but also for crafting a sense of self that resists or simply evades the prescribed roles made available to African Americans by the reigning cultural narratives of the day. Taken as a whole, my reading not only suggests a new way of understanding classics of African-American fiction but also brings them together with underread work in their collective attitude toward the American democratic system as it was perceived in the Cold War frame.

The Wright School and Naturally Organized Life

The first significant demonstration of how political uses of chance reflect race relations is in the most consequential African-American novel of the 1940s, Richard Wright's *Native Son* (1940). Those familiar with the novel may remember that when Bigger Thomas is on trial for murder, a point of contention is whether he "murdered Mary Dalton accidentally, without thinking, without plan, without conscious motive."[11] Bigger's Communist defense attorney, Max, is fond of offering his Marxist interpretations of society, and he argues to the jury that while Mary's murder was not premeditated, it cannot properly be called accidental because it was the inevitable result of accreted social forces. In his closing remarks, intended to convince the jury that Bigger's actions were the expression of these forces, Max in fact repudiates his client's own claim that the murder was accidental:

> Let us not concern ourselves with that part of Bigger Thomas' confession that says he murdered accidentally. . . . It really does not matter. What does matter is that he was guilty *before* he killed! That was why his whole life became so quickly and naturally organized, pointed, charged with a new meaning when this thing occurred. Who knows when another "accident" involving millions of men will happen, an "accident" that will be the dreadful day of our doom?[12]

In yoking Bigger's violent act to the promised violence of class revolution ("the dreadful day of our doom"), Max not only drains the murder of human agency but suggests also that we are all subject to the social forces that resulted in Mary's death. Max's passive construction—his insistence that "this thing occurred"—emphasizes Wright's general thinking at the time he wrote *Native Son*, that people are determined by the social forces buffeting them, an idea made especially visible in the United States by ever-tense race relations.[13] As a broadly drawn vulgar Marxist, Max must always handle "accident" with quotation marks because he believes that what looks like an accident or example of absolute chance is actually evidence of a "naturally organized" social universe that Marxism alone can describe.

The influence of Wright's Communist-inspired naturalism was found in what Robert Bone called in 1958 the "Wright School," African-American novels of the 1940s and early 1950s that showed how environmental forces virtually determined character responses, as in the famous opening scene of *Native Son*, when Bigger crushes a rat's head with a skillet.[14] His mother admonishes him for teasing his sister with the carcass: "I wonder what makes you act like you do," she asks, and readers realize that despite this seeming display of power, Bigger is just as reflexively programmed as the rat.[15] This idea is taken up in many other novels of the Wright School. William Demby's *Beetlecreek* (1950), for example, follows a young boy visiting relatives in West Virginia who, after falling in with the local scofflaws, finds himself burning down the house of a white man who has offered the black townsfolk the sort of kindness Mary offered Bigger. With this act, Johnny realizes he is oddly estranged from himself: "[H]e couldn't associate himself with the fire but then he soon realized he was still holding a gasoline can in his hand."[16] As in *Native Son*, Demby's protagonist finds himself acting as an expression of social forces. Abbie Crunch in Ann Petry's *The Narrows* (1953) describes Wright-style naturalism specifically in terms of chance: "Accident? Coincidence? No. It all depended on what happened to you in the past."[17] African-American writer Willard Motley's first novel, *Knock on Any Door* (1947), tells the story of Nick Romano, an Italian-American who is likewise a victim of circumstance, which eventually propels him, like Bigger, into the electric chair. Riffing on Bigger's encounter with the rat, Motley emphasizes that as a boy Nick is "like a little saint" with an anecdote about the time he rescued a mouse from the clutches of a cat and set him free.[18] Despite Nick's early reversal of Bigger's act, when his father loses his job and the family moves to the poorer area of town, gentle Nick finds himself caught in institutional and economic forces so profoundly that a life of crime seems not only natural, but indeed inevitable.

But however powerful was *Native Son*'s demonstration that Bigger is subject to external forces, another mode of thinking developed in postwar African-American writing that reflected a different sense of individuals' relationship to their environment, something only implied by Max's defense.[19] Because Max's argument is predicated on the notion that people must inevitably be organized by their social and economic environments, his logic also implies that, conversely, human agency is tied to chance.[20] After all, if there is no such thing as accident (only partial knowledge of social forces), then Bigger is both blameless and free from possessing his own agency. This idea that chance—in this case, deviating from what seems inevitable—is connected to human agency, and particularly African-American agency, is found in numerous works of the Cold War. In one well-known response to Bigger's killing the rat, for example, Gwendolyn Brooks suggests that quiet thoughtfulness and emotional engagement (in contrast to Bigger's loud actions and emotional distance) help one generate life by deviating from seemingly inevitable plots—what other writers would deem "the plan." There is in Brooks's short novel *Maud Martha* (1953), a chapter pointedly called "Maud Martha spares the mouse," in which she ironizes Wright's sense that there is an inevitable trajectory to a person's life. After empathizing with a mouse she has found in her home ("She wondered what else it was thinking"), Maud Martha asserts, as Valerie Frazier puts it, "her will and her ability to affect the external world."[21] Brooks writes: "A life had blundered its way into her power and it had been hers to preserve or destroy. She had not destroyed. In the center of that simple restraint was—creation. She had created a piece of life. It was wonderful. . . . Her eyes were mild, and soft with a godlike loving kindness."[22] Here one finds a personal thoughtfulness absent in Bigger Thomas, but that would come to characterize much postwar African-American fiction. The idea that "godlike" power could come not from blunt force but from a conscious choice is something explored in a range of work, from the most influential of all postwar African-American novels, Ellison's *Invisible Man*, to Wright's second published novel, *The Outsider*—which appeared thirteen years after *Native Son* and his turn from Communism—to John A. Williams's *The Man Who Cried I Am* (1967). By tracing an arc through these novels, we can mark a shift in the way they conceptualize U.S. and Soviet attitudes toward chance: in *Invisible Man*, Marxism is figured as manipulating chance, whereas the American democratic system seems to embrace it; in *The Outsider*, both systems are equally controlling with respect to both chance and to African-American identity; and in *The Man Who Cried I Am*, the specific control of chance has shifted to the United States and is indicative of its control of African Americans both at home and abroad.

Loose Ends and Great Potentialities

As complex and layered as it is, the basic plot of Ellison's *Invisible Man* concerns the eponymous narrator learning what it means to be an African-American male in the twentieth century. A recurring metaphor for this knowledge is game playing: if the Invisible Man ever hopes to gain a measure of control over his own life, he has to stop being a pawn in someone else's game. An older and wiser character advises him, "Play the game, but don't believe in it. . . . Play the game, but raise the ante."[23] The poker metaphor implies one aspect of his education: in learning to acknowledge the power of chance, he can also learn to acknowledge the power of his own agency in crafting identity. This idea helps explain why Jackson Lears, in his cultural history of luck in America, singles out *Invisible Man* as a novel that captures the "significance of the vernacular culture of chance."[24] As Lears observes, the novel takes an interest not only in African-American folk culture but also in the way that the "improvised life threatens devotees of control."[25] It is precisely this repudiation of social, political, and cultural control—manifest in a range of forms—that Ellison enacts by emphasizing the generative potential of chance.

In the opening pages of the novel, Ellison invokes the cliché of the accident of birth, but with a difference. The narrator writes: "Nor is my invisibility exactly a matter of a biochemical accident to my epidermis. That invisibility to which I refer occurs because of a peculiar disposition of the eyes of those with whom I come in contact" (3). Here accident seems only negative, as a threatening force that causes racial difference. As we saw in chapter 1, in this way Ellison may be read as a good Aristotelian, so that race is an accident of appearance, like height or weight, which is not essential to understanding a person's essence or substance. But as the second sentence indicates, in *Invisible Man*, what race "means" results from social norms, which insist that the particular accident of skin color is consequential. Viewed through the lens of chance, then, race becomes a paradox: it is both nothing (an accident of appearance) and everything (it causes a host of problems, from invisibility to contempt).[26] This unstable relationship between race and chance becomes increasingly important as the narrator becomes more attuned to the various games being played around—and on—him. If, for the Invisible Man, race has primarily meant social control, by the end of the novel, he has come to realize that acknowledging chance is a way for him to acknowledge likewise his own agency in the face of such mechanisms of control.[27]

In the first part of the novel, set in the Jim Crow South, there are numerous moments that suggest a connection between racial identity and chance. During the famous Battle Royal scene, for instance, in which young black men are blindfolded and made to box for the amusement of white spectators, the narrator writes: "Each of us was issued a pair of boxing gloves and ushered out into the big mirrored hall, which we entered looking cautiously about us and whispering, lest we might accidentally be heard above the noise of the room" (18). It is as if to have a voice as an African American in such a context would be mere accident. We later learn that the Golden Day, where the narrator takes Norton, a wealthy white trustee of the local Tuskegee-like college, is populated by black professionals now shunted off by society and was once a "fancy gambling house" (80). There one character tells the Invisible Man that "[t]he world moves in a circle like a roulette wheel. In the beginning, black is on top, in the middle epochs, white holds the odds, but soon Ethiopia shall stretch forth her noble wings!" (81). For this "student of history," the wise fool who speaks the truth, conceptualizing the world as a roulette wheel gives him hope that oppressive social norms will one day vanish, an idea that portends Frazier's observation that a God of Chance could displace other forms of belief. But in *Invisible Man*, chance is connected also to the potential of black power, even at a time when the white majority "holds the odds." In this way, *Invisible Man* confirms Henry Louis Gates's sense of African-American fiction as being deeply influenced by the circulation of the trickster figure in African myths, whose generative power was connected to chance. Quoting from an anthropological account of Legba, the important trickster figure for the Fon in Benin, Gates writes: "This power that permits man to escape his destiny—philosophically the personification of Accident in a world where Destiny is inexorable—is found in the character of Legba."[28] As I suggest throughout this chapter, the basic sense that the "personification of Accident" could help African-American characters evade the destinies written for them by various people in power runs through much fiction of the Cold War.

In *Invisible Man*, invocations of chance are counterpointed by kinds of design—as already mentioned, the Invisible Man invariably finds himself a part of someone else's game, whether Norton's "destiny" (168) or the toadying college president's secret schemes to keep him running. "Everyone," he observes, "seemed to have some plan for me, and beneath that some more secret plan" (194).[29] The damaging potential of such planning is taken to new levels in the second half of the novel, in which the narrator gets involved with the Brotherhood, Ellison's proxy for the CPUSA. As Max in *Native Son* summoned all his rhetorical powers to deny the operation of chance in the universe, so the members of the Brotherhood in Ellison's novel spend much of their time talking about their scientific plan that would likewise exclude such operation, thereby eliminating individual agency.

As Barbara Foley has shown, although Ellison was once much more sympathetic to Communism than many readers have supposed, as he reworked the drafts of *Invisible Man*, he "gradually . . . reduced his Communist characters, black and white, to the cartoonish exemplars of Stalinist authoritarianism appearing in the 1952 text."[30] One member of the Brotherhood, Brother Wrestrum, is in an earlier draft named Brother Elmo, and in the margins where he appears Ellison penciled: "a totalitarian type, eager to regiment all aspects of life."[31] Foley notes that such comments demonstrate Ellison's deliberate engagement with Cold War rhetoric—which made possible the sort of anti-Communist political sensibility that could recognize a "totalitarian type." In representing Communism, she writes, Ellison "routinely chooses highly anomalous details to perform the work of typification"; that is, he seizes on instances of control and manipulation that probably did occur at one time or another and makes them typical of the African American experience with CPUSA.[32] The overall effect is to emphasize the notion that the Brotherhood controls its members and fellow travelers and conscripts them to follow its own particular design.

If it is true that Ellison deliberately distorted what he knew of the CPUSA in order to align his novel with the mainstream anti-Communist norms of the Cold War, then it is worth pausing over how and why he characterizes the Brotherhood in this manner. In the published version of *Invisible Man*, when the members of the Brotherhood convene, their chief problem is that they are so invested in what the narrator calls their "science of history business" that they begin to confuse their theories with objective reality (311). "We are all realists here," says one, "and materialists. It is a question of who shall determine the direction of events" (307). As the narrator learns more about the Brotherhood—and, by implication, their Marxist inspiration—he gets the sense that this conflation of "realist" with "materialist" is actually a dangerous philosophical position that justifies authoritarianism in the name of freedom. Brother Jack, local Brotherhood leader, tells the narrator: "You will have freedom of action—*and* you will be under strict discipline to the committee" (360). Brother Jack's seemingly self-contradictory statement regulates freedom without seeming to do so; this sort of untenable logic—that the narrator might be both free and subject to the dictates of the committee—causes him to realize that his "life had been too tightly organized" (357). Despite their claims to social equality, the Brotherhood is for the narrator no better than the mainstream American alternative because its organization, its plan, is overly deterministic. As we have seen in much American writing of this period, one test for how much planning is too much is to ask how the plan handles chance—which is in *Invisible Man* tied to the narrator's potential for personal freedom.

The Brotherhood's commitment to the "scientific" plan is emphasized several times: "We are champions of a scientific approach to society" (350); "Don't worry . . . We have a scientific plan" (367); "we now have to slow them ["the Negroes"] down for their own good. It's a scientific necessity" (503); "We judge through cultivating scientific objectivity" (505).[33] This scientific sheen is at first comforting because it promises a plan that destabilizes the American status quo, which has consistently degraded the narrator and his bids for human recognition. It is the Brotherhood that first sees his gift for oratory and brings him into the fold to speak on various social issues. During this initial period of contact with the organized left, in fact, the narrator admires the Brotherhood's design: "I was dominated by the all-embracing idea of Brotherhood. The organization had given the world a new shape, and me a vital role. We recognized no loose ends, everything could be controlled by our science. Life was all pattern and discipline; and the beauty of discipline is when it works. And it was working very well" (382). Although the Invisible Man is at first enthusiastic about the Brotherhood's "pattern and discipline," he soon discovers that these aspects are precisely the problem and that he has become just another piece in another schemer's pattern. He has traded his place in Norton's destiny for a place in the destiny described by Marxist theory. With subsequent readings, the ironic distance between Ellison and his narrator become more clear: while the Invisible Man feels protected by the "all-embracing" nature of the Brotherhood, it is likewise sinister because he is simultaneously being "dominated." The problem is again a confusion between reality and materialist theories: the world itself has been given a "new shape," and this distorted sense of reality admits no chance operations or "loose ends." When the narrator marvels that "everything could be controlled by our science," he has not yet recognized that he is part of that "everything" and that the pattern and organization that marks the Brotherhood finds him as dispensable and interchangeable as any other person.

In the Brotherhood sections of *Invisible Man*, then, the narrator is learning to be suspicious of Marxist uses of pattern and control because they necessarily deny his own agency. All his adventures have built to this realization, and he articulates this insight again in terms of chance: a problem shared by both white mainstream Americans and the Brotherhood is that each control chance and foreclose any African-American agency outside the design of their respective plans. As the novel ends, the Invisible Man thinks more about the notion of "loose ends," and he decides that the world is all about these loose ends, the possibilities and "great potentialities" (511) that he calls the "real chaos" (499) opposed to the reality described by the Brotherhood. In this sense, *Invisible Man* is an attempt to articulate what a universe of loose ends and great potentialities would look like, and what it would mean for African Americans.

By the epilogue, the Invisible Man has gone underground, secreted in his hole so that he may tell the tale we have just read. But in the final pages of the novel, he has decided that he cannot simply disappear and resign from the world, but that he must rather "emerge" and engage the world in the terms he has learned through his varied experiences. His new sensibility is born from his surreal jaunt through the mid-twentieth century: "my world has become one of infinite possibilities. What a phrase—still it's a good phrase and a good view of life, and a man shouldn't accept any other; that much I've learned underground. Until some gang succeeds in putting the world in a strait jacket, its definition is possibility. Step outside the narrow borders of what men call reality and you step into chaos" (576). While the wise, experienced man at the novel's end concedes that it may seem sophomoric to speak of "infinite possibilities," he also realizes that the phrase expresses what is wrong with the various views of life he has encountered: they all manage, conscript, or otherwise control possibility. For the narrator, to define the world as possibility is to imagine a world of chance. When one recognizes that theories like the Brotherhood's pass for objective reality, but are actually false substitutes because they do not allow for possibility, one sees that "chaos"—that realm in which absolute chance is given free reign to operate—allows the possibility of self-definition.

The Invisible Man's model for this sort of existence is Rinehart, a cool Harlemite hipster who fluidly assumes different identities by playing on people's assumptive reliance on the surface of things. As Ellison remarked a couple of years after the novel was published, "Rinehart is my name for the personification of chaos. He is also intended to represent America and change."[34] It is significant that in Rinehart Ellison unites the idea of chaos and the idea of America because he thus represents the promise of what the country might be were it not beholden to excessive controls. Following Rinehart, the Invisible Man is attracted to chance because it allows him to recognize his own mind and his own "great potentialities" without being defined by scientific plans or the idiosyncratic destinies of other people.

In fact, as the Invisible Man wrestles with his own sense of self, he suggests that in order for a mind to function properly, it must recognize the chaotic nature of an unplanned universe, alongside the pattern given it by people: "In going underground, I whipped it all except the mind, the *mind*. And the mind that has conceived a plan of living must never lose sight of the chaos against which that pattern was conceived. That goes for societies as well as for individuals. Thus, having tried to give pattern to the chaos which lives within the pattern of your certainties, I must come out, I must emerge" (580–581). In contrast to Max's argument in *Native Son*, which linked Bigger's individual act to the inevitable rise of the proletariat, Ellison suggests that a governing principle of individuals, as well as societies, should be a recognition that chance reigns—it is not that absolute chance is in and of itself important, but that recognizing it leads one to the possibilities of an open reality unpatterned by others. The Invisible Man strives for his own kind of pattern that does not deny or replace the chaos of reality, but rather that acknowledges it in order to admit the possibility of human agency. The real world is characterized by chance, and recognition of such empowers the narrator to emerge into a new sort of consciousness so that he may define his own potentialities and possibilities without defining himself always against "the plan." The Cold War context, of course, makes this recognition of chance especially visible and urgent in the novel, for as much as the Brotherhood wants to hold a mirror against American race relations, one of Ellison's most damning criticisms of them is that they reproduce the same controlling logic as the good old boys in the novel's opening chapter. As I explain in the following sections, in its linkage of chance to human agency, *Invisible Man* underscores a way of thinking seen in other African-American works that likewise register the rhetorical demands of the Cold War.[35]

The Party Wants You to Obey!

Appearing the year after Ellison's triumph with *Invisible Man*, Richard Wright's second novel, *The Outsider* (1953), demonstrates how far he had moved away from the CPUSA, not only for its putative exploitation of black members but also for what he called in "I Tried to Be a Communist" its abiding "fear of the individual" and its ability to rival "the church and its myths and legends."[36] *The Outsider* in fact shares Ellison's critique of Communism as hyper-determined and distrustful of chance; it opens under an "invisible" sky and, as if taking a cue from the Invisible Man's remark that the Brotherhood appeared like "chance passengers in a subway car," has as its central moment a horrific subway accident that allows the protagonist to create a new identity.[37] In fact, Cross Damon's sense of self is possible because he embodies chance—he is, as one character remarks, "like an accident going somewhere to happen" (64), a phrase one could locate in other African-American fiction of the era such as John O. Killens's first novel, *Youngblood* (1954).[38] If the Invisible Man has learned by the novel's close to appreciate the chaos of reality, Cross seems his logical extension as he becomes adept at exploiting chance as an expression of his individualized identity.

When held against the vast amount of material that has appeared on *Native Son*, Wright's second novel has received comparatively little attention, but it merits discussion for the ways that it marks the shift not only in Wright's own thinking about Communism but also in African-American writing more generally. Those who have taken the novel seriously (some have dismissed it as turgid and flawed) have remarked on the centrality of chance—as I will show, this centrality has everything to do with the Cold War context outlined above.[39] Writing in 1960, for example, Kingsley Widmer sought to defend *The Outsider* against detractors by calling attention to its existential dimensions, which for him include randomness and contingency: "Though Cross Damon's destructive acts reflect psychological compulsions and the hostility of the social order, Wright insists repeatedly that they remain gratuitous, i.e. 'free' and random selection of sequences by 'a petty god' in 'a Godless world.'"[40] But as we have seen with *Invisible Man*, it is not so easy to simply equate the random with the gratuitous, and indeed in *The Outsider*, Cross's embrace of the random allows him to generate his own self-definition. It is true that this definition is not always clear, but this is part of the point. Sarah Relyea has written more recently that the "plot of *The Outsider* centers on attempts to decipher Cross as a signifier. . . . To other characters, Cross seems to be an indecipherable blur with contradictory racial, ideological, sexual, and geographical signs."[41] It is indeed tricky to decipher exactly what Cross means in and for the novel—he seems at moments to be heroic, and yet it is hard to think that the novel recommends mass murder in the name of self-actualization. Rather than wondering how we might clarify Cross's blurry identity, it is more profitable to ask how and why his appropriations of chance allow him to defy the expectations set for him by both Communism and the American democratic system because this question eventually makes legible the novel's broader engagement with Cold War culture.

As in *The Intuitionist* nearly fifty years later, *The Outsider*'s plot is driven by an accident. When Cross's subway car derails, it causes one of the worst accidents in Chicago history, but he emerges from the tunnel unscathed, and soon realizes that because the accident has rendered the remains of its victims physically unrecognizable, he would be presumed dead unless he reports otherwise to the authorities. As a devoted reader of existential literature, it quickly occurs to Cross to abandon his life by fleeing Chicago for New York City and living under an assumed name. Like an accident, Cross's actions thwart explanation by those who attempt to understand him and his plans, be they members of the CPUSA or the district attorney who investigates the string of murders he commits to keep his old identity hidden. Unlike Bigger Thomas, who finds himself forever caught in circumstances, Cross manipulates accident to manipulate his environment, thereby crafting his own sense of selfhood.

Early in the novel, before the subway accident that affords him a chance to assume a different identity, Cross's life is in turmoil. He is plagued by debt and alcoholism, he is estranged from his wife, and his 15-year-old mistress is pregnant and threatening to jail him for statutory rape. It is little wonder, then, that his "feelings were like tumbling dice" (12). Rather than allowing the situation to dictate his next move, however, Cross amplifies the tumbling dice of his feelings to embrace accident as fully as possible. This premise is introduced with a bizarre and disturbing scene in which Cross tries to force his wife, Gladys, to relinquish her "emotional authority" (50) and grant him a divorce. With this scheme, Cross thinks he can become an avatar of accident: "One afternoon in a bar, dawdling over a drink, he recalled how shocked Gladys had been when she had come home from the hospital with Junior and had found him in bed with the girl. That fantastic happening had now become accepted as an 'accident.' Well, why couldn't another 'accident' happen? One so fatal and unique that it would make her remember the last one as a guide by which to interpret it!" (51).[42] An accident is valuable for Cross's purposes because it is an event that lies beyond intention, and therefore beyond motive. His perverse insight here is that were he able to manipulate accident, he would likewise be able to control his wife's interpretation of events. By becoming an avatar of accident, Cross not only thinks that he can guide his wife into believing that her interpretations are "objective reality" (56), but he also comes to realize that aligning himself with chance confounds other people's interpretations of him, thereby creating an existential sense of self unanchored from social prescriptions.

As in *Invisible Man*, in *The Outsider*, the control rampant in contemporary American culture is highlighted through comparisons to the control evidenced in Communist views of the world. For the later Wright, Marxism functions as a sign of control, a view in which the nagging prospect of determinism trumps whatever concern for the working classes or racial minorities the CPUSA may claim. Cross learns this in New York, where he flees after surviving the subway accident. Playing on the racist expectations of white civil servants, he has easily acquired the papers of a recently dead man, Lionel Lane, and is able to assume his identity. Cross meets, by chance, a train porter named Bob Hunter, and once in New York Bob introduces Cross (as Lionel) around to members of the CPUSA.

The first person he meets is Gil Blount, a cartoonish sketch of the severe Communist intellectual who, like the members of Ellison's Brotherhood, insists that dialectical materialism encompasses the totality of human experience. A cold, almost inhuman presence, fishlike Gil seems always to be calculating the most effective way to insert people into the Party's design. Cross initially sizes him up like this: "He was not a little shocked at Gil's colossal self-conceit. He acts like a God who is about to create a man. . . . He has no conception of the privacy of other people's lives. . . . He saw Gil's eyes regarding him steadily, coolly, as though Gil was already seeing to what use his life could be put [Wright's ellipses]" (160). The sense that Communists have not merely dismissed the idea of God but have indeed supplanted it runs throughout *The Outsider* and suggests the degree to which Wright views them as attempting to control or manage objective reality. Cross thinks that Communist ideology drains people of their "privacy" and views them only in terms of their "use" value. Control is again conceptualized as at odds with individuality, an idea reminiscent of Kurt Mondaugen's insight in Pynchon's *V.* that politics engineers people into "raw material" or the Invisible Man's worry that The Brotherhood sees him not as a man but as a "natural resource" (303).

As if to confirm Cross's uncharitable first impression, Gil himself defines Communism against individual subjectivity: "We Communists do not admit any subjectivity in human life" (160). When Bob Hunter complains about the paces through which the Party has put him, Gil begins to tyrannically "act like a God":

> You are an instrument of the Party. You exist to execute the Party's will. That's all there is to it. . . . Goddamn your damned feelings! . . . Who cares about what you feel? Insofar as the Party is concerned, you've got no damned feelings! . . . What do you think men like Molotov do when they get a decision? They carry it out! Do you think the Party exists to provide an outlet for your personal feelings? . . . We're *Communists*! And being a Communist is not easy. It means negating yourself, blotting out your personal life and listening only to the voice of the Party. The Party wants you to *obey*! (168)

From one perspective, this is the classic Cold War critique of Communism discussed in the first chapter: the Red Menace is such because it means "negating yourself" in the name of Party ideology, an idea manifest in countless places, from Cyd Charisse's grave Soviet envoy in the film *Silk Stockings* (1957) who informs decadent Fred Astaire "Only by denying selfish interests can one properly serve the State," to the sci-fi classic *Invasion of the Body Snatchers* (1955), whose body-infiltrating space aliens seemed a transparent allegory for Communist assimilation over American individuality.[43] But Gil's rant is different because it is inflected by racial politics. As he is lecturing a black man, and a train porter no less, it is hard not to see real-world consequences of the Hegelian master–slave dialectic in Blount's exclamation that Bob "*obey*!" With racial difference in the mix, Gil's version of Communism, emphasizing as it does a desire for control so total that even "personal feelings" are obliterated, does not seem so far from mainstream American values, both of which are, from Cross's and Bob's perspective, systems of domination.[44]

The counterpoint to both systems is chance. Late in the novel, as Cross is thinking about why he does not feel part of mainstream American culture, with its "vast web of pledges and promises" (346), he muses, "It was not because he was a Negro that he had found his obligations intolerable; it was because there resided in his heart a sharp sense of freedom" (347). While Cross's race of course makes his particular web of social obligations more visible, the suggestion is that any person, regardless of his or her race, might find similar constraints on freedom, a notion that Wright himself underscored when he remarked that *The Outsider* "is anchored mainly in reflection and is concerned with problems that would beset anyone, black or white."[45] For Cross, the subway accident is a route to this realization, and by embodying accident, he replaces the inevitability associated with Marxism or the social norms underwritten by American attitudes toward race with the inevitability of personal action: "[A]ccident had made possible his decision to dishonor those unwritten vows that he had been made to promise, but his eagerness in embracing the opportunities presented by that subway accident had robbed that accident of its element of contingency, and the rest had flowed naturally and inevitably" (347). The accidental is ironically elevated to the necessary through Cross's intention and action.

This turn to chance is Cross's way to frustrate both American social norms and the CPUSA's plan for him. Musing about the Communists, for example, he could well be thinking about democratic norms: "He understood now the hard Communist insistence on strict obedience in things that had no direct relation to politics proper or to their keeping tight grasp of the reins of power. Once a thorough system of sensual power as a way of life had gotten hold of a man's heart so that it ordered and defined all of his relations, it was bound to codify and arrange all of his life's activities into one organic unity" (185). For Cross, the problem is the system that conscripts individuals into "one organic unity," thereby quashing chance and choice. Indeed, while *Invisible Man* was comparatively optimistic about the power of the American democratic system to accommodate potentialities (though imperfect, this system is better than the one proposed by the Brotherhood), *The Outsider* is much more critical of the system, as it is shown to rival Communism in its controlling tendencies.[46]

It is ultimately not that *The Outsider* underwrites Cross's actions—in the course of embodying accident, he abuses his wife, murders four people, burns down a church, and causes one of his lovers to commit suicide—but rather that it analyzes the ways in which African-American free will is caught between the opposing demands of the American and Communist systems. It could well be, in fact, that there is no good, viable solution to this situation: embracing chance is one route to self-definition (at the novel's close, when the district attorney recognizes the extraordinary self-possession required to commit these various crimes, Cross is, if nothing else, his own man), but certainly not the ideal route. But the emphasis on accident throughout *The Outsider* suggests just how important Wright considered chance to be when challenging the reign and legitimacy of the various plans and systems that existed to make the life of an African American not his own.

King Alfred's American Dream

The suspicion of the plan, whether the Invisible Man's realization that he is being gamed by those in power, or Cross Damon's repudiation of both the American and Communist plans for his life, perhaps reached its apex in John A. Williams's *The Man Who Cried I Am* (1967), which shifts overt suspicion from Communist norms to American ones. Williams, an African-American novelist and journalist who lived in the same Parisian expatriate circles as Wright and James Baldwin, was acutely attuned to the sinister side of American planning required by the Cold War. Drawing on some of his own experiences, he created Max Reddick, a writer who moves through the global scene carved out by the Cold War. Like Cross, "Reddick fitted no exact pattern," yet as the novel unfolds, he learns of the systematic control not of the Soviets or the CPUSA, but of the American democratic machine bent on suppressing or otherwise containing Communism at any cost.[47] In *The Man Who Cried I Am*, in other words, the explicit threat has moved from Communism to the equally shadowy machinations of the American government.[48]

There is a taste of such shadowy control early in the novel, when a representative of a U.S. "government agency" (the CIA) pays a visit to Harry Ames, a famous African-American writer modeled on Richard Wright, in Amsterdam. Ames, who like his real-life counterpart has been writing essays openly critical of American foreign policy and domestic life, is informed by the agent: "In foreign countries, particularly those with strong attractions to communism . . . we'd like all Americans to be careful in their criticisms" (22). This seemingly innocuous injunction is revealed over the course of the novel as merely the face of a much larger and complicated web designed to maintain both the racial status quo and America's prominent position on the global stage. Just as the Invisible Man learns to "[p]lay the game, but don't believe in it," Max learns that "[p]olitics was some American game; it had its pauses, but never an end. It was the Ultimate Game, while you lived" (166). As it turns out, the final clause has special resonance in *The Man Who Cried I Am*, as the novel's denouement comes not when Max dies from the aggressive rectal cancer that has plagued him throughout the book, but when he is killed by American undercover agents: having been given information pertaining to secret American plans, he is assassinated by black CIA agents who arrange it so his death appears to be an accidental drug overdose (402).

From one point of view, the information Max discovers represents the logical conclusion to all the various—though uncollected and perhaps unconfirmed—inklings that American systems of control outstrip Communist ones in their impact on African-American citizens. Upon Harry's death, Max is given a case containing a detailed dossier of information first "stumbled on" by Jaja Enzkwu, a Nigerian official, concerning something called the King Alfred Plan (319). This chance discovery uncovers an elaborate plan, developed in secret by the U.S. government, that is named after the king who "directed translation from the Latin of the *Anglo-Saxon Chronicle*" (371), and has as its aim the systematic extermination of the country's African-American population. Ultimately, this plan would help bolster the United States' standing in the Cold War world, as the goal is to "terminate, once and for all, the Minority threat to the whole of the American society, and, indeed, the Free World" (372). As Max reads through the documents detailing the King Alfred Plan, he finds a disturbing coordination among six federal agencies, working in collusion with state and local authorities, to accomplish this termination. The idea is that African Americans are merely present in a geographical, ideological, and bureaucratic space of and for white citizens. What marks the King Alfred Plan is its attempt to leave nothing to chance in the face of the "inevitable" "racial war" it forecasts (372): not only are there instructions to detain the leaders of such groups as the Student Nonviolent Coordinating Committee and the NAACP, but there are also provisions for the unhappy fact that, in places like Harlem, "[l]ocal law enforcement officials must contain the Emergency until help arrives, though it may mean fighting a superior force" (375). Throughout *The Man Who Cried I Am*, there is a sense of a ubiquitous state presence dedicated to maintaining the (white) status quo; however visibly or invisibly it may effect this goal, the novel is saturated by the feeling that Max's free movement is a fiction that can be curbed at any time by the actions of the government agents who float around the margins of his life.

Although the King Alfred Plan is shocking in its scope and thoroughness, it is not entirely surprising to either Max or Harry Ames, both of whom have had numerous occasions to witness American racism in forms that are less systematically engineered. When, for example, Harry is ultimately refused a prestigious fellowship even though a panel of his peers selected him, he chalks it up to his having been a vocal critic of American policies and imagines equally "outlandish" scenarios—that, for instance, "He was part of a Communist-inspired plot to create a web of interracial affairs and marriages along the Eastern seaboard" (136).

When, later in the novel, Max is appointed as the White House's liaison for African-American affairs, he meets the president himself (a youngish liberal modeled on John Kennedy), but finds that, once again, he has no real power. Max in fact discovers that when a fully qualified African-American man tried to enroll in the University of Mississippi, agents from the administration found him and urged him to give up the fight for the moment because the timing was off. As one of the president's advisors explains to Max: "It's been a bad time: Cuba, the Russians in space, and now this. . . . I know the President is sincere in wanting to keep his promises to American Negroes. But he's got almost a complete term left and when he makes his move, he wants to lock it up, not lose. You know that sometimes the individual has got to be sacrificed for the group" (312). This is an extraordinary—though unsurprising—passage because it represents an American political logic that puts the needs of its citizenry far behind re-election priorities and that culminates with a sentence that could have come from the mouth of a cartoon Marxist in any anti-Communist work of the Cold War. As far as Max is concerned, giving into the demands of American politics is tantamount to yielding to Communist ones, and with this exchange he realizes that the maintenance of the white status quo will always take precedence over effecting meaningful social change.

Given such intimate contact with those in political power, by the end of *The Man Who Cried I Am*, the King Alfred Plan is somehow expected. Harry, who has been intimate in his own way with Cold War politics, is compelled by the terrible "truth" of official governmental policy with respect to African Americans:

> The material fascinated me. I'd spent so much of my life writing about the evil machinations of Mr. Charlie [white America] without really *knowing* the truth, as this material made me know it. It was spread out before me, people, places and things. I became mired in them, and I *knew* now that the way black men live on this earth was no accident. And yet, my mind kept telling me that Jaja's death [at the hands of CIA agents] was a coincidence, a mere coincidence. I could not believe that I, too, soon would be dead. (369)

In this conception, "coincidence" means two apparently chance events coming together in a way meaningful to the observer. For Harry, the King Alfred Plan confirms that as far as the American government is concerned, there is no such thing as chance for African Americans. When he muses that "the way black men live on this earth was no accident," he echoes both the latent power that chance has held in other African-American narratives and recognizes the sense that in order to maintain control, the U.S. government must actively seek to destroy any power accident might have—Ellison's "potentialities."[49] As the lengthy catalogue of the various procedures and agencies involved in the King Alfred Plan indicates, those in power are obsessed by systems of control, which the very fact of racial difference apparently threatens.

In terms of a black perspective on the Cold War, "Mister Charlie and the engineers of King Alfred" (388) represent merely another version of totalitarianism; as Harry remarks, "I quit the Party because I became damned sick and tired of white men telling me when I should suffer, where and how and what for.... Karl Marx was not thinking about niggers when he engineered *The Communist Manifesto*" (50). That both systems—the King Alfred Plan, a culmination of an American democratic experiment, and *The Communist Manifesto*, founding document of international Communism—are threatening because they are "engineered" points again to the generative power of that which is not engineered, the flip side to the claustrophobic "no accident" of African-American life.

With its inclusion of the King Alfred Plan, the final solution to the Negro Problem in the United States, *The Man Who Cried I Am* holds little hope for African-American self-definition—American life is too plotted, too fraught with the fact that, as it is put in *Invisible Man*, "white holds the odds." But as a novel about the global reach of the Cold War, *The Man Who Cried I Am* looks beyond the promise of the United States to Africa; in its awareness of the third world "stakes" of the global power struggle between the United States and the Soviet Union, it suggests that, even in the face of the Alliance Blanc (a consortium of nations working to maintain white domination in the world), Africa might afford freedom and true self-definition without the machinations of Mister Charlie. There is buzz about Africa early in the novel, even before Max goes there, as Harry calls it "a continent where freedom was going to break out with a bang. . . . Can you imagine that? A free Africa. Big, rich, three hundred million people, untold wealth. Can't you see what will have to happen to the white man's politics?" (96–97). Later, as political events such as the Mau Mau Rebellion in Kenya (1952–60) focus attention on the continent, Kwame Nkrumah declares Ghana a free state and travels to the United States, where the excitement Max witnesses is palpable: "Africa. Af-rica. Freedom. Free-dom! / Africa gave back a reflection. Africa was becoming free and her first black prime minister in modern times was coming to Washington. In triumph" (262).[50] While the promise of African freedom is not as uniformly naive as these chants of freedom suggest— after all, Jaja Enzkwu is assassinated and both the CIA and Soviets have their presence in these countries—Africa is imagined as a space that might have potential to be free from the hyper-engineering and control that marks life under the major political systems of the Cold War.

Despite the generally bleak tone of *The Man Who Cried I Am*, what is perhaps most significant about the awareness and exploitation of chance in Cold War African-American fiction is how it bonds black characters to a mainstream American experience. Although chance may be an especially important concept for African Americans caught between democratic and Communist systems of control, as we have seen in works by Pynchon and Nabokov, chance was also relevant in its expression-making capacity for those who were (at least visibly) more mainstream. Otherwise put, by demonstrating the unique relationship between chance and African-American identity, mid-century authors ironically "mainstreamed" their black characters, who could share with any American of any race the uneasy sense of being subject to control or hyper-systemization— even if not to the extent of something like the King Alfred Plan. Thus, *Invisible Man*'s famous last line, "Who knows but that, on lower frequencies, I speak for you?" (581) addresses Ellison's predominately white audience, who not only appreciated the novel's anti-Communism, but who would have also recognized the narrator's desire for personal agency and his emphasis on the diverse nature of the American experience. Similarly, when Wright insists that *The Outsider* is concerned with "problems that would beset anyone, black or white," he reminds readers of Cross's position as human being first and African American second ("What's a man?" asks Cross, "He had unknowingly set himself a project of no less magnitude than contained in that awful question" [83]). In *The Man Who Cried I Am*, Max's discovery of the King Alfred Plan and his chilling assassination not only implicate all Americans in racial discord, but as the ubiquitous presence of the shadowy CIA agents suggest, any American could be the subject of such control. While race is, of course, an integral aspect of each of these books, the authors refuse to essentialize race—it remains something significant but also ever-shifting. Chance is an ideal concept to articulate this sense of race because by its very nature it cannot be pinned down or fit into a scheme or plan, even a racially aware one. Thus, one thing the Cold War did to African-American writing was encourage writers to innovate strategies of representation that would retain a sense of African-American identity while simultaneously aligning an African-American experience with a mainstream American experience.

5

The Game Theory Narrative and the Myth of the National Security State

> With the Soviet Union, you did get the sense that they were operating on a model that we could comprehend in terms of, they don't want to be blown up, we don't want to be blown up, so you do game theory and calculate ways to contain.
> —Barack Obama, September 2004

> A state's ability to wage war is measured only loosely in kilotonnage. A better indicator is a country's ability to wage randomness, to impose a signal-to-noise problem on the enemy, render his informational stockpile incoherent.
> —Richard Powers

"You can never underestimate the willingness of the state to act out its own massive fantasies." So says Eric Deming in the novel *Underworld* (1997), Don DeLillo's weighty stocktaking of postwar American culture.[1] As Matt Shay listens, Eric, stoned and introspective, repeats this statement: *"You can never unterestimate the villingness of the shtate. . . . To ahkt out its own massif phantasies."* The accented repetition signals that this is a clichéd phrase, likely lifted from some half-remembered antifascist B-movie. But the following day, as Matt thinks about the phrase, he wonders if it was not "paying tribute" to "all those émigrés from Middle Europe . . . [who] came to do science in New Mexico during the war." This speculation is occasioned by a rambling reference Eric wedges between the first statement and its repetition: "Eric went on in his stupid voice, talking about problem boxes and minimax solutions, all the kriegspielish stuff they'd studied in grad school, theory of games and patterns of conflict, heads I win, tails you lose." With this pairing, DeLillo implies a connection between game theory—"minimax solutions, all the kriegspielish stuff"—and fantasies of state control. Although paranoid narratives about the hand of the state manipulating individual lives are familiar aspects of Cold War rhetoric, scholars of mid-century American culture have paid less attention to what such narratives have to do with game theory.[2] The connection is a vestige of what I call the "game theory narrative," a cultural narrative that told the story of game theory's potential to prevent nuclear exchange by conceptualizing the Cold War as a game, and by playing this game according to specific rational strategies.

As the Cold War got underway, the white-coated scientist and the horn-rimmed mathematician became symbols of the new war effort's intellectual heft.[3] In the Atomic Age, eggheads found themselves the most consequential of soldiers, an idea that survives in recent reconstructions of the era. *A Beautiful Mind* (2001), for example, the Oscar-winning biopic of mathematician and sometime game theorist John Nash, opens in the Princeton mathematics department in 1947. Professor Helinger (Judd Hirsch) stirs the patriotism of the new class: "Mathematicians won the war. Mathematicians broke the Japanese codes and built the A-bomb. Mathematicians like you. The stated goal of the Soviets is global Communism. In medicine or economics, in technology or space, battle lines are being drawn. To triumph, we need results. Publishable, applicable results. . . . Who among you will be the vanguard of democracy, freedom, and discovery?"[4] This narrative, that "global Communism" would be defeated only if seemingly pure disciplines such as mathematics yielded "applicable results," had its singular expression in game theory, a system of rational decision making that would, it was claimed, give Americans an advantage in the global game against the Soviets.

Although game theory's mathematical underpinnings were complicated enough to flummox a nonspecialist, in the late 1940s and early 1950s, it was popularized in the print media as America's "secret weapon."[5] In 1950, John McDonald, a journalist who first brought the game theory narrative to the reading public, described game theory in almost messianic terms: "Mathematicians are discovering a perfect, fool-proof system for playing all cut-throat games including poker, business—and war."[6] McDonald's sweeping assertion is a visible manifestation of the game theory narrative, a popularized (if imperfect) understanding of game theory's capabilities that gained significant authority and privilege in American culture in the early 1950s.

Thus far in *No Accident, Comrade*, I have explored the circulation of chance in Cold War culture mainly through the intersections among various kinds of political and fictional narratives. This chapter shifts focus to how the game theory narrative ironically promised to manage major threats of the Cold War—the menace of an unknown enemy and the specter of an accidental nuclear exchange—by incorporating random strategies. The following sections explore how this popularized narrative was both exemplified and criticized by a variety of creative works and other artifacts of Cold War culture.[7] Taken together, these sections show how, in the game theory narrative, the promise of scientific redemption combines with the power of rationality to triumph over the threat of chance, and, ultimately, with the power of the United States to triumph over the

Soviets and their perceived goal of global Communism. Attention to this narrative helps us understand classic Cold War texts in a new light—it demonstrates, for example, that Stanley Kubrick's *Dr. Strangelove* (1964) is a satire not only of nuclear brinksmanship but also of the particular game-theoretic rationality that was claimed to prevent such escalation from actually coming to war; or that Philip K. Dick's first novel, *Solar Lottery* (1955), offers a critique of postwar politics by imagining a future universe whose fundamentally flawed political systems are governed by the dictates of the game theory narrative; or that Joan Didion's *The Last Thing He Wanted* (1996) posits an opposition between the workings of the "real world" and those of a game theoretic model. In these and other works, writers and cultural observers registered the pervasiveness of the game theory narrative but also probed the potential dangers of relying on it too exclusively when engaging real-life problems.

In many ways the game theory narrative was a perfect fit for the culture of the Cold War, and as such it explains some of its peculiarities. As a narrative that both exploits and presupposes the dominance of certain subjectivities, it is insistently rational, it forecloses possibility by managing chance, and it seems an extension of what Suzanne Clark calls the "hypermasculinity of [Cold War] national policy."[8] At the end of this chapter, I suggest that these features help explain why the Cold War has tended to be conceptualized as a two-person contest, but then take Didion's novels about American intervention in the Third World as exemplars of how the game theory narrative's limitations were exposed. By emphasizing the role of "non-state actors" in the real operation of Cold War politics, Didion describes what is left out by the game theory narrative, a general critique that became widespread after the early 1960s.

The Game Theory Narrative Explained

The development of game theory owed much to the needs—and financial backing—of the American military, which by the late 1940s found itself waging a new sort of war. Philip Mirowski has articulated the conflicted relationship game theory had with the Cold War:

> In the first two decades of its existence, to discuss game theory was to discuss "strategy," and from there attitudes toward militarism and the arms race rapidly took over. Some laid the blame for the escalation of nuclear weaponry directly at the door of game theory; other, cooler heads claimed that game theory was symptomatic of an apologetic bias in favor of the military–industrial complex; still others asserted it was an expression of abstract rationality ideally tuned to the technological character of the Cold War.[9]

Whatever the specific material connections between the military–industrial complex and the rise of game theory, we might take Mirowski's point to be that game theory was linked to the special demands of the Cold War, and in this connection made concepts like "strategy" and "abstract rationality" especially urgent in their power to manage the nuclear age.[10]

For a reasonably informed nonspecialist in 1950, game theory was a language used by scientists—in comforting collusion with the government—to help control the inherent risk of war. Although game theory had its most influential and far-reaching articulation in John von Neumann and Oskar Morgenstern's *Theory of Games and Economic Behavior* (1944), this book, dense with mathematical proofs, was not widely read by nonprofessionals.[11] But by the late 1940s and early 1950s, discussions of game theory began to appear in magazines like *Fortune*, *Scientific American*, *Newsweek*, and *Time*, many of which echoed the *New York Times* review of *Theory of Games and Economic Behavior*, which was quick to note game theory's potential "military application."[12] In 1948 and 1949, *Fortune* published a pair of articles by John McDonald, "Poker: An American Game" and "A Theory of Strategy," that would later form the core of his cartoon-illustrated introduction to game theory's potential, *Strategy in Poker, Business and War* (1950).[13] As this title implies, McDonald's principal claim is that game theory demonstrates affinities among poker, business, and war because it offers a theory of strategy for excelling in all three arenas. By emphasizing the link between poker scenarios and nuclear war, McDonald not only suggests that the latter is manageable but also that the ultimate importance of game theory is its potential for real-world military application. It is this seemingly necessary connection between game theory and American military strategy on which most public conceptions of game theory rested. In the opening paragraph of "A Theory of Strategy," for example, McDonald draws the association between game theory and national security that would come to dominate the public's conception for the next decade:

> In the spartan surroundings of a Pentagon office a young scientist attached to the Air Force said, "We hope it will work, just as we hoped in 1942 that the atomic bomb would work." What he hoped and in some sense implied will work is a newly created theory of strategy that many scientists believe has important potentialities in military affairs, economics, and other social sciences. The theory is familiarly known to the military as "Games," though its high security classification wherever it has actual content is a sign that its intent is anything but trifling.[14]

Here, as in *Strategy in Poker, Business and War*, McDonald emphasized that the American military was relying on game theory as a key weapon in the global game of the Cold War. Whereas von Neumann and Morgenstern's innovation was to link game theory to economic behavior, McDonald's dramatic sense that scientists and the military alike were putting all their "hope" into game theory intimates what many game theorists in the 1950s found themselves pursuing: a winning military strategy. However simplified the mathematics were, articles and books like McDonald's suggest game theory's defining characteristic became its potential real-world application to military strategy in a nuclear age.[15]

The association of game theory with military strategy was cemented by the connection both had to the RAND Corporation. Founded in 1946 with support from the Air Force, RAND was a nonprofit "brain factory" where much of the theoretical work was performed with an eye toward practical, military application. As historian Fred Kaplan has succinctly put it: "Game theory caught on in a very big way at RAND in the late 1940s."[16] And it was at RAND where game theory and military strategy were united by the media in the early 1950s. A 1953 *Newsweek* article suggested that "the average man might not understand Rand's preoccupation with the new and highly mathematical 'theory of games.' Yet games are vital to Rand's work, for the theory of probability, in its risk-versus-gain aspect, looms big in modern scientific warfare."[17] The adjective that the *Newsweek* writer appends to "warfare" is significant: in this view, game theory has helped to make war "scientific"—that is, less risky, more controllable. This early sense that RAND experts would employ game theory to manage the randomness of war—randomness that became more acute as the arms race escalated—was an important aspect of the game theory narrative. By the early 1960s, RAND was even more well-known to the public as the "Brain Power for the Air Force," as one 1960 *New York Times* article asserted.[18] Despite such laudatory press, the more exposure RAND received, the more skepticism mounted about its ties to the military, and about their combined ability to head off accidental nuclear war, an idea I return to in the last section of this chapter.

But in the early 1950s, game theory was attractive to those looking for a way to "reduce war by accident." John McDonald was especially optimistic; he closes *Strategy in Poker, Business and War* by imagining that a nuclear strike has been launched against the United States, and that it "cannot be assumed that every rocket contains an important bomb—a large proportion of them are likely to be feints, or bluffs."[19] A dire scenario indeed, but by noting the strategic parallel to a game of poker (the dummy bombs are "bluffs"), McDonald begins to suggest that minimax, one of game theory's most well-known concepts, would help the United States win the hand: "War is chance and minimax must be its modern philosophy."[20] McDonald thus anticipates the *Newsweek* article proclaiming that "modern scientific warfare" is war in which chance can be managed by the "modern" philosophy of minimax. McDonald writes:

> In brief, then, the theory of games says this: Strategical games give a player a choice of action in a situation where all the players are

interdependent. Uncertainty in a game may derive merely from a practical limitation on foresight, as in chess. But more often it derives from a chance element (controllable by the theory of probability) and from imperfect information on the part of one player regarding what his opponents may do (uncontrollable except in the theory of games). Strategy is a policy devised to reduce and control these uncertainties. Strategy may require the introduction of chance moves by the players to prevent their pattern from being discovered, that is, to increase the imperfection of information. Good strategy requires the use of the principle of "minimax," that is, a policy in which a range of possible high and low gains is adopted on the assumption that one might be found out. But to avoid being found out one obscures the specific pattern of play by randomizing the strategy with chance plays.[21]

As McDonald explains it, minimax's relationship to chance is paradoxical: it controls chance (war) by invoking chance (random moves). Minimax is therefore simultaneously pro- and anti-chance. To meet the unknown, random aspect of war—or business, or poker—a good strategist becomes himself an avatar of the unknown by incorporating randomness. The narrative of game theory—that it was a "fool-proof system" for allowing the United States to gain a strategic advantage in the Cold War—was thus tied to its perceived ability to both manage and incorporate chance. Such was the popularity of this idea that by 1949, the *Reader's Guide to Periodical Literature*'s entry for "Chance" directed readers to "Games, Theory of." If the prospect of an accidental nuclear exchange came to weigh heavy on the minds of the American public, then game theory's promise seemed so powerful because it could erase this chance by rational means.

The Game Theory Narrative Explored

Reverberations of the game theory narrative can be heard throughout Cold War culture. With respect to game theory's relationship to chance, for example, one might note how William S. Burroughs described the origins of the infamous "cut-up" method I mentioned briefly in the first chapter: "*Theory of Games and Economic Behavior* introduced the cut up principle of random action into military and game strategy. . . . The cut up method was used in *Naked Lunch* without the author's full awareness of the method he was using."[22] In Kurt Vonnegut's first novel, *Player Piano* (1952), the symbolic role of a character named Professor von Neumann would have been clearer to those readers familiar with his real-life namesake.[23] In 1963, Milton Cannif explored the military's use of games in his popular *Steve Canyon* cartoon strip.[24] In a 1955 essay for the magazine *Astounding Science Fiction*, editor John W. Campbell, Jr.—one of the most important champions of science fiction in the twentieth century—suggested how the game theory narrative encouraged Americans to conceptualize life as a specific type of game: "Now Game Theory has considered two essentially different types of games; the open game, and the concealed game.... Poker... is a concealed game; the rules are known, but the actual situation at any instant is not known to *any* player.... The Game of Life as currently played by this culture is, in essence, a concealed game; it's based on Privacy of Action.... People raised in a concealed game culture are going to have some horrendous psychic problems."[25] The problems Campbell has in mind concern the civic logic such a concealed game encourages: citizens are left to second-guess their own actions and regard the behavior of others with suspicion. This analysis in fact implies a fundamental critique prevalent among those who engaged and criticized the game theory narrative. Campbell suggests that although the narrative passed for a natural or scientific aspect of reality (like gravity), it was really a metaphor that would prove itself imperfect when pressure was applied. Whether the specific metaphor was poker or rational game playing, this pervasive critique concerned the nature of the metaphor itself, which normalized the abnormal by viewing real life only through the strictures of a bounded game. To suggest the various ways the game theory narrative came to be viewed in Cold War culture, I want to turn now to some of the more sustained and complex ways it was explored.

The connections among game theory, national security, and chance come together in what is, to my knowledge, the first full-scale fictional engagement with the game theory narrative, Philip K. Dick's novel, *Solar Lottery* (1955). A prolific science-fiction writer whose work was the basis for the film *Blade Runner* (1982), Dick became interested in the promise of game theory in the early 1950s. In *Solar Lottery*, Dick imagines a universe in which political structures are based on the principles of game theory as articulated not by its expert practitioners, but by John McDonald, the journalist who popularized the game theory narrative. The novel's epigraph is in fact taken from McDonald's *Strategy in Poker, Business and War*. Building on McDonald's sense of game theory, Dick's universe is set in 2203, when every inhabitant of every planet has a "power card" with a unique number. In the great solar lottery of the title, a specially constructed bottle, "the socialized instrument of chance," twitches at random and delivers a power card number.[26] Whoever holds this power card, no matter what his or her status, background, or education, is immediately elevated to the universe's most powerful position, Quizmaster. Although it is not quite an example of democratic freedom, the system is intended to forestall despotism since no person, in theory, "can plan to be a dictator: it [the bottle system] comes and goes according to subatomic random particles" (38).[27]

This system is the logical extension of what Dick perceives to be the marriage of game theory and military policy during the early 1950s. He prefaces the novel in this way:

> I became interested in the Theory of Games, first in an intellectual manner (like chess) and then with a growing uneasy conviction that Minimax was playing an expanding role in our national life. Although specialists in related fields (mathematics, statistics, sociology, economics) are aware of its existence, the Games Theory has been little publicized. Yet it was instrumental in the Allied strategy in the Second World War. Both the U.S. and the Soviet Union employ Minimax strategy as I sit here. While I was writing SOLAR LOTTERY, Von Neumann, the co-inventor of the Games Theory, was named to the Atomic Energy Commission, bearing out my belief that Minimax is gaining on us all the time. (no page)

For Dick, Dwight Eisenhower's appointment of von Neumann to the Atomic Energy Commission was a symbolic event that implied the power game theory had—and would come to have—over U.S. political life.[28] He understands game theory as intimately tied to Cold War "strategy," a situation that the novel analyzes as it explores the ways game theory manages what one character calls the "universe of chance" (34). One running theme is the sense that game theory has imposed its own set of rules onto the universe, and that when those artificial, perhaps arbitrary, rules become codified by governments, people have trouble distinguishing the narrative from the laws of the universe. Discussing the theory of minimax (or the M-Game, as the lottery is called), one character remarks, "The whole system is artificial. This M-Game was invented by a couple of mathematicians during the early phase of the Second World War" (57). This notion is countered with the argument that minimax is a law of the universe: "You mean discovered. They saw that social situations are analogues of strategy games, like poker. A system that works in a poker game will work in a social situation, like business or war" (57–58). This dispute over whether game theory and minimax are accurate discoveries of universal laws, or merely arbitrary impositions onto the universe reflects a growing reservation that many observers would come to have about the promise of the game theory narrative. We might understand Dick's critique as a more complex version of Campbell's concern about how metaphors are confused with objective reality so it becomes hard to say whether game theory was "invented" or "discovered."

Although the universe Dick has imagined may seem at first to endorse the potential of game theory to become "the basis of Government" (20), the novel also suggests the danger of confusing metaphor with objective reality, a danger intimated in the author's note, with its ominous sense "that Minimax is gaining on us all the time." Minimax indeed holds as much promise in Dick's future as it does in his present. One character explains it this way: "Minimax was a brilliant hypothesis. It gave us a rational scientific method to crack any strategy and transform the strategy game into a chance game, where the regular statistical methods of the exact sciences function" (58). In this conception, minimax promises to convert the chance inherent in poker or war into a scientifically managed aspect of the conflict. Yet minimax and the game theory narrative are ultimately viewed with skepticism in *Solar Lottery* because in the end chance cannot be manipulated; Dick's universe is subject to chance, and we learn that the "Uncertainty Principle is on the level" (177). As an early engagement with the game theory narrative, *Solar Lottery* expresses ambivalence about its promise. In debating whether the narrative was "discovered" or "invented," the novel also poses questions about the role of chance in the universe, and the way that the popularized versions of mid-century strategy engaged this universe.[29]

Eight years after *Solar Lottery*, Robert Coover published one of his earliest short stories, "The Second Son," about a solitary accountant who entertains himself with an absurdly complicated baseball game played with dice, in the *Evergreen Review*. "Second Son" forms the germ of Coover's second novel, *The Universal Baseball Association, Inc., J. Henry Waugh, Prop.* (1968).[30] This novel explores the tensions between chance and design in J. Henry Waugh's imagined world and derives much of its force—and its plot—from its metafictional meditation on the natures of fiction and reality, a meditation that is explicitly extended to the game theory narrative. Waugh creates a fictional universe dominated by the game of baseball and governed by the roll of three dice. Although Waugh is responsible for the rules of this universe—he has elaborate charts and meticulous record books—the outcomes of each season are ultimately "committed" to the chance roll of the dice.[31] While Waugh's lackluster real life occupies some of the novel, most of the book is concerned with the baseball association and its colorful players—characters who have not only backstories, but complex personal histories, loves and inner lives. The crisis of the novel occurs when, at a crucial point in a game, Waugh tosses three ones, which means that Damon Rutherford, one of the Association's stars, is "struck fatally by [a] bean ball" thrown by pitcher Jock Casey (70). The turning point of the book, in other words, hinges on a moment of chance—although this is Waugh's universe, he is still beholden to the chance roll of the dice. After this "one chance in 216," an emotionally affected Waugh struggles with whether he should violate his own rules by deliberately positioning the dice to determine an outcome (70). Ultimately, when Jock Casey comes to bat in a later game, Waugh rigs the system: "holding the dice in his left palm, he set them down carefully with his right," so Casey too is killed by an errant pitch (202).

It may be apparent from this description that Coover's novel is a canny engagement with some of the questions the game theory narrative invited: in the universe of the Baseball Association, the results of Waugh's intervention are paradigm-shifting because a chance roll was converted into a willful strategy. The novel is about the veils between fiction (or myth) and reality: once Waugh intervenes to adjust the dice, the characters in his universe intimate the guiding hand of the Association's author, and deify the players involved.

The novel's final chapter thus invites readers to consider how the Universal Baseball Association could be an allegory for religious narratives—after all, J. Henry Waugh, an echo of Yahweh, has created the rules of his universe, but has (for a time) allowed chance to mimic free will and ability in the rolls of the dice.[32] Once Waugh intervenes, predetermining an outcome, the players themselves wonder "if there's really a record-keeper up there or not" (239). Although the affinities between J. Henry Waugh and Yahweh or a deist clockmaker are manifest, the game theory narrative helps us see how *The Universal Baseball Association* concerns also Cold War politics—between baseball games, Waugh reads newspapers with headlines about the "Makings of another large war," and he contemplates a game about the "space race" (130, 132). By the final chapter, in which pseudo-religions and mystery cults have proliferated in Waugh's imagined universe, one available faith is "the folklore of game theory" (234). As the yoking of religion to folklore to game theory implies, Coover's critique of the ways that religious myths govern reality extends to the game theory narrative. One recurring element is how the Cold War is figured as a game:

> [Waugh had] always played a lot of games: baseball, basketball, different card games, war and finance games, horseracing, football, and so on, all on paper of course. Once, he'd got involved in a tabletop war-games club, played by mail, with mutual defense pacts, munition sales, secret agents, and even assassinations, but the inability of the other players to detach themselves from their narrow-minded historical preconceptions depressed Henry. Anything more complex than a normalized two-person zero-sum game was beyond them. (44)

The "war-games club" plays out a modern military conflict on paper, a pastime that is a wink to the tendencies of game theorists to play out their versions of conflict on paper.[33] This particular war game in fact exudes the very language of game theory—the "normalized two-person zero-sum game"—that is used in numerous books like Duncan R. Luce and Howard Raïffa's *Games and Decisions: Introduction and Critical Survey* (1957).[34] That Waugh thinks of such language as "narrow-minded historical preconceptions" is in keeping with the notion that the game theory narrative was tied to a specific historical and political moment. Although the theory was supposed to have been discovered rather than invented, Waugh finds its particularized games so depressing because they lack the rich and multilayered imagination he displays throughout the novel.

The Universal Baseball Association ultimately suggests that the promise of salvation through control is a feature common to both religious and game theory narratives. The critique, in other words, has affinities with numerous positions we have seen throughout *No Accident, Comrade*: although we live in a universe of absolute chance, the game theory narrative, like religion, offers unverifiable methods for controlling or managing chance as such. When the Chancellor of the Association, Fennimore McCaffree, ruminates about the nature of baseball, he thinks about it in the terms of the game theory narrative: "He was forever yakking about distribution functions, the canonical form of M, compound decision problems, relations of dominance; like Fenn had somehow forgot the game was baseball" (146). Fenn forgets "the game was baseball" because he is actually meditating on game theory and its relation to real-life problems. In *The Universal Baseball Association*, baseball functions as a metaphor of both religious control and of the control of game theory: "the canonical form of M," like the M-Game in *Solar Lottery*, alludes to minimax, the notion of balance and equilibrium, so that "old strategies, like winning ball games, sensible and proper within the old stochastic or recursive sets, are, under the new circumstances, *insane!*" (148). In a world in which Waugh has loaded the dice, former normative standards ("old stochastic or recursive sets") become irrational—"insane"—because the rules of the game are no longer chance governed. While manipulating the dice is a way out of the "loneliness" that came when "pattern dissipated, giving way to mere accident," this control of accident has religious reverberations, as well as secular ones. In Coover's world, many Americans, like the fans of the Universal Baseball Association, looked to the "folklore of game theory" to salve their anxieties about the game being played with atomic bombs instead of baseballs.

The Game Theory Narrative and Irrational Rationality

By the early 1960s, another aspect of the game theory narrative had found important expression in popular culture. Game theory, this story went, relies on rationality, and rationality alone will cope with the nuclear situation—if not ultimately to prevent nuclear exchange, then to manage its effects. This narrative is best illustrated by looking at how one landmark treatise, Herman Kahn's *On Thermonuclear War* (1960), was satirized in a landmark film, Stanley Kubrick's black comedy *Dr. Strangelove, or: How I Learned to Stop Worrying and Love the Bomb* (1964). Although *On Thermonuclear War* is not about game theory in the way that *A Theory of Games and Economic Behavior* is, it is still an important part of the game theory narrative, since it aims to work through several rational "national strategies" to deal with hypothetical situations created by the arms race and the ascendance of fail-safe systems.[35] As one letter writer put it to the *New York Times* in January 1965, "'The Return of Dr. Strangelove' might have been the title of the [recent] . . . interview of . . . Herman Kahn. . . . It is great comfort to see that the advanced techniques of mathematical operations research and war games theory have finally reduced the baffling complexities of nuclear war to the simple equation of tit-for-tat."[36] This comparison of Kahn with Dr. Strangelove was on the mark: as numerous historians have shown, in the early 1960s, Kubrick read widely in the literature of nuclear strategy and carefully studied Kahn's work as he conceived the film that would become *Dr. Strangelove*.[37] As Kubrick absorbed the arguments of real-life strategists, he became convinced that the insistent rationality of a thinker like Kahn was actually irrational and that "the only way to tell the story was as a black comedy, or better, a nightmare comedy, where the things you laugh at most are really the heart of the paradoxical postures that make a nuclear war possible."[38]

Kubrick's principal target is Kahn's basic insistence—so measured and rational as to be chilling—that global thermonuclear war would not result in complete annihilation of the human race. By implementing the right strategy, Kahn argued, human life would survive: "[I]f proper preparations have been made, it would be possible for us or the Soviets to cope with all the effects of a thermonuclear war, in the sense of saving most people and restoring something close to the prewar standard of living in a relatively short time."[39] This premise demands that the United States think strategically about both the escalation building to nuclear exchange and the aftermath of this exchange. In what is perhaps the most notorious section of *On Thermonuclear War*, Kahn analyzes how many human losses are "acceptable" in a nuclear war, and includes tables like this:

Tragic But Distinguishable Postwar States

Dead	Economic Recuperation
2,000,000	1 year
5,000,000	2 years
10,000,000	5 years
20,000,000	10 years
40,000,000	20 years
80,000,000	50 years
160,000,000	100 years

Will the survivors envy the dead?[40]

The sort of no-nonsense scientific clarity embodied by this table characterized Kahn's argument as a whole. Even though Kahn's professed goal was to increase the prospects for peace by outlining the practical aftermath of nuclear war, many people were shocked and offended by the pointed way he incorporated human lives (and deaths) into his strategic analyses. James R. Newman, for example, writing for *Scientific American* in 1961, asked: "Is there really a Herman Kahn? It is hard to believe. . . . No one could write like this, no one could think like this. Perhaps the whole thing is a staff hoax in bad taste."[41] Newman was not alone in recoiling from the bad taste left by Kahn's emotionless charts and statistics.[42] In fact, *On Thermonuclear War*—connected as it was to RAND and to the game theory narrative's promise of rational control over an irrational global situation—came to stand for the way that the concept of "strategy" became linked to the game of the Cold War. In sober treatments of Kahn's scenarios like Sidney Lumet's film *Fail-Safe* (1964), the bad taste of rationality lingers. *Fail-Safe* follows the agonizing decisions required of the president after an accidental nuclear strike against the Soviet Union. In discussing the best strategy for responding to the accident, Professor Groeteschele (Walter Matthau), resident Kahn-like expert in the war room, lays out the situation in game theoretic terms: "naturally [war] means taking risks, but our intention has always been to minimize those risks. Of course we can only control our own actions. Our concept of limited war is based on an equal rationality on the part of the Russians; it also presupposes there will be no accidents on either side." The Cold War is figured as a game of risk in which each player must assume equal rationality on the part of his opponent—but as many commentators were arguing by the early 1960s, this metaphor was flawed enough to be dangerous.[43]

Whereas *Fail-Safe* dramatizes a straight version of Kahn's warnings, *Dr. Strangelove* skewers his dogged rationality by showing what happens when rationality itself is exposed as contingent and contextual. *Dr. Strangelove* shares its basic plot with *Fail-Safe*: a nuclear attack is accidentally launched against the Soviet Union, and the American president must work with the Soviet leader to avert an all-out nuclear exchange. But in *Dr. Strangelove*, the idea of "rationality" is not so stable as it is in *Fail-Safe* (or indeed in *On Thermonuclear War*), and Kubrick emphasizes that the nuclear strike is only accidental from the perspective of what the president calls "national policy."[44] From the perspective of General Jack D. Ripper (Sterling Hayden), the Air Force commander who ordered the strike, it was not accidental at all. This difference in perspective points to the problem with the stridently rational approach insisted on by Kahn. Ripper, who is, as British Group Captain Mandrake (Peter Sellers) observes, "as mad as a bloody march hare," nevertheless proceeds from a rationality of sorts. His motive for launching the strike against Russia is a parody of the paranoid civic logic encouraged by the Cold War: he believes it is necessary to strike the Russians pre-emptively because they are actively conspiring to sap "our precious bodily fluids." Kubrick links this initially outlandish statement to actual Cold War controversies about water fluoridation: "Do you realize," says Ripper, "that fluoridation is the most monstrously conceived and dangerous Communist plot we have ever had to face?"[45] This technique of connecting the absurd to the real is used throughout *Dr. Strangelove* to suggest the dishearteningly familiar brand of rationality employed not only by Ripper but also by the world's two superpowers.

The sense that the people in charge of preventing nuclear war are blind to their own irrationality is tied to a critique of the game theory narrative, which is rooted—insistently so—in rational decision making. *Dr. Strangelove* shows that what game theory dictates is good strategy does not necessarily translate to favorable outcomes in the real, human world. A central idea of the game theory narrative as inflected by Kahn—that the Cold War is a global game—is visually present in *Dr. Strangelove*'s famous War Room set. According to production designer Ken Adam, even though the film was shot in black and white, Kubrick wanted the enormous round conference table covered in green baize "to give the impression that these characters sitting around this table are involved in a gigantic poker game for the fate of the world."[46] It is around this enormous poker table that Kubrick most devastatingly skewers *On Thermonuclear War*. A parody of the hypermasculine Cold Warrior, Buck Turgidson (George C. Scott) is a hawkish, gum-smacking general who echoes Kahn's substance and style as he tries to convince the president to launch a full-scale nuclear strike:

> Now, the truth is not always a pleasant thing, but it is necessary now to make a choice, to choose between two admittedly regrettable, but nevertheless distinguishable postwar environments: one where you got twenty million people killed, and the other where you got a hundred and fifty million people killed. . . . Mr. President, I'm not saying we wouldn't get our hair mussed. But I do say no more than ten to twenty million killed, tops. Uh, depending on the breaks.

Turgidson's notoriously folksy metaphor for nuclear annihilation ("I'm not saying we wouldn't get our hair mussed") lampoons a cowboy sensibility that couched the absurdity of Cold War logic in a straight-talking, matter-of-fact style that was meant to make such logic seem reasonable.[47] If the game theory narrative had elevated a particular kind of "abstract rationality" to the forefront of nuclear strategy, then speeches like Turgidson's demonstrate how this logic was crumbling by the early 1960s—it was sensible only given the bounded terms of the Cold War "poker game," but irrational and irresponsible from a real human perspective.

The notion of insane rationality is embodied by the eponymous Dr. Strangelove, played by Peter Sellers as a wheelchair-bound ex-Nazi. Strangelove is the president's expert consultant who represents what Kubrick saw as the increasingly alarming logic of Kahn and the RAND crowd. Asked about the viability of building an Earth-destroying "Doomsday" machine (an idea lifted from the pages of *On Thermonuclear War*), Strangelove informs the president: "Under the authority granted me as director of weapons research and development, I commissioned last year a study of this project by the BLAND Corporation. Based on the findings of the report, my conclusion was that this idea was not a practical deterrent, for reasons which, at this moment, must be all too obvious."[48] If the favorable responses to *Dr. Strangelove* are any index of public opinion on nuclear strategy, the not-so-subtle allusion suggests that RAND's cultural star had plummeted since the late 1940s.[49] By the end of the film, when it is clear that a Soviet-built Doomsday device will be triggered as soon as the American bomb strikes, Strangelove advises retreating into "some of our deeper mineshafts." In a manic plan that unites Kahn-like rationality with Nazi ideology (Strangelove is prone to absentmindedly addressing the president as "mein Führer"), a nuclear holocaust becomes an opportunity to cherry pick the human race: "a computer could be set and programmed to accept factors from youth, health, sexual fertility, intelligence, and a cross section of necessary skills. Of course it would be absolutely vital that our top government and military men be included to foster and impart the required principles of leadership and tradition." Strangelove's reliance on an emotionless, calculating computer demonstrates the flip side to the game theory narrative's elevation of science—in 1953, as we have seen, *Newsweek* lauded the promise of "modern scientific warfare"; in 1964, the science of selecting survivors was a disturbing corollary to Kahn's approach to the arms race. *Dr. Strangelove* argues, then, that far from preventing nuclear war, the rationality of the game theory narrative could actually precipitate it.

A year after Kubrick's wild vision of game theory gone awry, the *New Yorker* published an early story by Donald Barthelme, who would become one of the more respected practitioners of what was soon labeled postmodernism. Like *Dr. Strangelove*, "Game" puts a surreal spin on the rationality of deterrence. The story is simple and repetitive: the narrator explains that he is one of two men tasked with manning an underground missile bunker. Inadvertently forgotten by their superiors, the men have been locked together for 133 days, and the rational decision making that is supposed to govern their behavior has begun to break down. Writing in the context of game theory's history, Philip Mirowski remarked that Barthelme's story "captures in a concise way what game theory meant to someone living in the United States in the early 1960s."[50] "Game" is governed by the logic of the game theory narrative, and the story is interested in how such logic was proving itself increasingly absurd. Here is how the narrator describes his stalemate with his fail-safe partner, Shotwell:

> Shotwell and I watch the console. Shotwell and I live under the ground and watch the console. If certain events take place upon the console, we are to insert our keys in the appropriate locks and turn our keys. Shotwell has a key and I have a key. If we turn our keys simultaneously the bird flies. But the bird never flies. . . . Meanwhile Shotwell and I watch each other. We each wear a .45 and if Shotwell behaves strangely I am supposed to shoot him. If I behave strangely Shotwell is supposed to shoot me.[51]

The game of the Cold War is dramatized by the edgy standoff between Shotwell and the narrator. This connection implies not only that both situations are absurd but that they are absurd because the situation itself stalls linear progression (or, in narrative terms, plot). To tell a story about the rational situation created by the Cold War, conventional plots are insufficient: the repetition of this passage characterizes the story as a whole and implies how the game theory narrative has imposed a set of norms no longer sustainable. "In the beginning," writes the narrator, "I took care to behave normally. So did Shotwell. Our behavior was painfully normal. Norms of politeness, consideration, speech, and personal habits were scrupulously observed. But then it became apparent that an error had been made, that our relief was not going to appear. . . . the norms were relaxed. Definitions of normality were redrawn in the agreement of January 1st, called by us 'The Agreement.'"[52] "Game" suggests that the military demands of the Cold War (being stationed in a missile bunker) are so inflected by the demands of the game theory narrative (Shotwell's behavior must be rationally evaluated, even as he reads, in another echo of McDonald's connection between business and war, "*Introduction to Marketing* by Lassiter and Munk") that the whole situation amounts to a stalled narrative. As in *Dr. Strangelove*, when the U.S. president and the Soviet premiere endlessly talk past each other on the hotline phone, genuine human communication has broken down between Shotwell and the narrator because both men have defined themselves according to the game theory narrative and so have become players instead of people.

Throughout the 1960s, the sense that the game theory narrative had stalled was explored by game theorists themselves. Among the more vocal critics was Anatol Rapoport, an academic who also wrote for a more general audience with the aim of correcting what he perceived as the unrealistic popularization of game theory. In his professional work, Rapoport became increasingly interested in arguing against the notion that pure rationality in strategic decision making was possible or even desirable; in writing for nonprofessionals, he explicitly engaged some of the signal features of the game theory narrative I have been describing. To cite one example: in a 1962 *Scientific American* article, Rapoport challenged the notion that the "fashionable technique" of game theory can "really be used to solve the problems of human conflict."[53] Rapoport's opening move returns us to the paeans to scientists one encountered in the early 1950s: "We live in an age of belief—belief in the omnipotence of science."[54] For Rapoport, allegiance to science's power and potential had led to game theory's promise being exaggerated in public discourse for reasons that, as we have seen, were met with resistance in numerous creative engagements. "A thorough understanding of game theory," Rapoport wrote, "should dim these greedy hopes. Knowledge of game theory does not make one a better card player, businessman or military strategist."[55] Here he is not necessarily arguing against the uses of game theory as articulated by von Neumann and Morgenstern and in RAND working papers, but rather against the "misuse" of game theory as it was popularized in the game theory narrative.[56]

From about the mid-1960s, many professional observers came to concur with Rapoport's more tempered view of game theory's promise, and its specific effect on U.S. foreign policy had waned considerably since the early 1950s.[57] Over the next few decades, in fact, the uses of game theory were evident less in foreign policy or military strategy and more in complex economics and social science. Still, it is tempting to locate some lingering effects of the game theory narrative even in the 1980s, when the Reagan administration acted from the belief that a nuclear war was winnable given the use of rational strategies.[58] It seems worth noting, for example, that some critics of the Reagan administration's stance on nuclear strategy gestured toward the earlier conceptualizations of the Cold War as a game that I have been describing. In 1984, Robert Jervis wrote about the "illogic" of a nuclear strategy that supposes a winnable nuclear war: "A rational strategy for the employment of nuclear weapons is a contradiction in terms"; from this premise, he concludes that "the poker game model of bluffing is misleading."[59] In his critique of contemporary applications of "abstract rationality," Jervis alludes to the ways that the game theory narrative linked war with poker, and how it promised to control nuclear war by making chance manageable. By the 1980s, this promise was largely viewed as false, policy-makers were turning elsewhere to manage a new era of nuclear relations, and the game theory narrative was beginning to be associated with the bygone era of the early Cold War.

While the Reagan administration engaged in new varieties of rhetorical brinksmanship, one novel discussed the game theory narrative as a historically bounded phenomenon that had lost its real-world potency by the 1980s. Richard Powers's *Prisoner's Dilemma* (1988), with the benefit of hindsight, explores how the game theory narrative was linked to the pressures of the early Cold War. Powers takes his title from the most well-known of game theory's puzzles and uses it as an extended metaphor for the nature of narrative itself.

Prisoner's Dilemma is centered on the patriarch of the Hobson family, Eddie, Sr., who is dying from an unknown disease. Because the illness only manifests itself with occasional fainting spells, and because Eddie, Sr. has long refused medical treatment, his family members are left to deal with his slow decline in their own ways. Through Eddie, Sr.'s puzzling behavior, the matrix of the prisoner's dilemma becomes the guiding metaphor of the novel. Ever the high school history teacher, Eddie, Sr. avoids discussing his illness by filling table conversation with quizzes and thought experiments: his "miniature classroom was a prisoner's matrix all its own. Dad diverted them from addressing the real catastrophe by drawing them into this game of defection and cooperation. They had to play his dilemma if he was to play theirs."[60] Connecting the Hobson family history to the history of the United States—with special attention to their respective involvement in WWII—Powers suggests that the game theory narrative distracts from "real catastrophe"—be it Eddie, Sr.'s illness, the development of the atomic bomb, or the internment of Japanese-Americans. In other words, the game theory narrative can mask the truths of reality rather than make them evident.

Early in the novel, Eddie, Sr. again demonstrates how the game theory narrative was linked to high Cold War concerns:

> I've been doing a little reading on a puzzle called The Prisoner's Dilemma. The modern form of the paradox comes from a guy at the Rand Corporation, 1951, a year wedged between a couple of dates that ought to go off like bells in your brains. . . .
>
> Two guys are up in Senator Smoking Joe McCarthy's office, sometime in the early 1950s. The gentlemen are both prominent public servants. The senator says, "Fellas, we know that you are both Reds. I've got plenty of evidence for an indictment, but not enough to guarantee the conviction you deserve. Let's make a deal. If either of you comes forward with the dope on the other, the man who talks will go free and the other will fry. If neither of you spills the goods on the other, you'll still suffer public humiliation at the very least."[61]

This is the classic prisoner's dilemma as discussed in nearly every book and article related to the game theory narrative in the 1950s and 1960s—for Powers, by the 1980s, this puzzle had passed into a historical association with that embodiment of Cold War paranoia, Joe McCarthy. In this conception, the prisoner's dilemma is a story distinctly of the Cold War, and one that can never be completely understood or solved. When, late in the novel, Eddie, Jr. asks whether the "two guys in the bind ever get it together," his father replies, "[E]ven if the game stabilizes with two players, it's certainly hopeless at four billion."[62] This connection between the prisoner's matrix of his own life to the global struggle of "four billion" people is underscored in the conclusion when we learn that Eddie, Sr.'s lingering illness was caused by radiation poisoning as a result of his having witnessed an atomic bomb test.

Although the metaphor of the prisoner's dilemma unites game theory with the menace of the atomic bomb, the novel also asks whether the game theory narrative might not have a positive function if recognized as a narrative rather than as a vocabulary for articulating objective reality or a "perfect, fool-proof system" for dominating conflict situations. There are no winners and losers in *Prisoner's Dilemma*, yet the process of engaging the puzzle becomes itself therapeutic. The novel ends with an association of the prisoner's dilemma with stories that literally cope with death: in *The Decameron*, "one of Pop's favorites," we are told that "a handful of people escape the Black Death and keep themselves alive and entertained in their exile by telling one another fantastic stories."[63] The idea that stories are intertwined with life, even in the face of plagues (and Eddie, Sr.'s radiation poisoning pointedly shares physical characteristics with the bubonic plague), suggests that a powerful way to understand the culture of the Cold War is as a matrix of narratives describing a reality that cannot ever be fully known. Recognizing these narratives as such allows Eddie, Sr. to understand his place in the tide of mid-century history, which for him is the story of stories vying for primacy.

Wild Cards and Non-State Actors

One implication of this discussion is that the game theory narrative was another manifestation of the widespread cultural apprehension about the atomic bomb. This narrative promised to defer endlessly the threat of nuclear annihilation by managing the chance inherent in war. If it is true that the twin specters of an accidental nuclear exchange and the psychic incomprehensibility of such an exchange were signal features of the early Cold War experience, then the game theory narrative softened these dangers by treating an unknowable, unnatural conflict as knowable and natural—as familiar as a poker game. And yet, as we have seen, the narrative did not always succeed in this regard, as many writers and cultural observers challenged its pretense of existing outside ideology as a purely rational law of the universe.

Because scholars of Cold War culture have long recognized the profound effects of the atomic bomb, there has been a tendency to view the period only as a contest between the two superpowers that might wield such a weapon. As I discussed in the first chapter, however, some scholars have called for analyses that complicate our sense of a U.S.–Soviet struggle underwritten by the bomb. Christina Klein, for example, has demonstrated how a "global imaginary of integration" was a corollary to the norms of containment that demanded a binary, friend/foe mentality, and Leerom Medovoi has urged us to think of the Cold War as "the age of three worlds."[64] Expanding on the work of Carl Pletsch and others, Medovoi has persuasively argued that the "U.S.–Soviet rivalry ... took the form of a triangulated rivalry over another universe that only now became known as the 'third world.' ... By the mid-1950s, the 'three worlds concept' has become the globe's dominant topological imaginary."[65] While work like Medovoi's and Klein's has given us ways to understand the scope of a global conflict, the game theory narrative helps explain why the Cold War has conventionally been seen only as what Coover called in *The Universal Baseball Association* a "normalized two-person zero-sum game." Coover's appropriation of game theory's language indicates the way in which people were encouraged to see the global conflict involving the fates of many nations as a two-person game of the highest stakes. To view the stakes as the hearts and minds of third world countries is to note one consequence of the game theory narrative: these countries were viewed largely in terms of how they related to the game being played.

Consider, for example, a drawing by the well-known cartoonist Bill Mauldin that appeared in *The New Republic* in 1965 (see figure 3).

"Call, Raise, Draw or Fold?"

Figure 3. Bill Mauldin, "Call, Raise, Draw or Fold?" *The New Republic* (March 6, 1965): 24

With the United States becoming ever more entangled in Vietnam, Mauldin pictures stone-faced Lyndon Johnson, decked out in his cowboy hat, playing poker with an embodiment of a rank-and-file Viet Cong soldier. The metaphor of international conflict as a poker game has moved from the war room of *Dr. Strangelove* to an intimate game with two players. But even at this early stage of a war about checking Communist influence, Johnson is not playing with his Soviet counterpart, but rather with a generic Viet Cong soldier. Particular identities or subjectivities are erased, and what becomes important is the soldier's status as an opponent. We might then read this cartoon as a visual example of one way the game theory narrative viewed the Cold War world: as a two-person game that not only downplayed the "dominant topological imaginary" of three worlds but also the workings of other forces outside or beyond the two super states.

Although Mauldin's visual representation is an especially vivid example of how the game theory narrative encouraged the notion that U.S. adventures abroad amounted to a two-person zero-sum game, other fictional treatments of this theme parsed the phenomenon with more subtlety. In the late 1940s, Gore Vidal—who would become one of the most persistent political critics on the postwar literary scene—left New York for Guatemala, where he bought a dilapidated convent as a space to finish his third novel, *The City and the Pillar* (1948). In Guatemala, Vidal witnessed an unstable national politics that gave him the germ of a new novel, *Dark Green, Bright Red* (1950). Set in the years immediately following WWII, the book takes readers to a fictional Central American country in the throes of an incipient revolution. The third-person narrator is aligned with the perspective of Peter Nelson, an American soldier of fortune who has come to the country to assist General Alvarez in his coup; Vidal spends nearly three hundred pages detailing the strategic moves and counter-moves between Alvarez and the sitting president, Ospina, who had ousted Alvarez some nineteen years prior. With Nelson watching on and then taking an active lead, Alvarez raises an army and begins to occupy towns in advance of the capital. Vidal describes the internal power struggles as a kind of game unfolding always under the watchful eye of the United States, which is why Alvarez, who would want "a loan from the United States" had to "prove, reasonably well, that he's only slightly left of center and that his government is not only legitimate but popular"—and why he frames local politics in terms that anybody up in the States could understand: "Ospina is, basically, a Latin version of a Bolshevik dictator."[66] Yet if such remarks seem to make plain the role of a tiny Central American country in the larger Cold War struggle for dominance, the novel's final pages introduce another force that is American in character but not quite of a piece with the U.S. government.

After Alvarez—with the help, pointedly, of Nelson's strategic and tactical expertise—makes some important strides in the interior of the country, he is ready to move on the capital and seize control of the government. But when, at this late stage of his plan, one of his colonels begins to dodge orders, Alvarez finally learns the truth about his coup, that it was being staged by the American-owned Company (based on the United Fruit Company) that had significant investments in the country. As his former colonel, Aranha, explains to the stunned Alvarez: "Mr. Green [head of the Company], my old friend, my adviser and companion, Arthur Green, was behind this entire plot . . . this army and this movement and all of you, too: you're all a part of this scheme of his. You're victims just as much as I."[67] With Alvarez still in disbelief, Colonel Aranha spells out the real politics behind "this entire plot," the game behind the game:

> About a year ago Ospina put a heavy tax on equipment, on the Company's equipment, and Mr. Green decided it was time to replace Ospina. There were two reasons for Rojas [who was to replace Ospina as president in Green's plan] not doing anything outright: first, he was almost unknown among the people and has no following and, second, we couldn't tell what line the State Department in Washington might take if one of their favorite governments . . . was thrown out by a military junta headed by an unknown officer with definite Left, far Left, tendencies . . . assisted by the Company which, as we all know, is far to the Right. . . . Then Mr. Green . . . hit on the plan of allowing you to come back, knowing perfectly well that you'd try to seize the presidency. We decided you were the logical man to head a mock revolution.[68]

With the revelation that regime change was underwritten by the Company, *Dark Green, Bright Red* famously anticipated the Guatemalan coup of 1954, in which the sitting government was overthrown by a colonel whose army had been trained by the CIA at least partly because of pressure from United Fruit.[69] Reflecting on the prescience of *Dark Green, Bright Red* in 1995, Vidal described these events, four years after his novel's publication, like this: "Senator Lodge [Jr., of Massachusetts] denounced Arévalo's popularly elected successor, Arbenz, as a communist because, in June 1952, Arévalo had ordered the expropriation of some of United Fruit's unused land, which he gave to 100,000 Guatemalan families. Arévalo paid the company what he thought was a fair price, their own evaluation of the land for tax purposes. The American Empire went into action, and through the CIA, it put together an army and bombed Guatemala City."[70] In this narrative, the U.S. government acts as the military wing of the United Fruit Company, an idea that adds another dimension to the game theoretic story of Cold War geopolitics.

What is in fact more relevant in the context of this chapter is how Vidal undermines the sense that the complexities of global politics could profitably be reduced to a zero-sum game. In *Dark Green, Bright Red*, the clear profit motive of the Company takes on a more prominent role than fears of Communist ideology in and of itself. It is Mr. Green who controls the terms of the game, not the U.S. government and its intelligence agencies. For Vidal, it would be naive to assume that U.S. intervention in the third world amounts merely to the amassing of stakes as suggested by Mauldin's cartoon. Not only do Alvarez, Nelson, and a host of other characters have their own motivations and interests, but so does Mr. Green, who does not exactly erase the subjectivities of these other characters, but certainly does invalidate their agency as they become pawns in his game. In this sense, the fictional Central American country in *Dark Green, Bright Red* becomes the board on which Americans play out a game—at the expense of the local population, who are conscripted into the opposing armies, and who die for the sake of theater—and yet the players are not imagined as only the monolithic camps of the United States and the Soviet Union.

Vidal demonstrates the limitations of conceptualizing Cold War geopolitics according to the logic of the game theory narrative without necessarily engaging the particulars of this narrative (partly because *Dark Green, Bright Red* was written as the narrative was gaining cultural traction); a specific critique of the narrative with respect to the United States' relationship with the third world is more visible in the work of Joan Didion. Like Vidal, Didion has been an incisive political and cultural critic since the 1960s and tends to write novels with explicitly political themes. And like Vidal, she has spent much of her career exposing what she takes to be the real players behind the patina of official history. In her 1977 novel, *A Book of Common Prayer*—which is, like *Dark Green, Bright Red*, set in a fictional Central American country—revolutions are a matter of course, but they are not entirely homegrown phenomena. The book's narrator, Grace Strasser-Mendana is, in her fraught blend of distance and complicity, a typical Didion narrator: a native of Colorado, she has married into the Boca Grande ruling class, and thus controls much of the country's wealth, although she claims to stand outside the power struggles of her extended family. As she observes:

> I know for months before the fact when there is about to be a "transition" in Boca Grande. . . . A game is underway, the "winner" being the player who lands his marker in the Ministry of Defense, and the play has certain ritual moves: whoever wants the Ministry that year must first get the *guerrilleros* into the game. The *guerrilleros* seem always to believe that they are playing on their own, but they are actually a diversion, a disruptive element placed on the board only to be "quelled" by "stronger leadership." Guns and money begin to reach the *guerrilleros* via the usual channels.[71]

Just as Grace's ironic quotation marks suggest the rhetorical violence done when couching real violence in euphemistic political-speak, the novel as a whole analyzes the complex relationship the United States would have with a country like Boca Grande—and indeed, the "guns and money" of the final line turn out to mean everything for the success or failure of a given regime change. The "ritual moves" being played in Boca Grande may be at the hands of the rival brothers, but this game is again underwritten by U.S. power—for Didion, such power is not necessarily directly linked to the U.S. government but rather to a whole network of people who exist on the margins of official political power.

One such person in *A Book of Common Prayer* is Leonard Douglas, a prominent American attorney and estranged husband of Charlotte Douglas, the enigmatic woman who drifts into Boca Grande after her privileged daughter, Marin, has disappeared after hijacking an airliner in the name of a people's revolution front. In his capacity as an attorney, Leonard Douglas has occasion to defend those accused of high profile acts of sedition or terror, but in his ties to various revolutionary organizations around the world, his profession may be more accurately summarized by Charlotte's pithy phrase: "He runs guns."[72] Throughout the novel, for example, there is mention of an emerald ring "Leonard had brought her from wherever he had gone to meet the man who financed the Tupamaros [a revolutionary group in Uruguay]"—and it turns out later that Grace's husband was this point person, thus binding her to back-channel politics she knew little about.[73] In his shadowy mix of legitimate and illegitimate dealings, Leonard Douglas represents a character type in Didion's fiction, those men who may or may not work for the U.S. government, but who certainly work in collusion with covert agents of one or another country when appropriate, and who can help provide the material means to make a "transition" effective. Like

Leonard Douglas, Jack Lovett in *Democracy* (1984), and Dick McMahon in *The Last Thing He Wanted* (1996) operate outside the purview of official history or above-board politics, and in so doing have a hand in some key events of the global Cold War: in Lovett's case, the escalation in Vietnam and Cambodia, in McMahon's, the Iran-Contra affair.

In each of these novels, the men in the margins of history are associated both with game playing and with an almost obsessive need to control the game; Leonard Douglas is "a man who prized control," and Jack Lovett goes so far as attempting to eliminate the operation of absolute chance.[74] As the narrator of *Democracy* (called Joan Didion) explains:

> I said that Jack Lovett was one of those men for whom information was an end in itself.
>
> He was also a man for whom the accidental did not figure.
>
> Many people are intolerant of the accidental, but this was something more: Jack Lovett did not believe that accidents happen. In Jack Lovett's system all behavior was purposeful, and the purpose could be divined by whoever attracted the best information and read it most correctly. A Laotian village indicated on one map and omitted on another suggested not a reconnaissance oversight but a population annihilated, x number of men, women, and children lined up one morning between the maps and bulldozed into a common ditch. A shipment of laser mirrors from Long Beach to a firm in Hong Kong that did no laser work suggested not a wrong invoice but transshipment, re-export, the diversion of technology to unfriendly actors. All nations, to Jack Lovett, were "actors," specifically "state actors" ("non-state actors" were the real wild cards here, but in Jack Lovett's extensive experience the average non-state actor was less interested in laser mirrors than in M-16s, AK-47s, FN-FALs, the everyday implements of short-view power, and when the inductive leap to the long view was made it would probably be straight to weapons-grade uranium), and he viewed such actors abstractly, as friendly or unfriendly, committed or uncommitted; as assemblies of armaments on a large board. Asia was ten thousand tanks here, three hundred Phantoms there. The heart of Africa was an enrichment facility.[75]

The comparison of non-state actors to wild cards not only extends the poker playing metaphor seen in *Dr. Strangelove* and the Mauldin cartoon but suggests also that state actors alone are insufficient to account for the ways the world actually works. Although, as we have seen, the Cold War rhetorical field generally—and the game theory narrative specifically—encouraged the notion that only state actors were consequential, in Didion's fiction, this represents an incomplete understanding of global politics. In *Democracy*, Jack Lovett is himself a non-state actor, a wild card who does not "believe that accidents happen." Perhaps it is the case that he works for some government agency, perhaps he just works between them, but as a master of information that cannot by necessity be part of the official historical record, Jack Lovett is shown as having the most direct power of anyone in the novel. He is compared, for instance, to Senator Harry Victor, who was elected on the strength of his interest in grassroots change, but who has since become defined by media images and sound bites; unlike Jack Lovett, he has comparatively little power when it comes to the real world.

There is much made of the "real world" in Didion's most recent novel about U.S. intervention in the third world, *The Last Thing He Wanted* (1996). That novel focuses on Elena McMahon, the daughter of another non-state actor, Dick McMahon, who has spent his career dealing arms and engaging in other illicit activities around the world; it is suggested, for example, that in November 1963 he was involved with those who wanted to "make the deal" with Fidel Castro.[76] In the novel's present, Dick is dying and asks Elena to escort an arms shipment to an unknown Central American country, which will be his last, million-dollar deal (and which, not incidentally, he describes in terms of poker: "This one turns out the way it's supposed to turn out, he said, I'll be in a position to deal myself out, fold my hand, take the *Kitty Rex* down past Largo and stay there.")[77] Elena—like General Alvarez in *Dark Green, Bright Red*—thinks she has all the players figured, but does not in fact fully realize the complexities of the game she has agreed to play. After landing in Central America, she does not immediately receive payment as planned, and so at the suggestion of her father's shadowy contacts, winds up on an unnamed Caribbean island overrun with American intelligence officers, and at the end of the book is assassinated without ever having comprehended exactly what was going on. It thus falls to the narrator, a journalist by trade, to piece together what had happened even though, as she writes at the outset, "The facts of Elena McMahon's life did not quite hang together. They lacked coherence. Logical connections were missing, cause and effect."[78] In detailing this world of American intervention some twenty years after *A Book of Common Prayer*, Didion imagines the subtle, sometimes fuzzily motivated human side to the splashy, large-scale scandals of the Cold War (it is suggested, for example, that the McMahons' arms deal plays some part in what would become the Iran-Contra affair).

In exploring Cold War power with an eye toward the role of non-state actors, Didion refers to some of the key tropes of the game theory narrative and suggests that despite all the rational projections and RAND modeling, there are "situations" that lie beyond the calculations of such thinking. This argument is emphasized by the novel's dismissal of the "zero-sum" view of the world, which is described as part of "the rhetoric of the time in question":

This wasn't a situation that lent itself to an MBA analysis.
This wasn't a zero-sum deal.
In a perfect world we might have perfect choices, in the real world we had real choices, and we made them, and we measured the losses against what might have been the gains.
Real world.

. . .

Add it up.
I did that.
I added it up.
Not zero-sum at all.
You could call this a reconstruction. A corrective, if you will, to the Rand study. A revisionist view of a time and a place and an incident about which, ultimately, most people preferred not to know.
Real world.[79]

The narrator recirculates contemporary rhetoric that was itself critical of RAND-type studies—these italicized, disembodied voices, which are meant to recall the players such as Dick McMahon (who, like his cohort, speak in terms of the "deal"), suggest a critique that is descendent of Kubrick's critique in *Dr. Strangelove* about the limitations of rational decision making when it comes to the complexities of the Cold War environment. In Didion's case, these limitations are best illustrated by looking at the third world, which does not fit so neatly into the zero-sum model. Those non-state actors who see themselves as operating in the "real world" think of themselves as making "real choices," whereas the "MBA analysis" assumes, like much of the game theory narrative we have seen throughout this chapter, a world of "perfect choices" for negotiating the "zero-sum deal." *The Last Thing He Wanted*, in this view, is about how U.S. adventures in the third world—both in official and unofficial capacities—cannot be understood solely by such analysis. The narrator's insistently subjective "reconstruction" becomes a "corrective . . . to the Rand study" insofar as it probes those other possibilities rather than attempting to control or manage chance as the game theory narrative or those broadly drawn RAND studies might.[80] As the excerpt above indicates, the novel, by contrast, relies on a highly elliptical narrative style that allows for the operation of chance and the play of possibility—hence the acknowledgment that *"we were dealing with forces that might or might not include unpredictable elements."* Didion's narrative swirls around identifiable facts as reported not only by the RAND study but also by newspaper accounts, investigatory Senate reports, and oral interviews, but is itself only suggestive of these final facts (we never learn, for example, exactly who took possession of the arms Elena delivered to Central America). The novel remains suspended in a subjunctive state that implies motives that "might or might not" have been the case, and as such avoids the reductive folly of something like a RAND study, which must necessarily operate by conceptualizing geopolitics in knowable terms.[81]

The part of the novel that leaves the worst taste in the reader's mouth comes in the final pages, when, after briefly describing what happens to one of the principals, the narrator shifts into a recollection of a *New York Times* article "about a conference, sponsored by the John F. Kennedy School of Government at Harvard, at which eight members of the Kennedy administration gathered at an old resort hotel in the Florida Keys to reassess the 1962 Cuban missile crisis."[82] Here the narrator has a chance to reflect on the official narrative of the Cold War, as the article is about the moves and counter-moves made by those in the inner circle of power during one of the tensest moments of the postwar period. This conference, tinged for the participants with nostalgia (a view that, as we will see in the next chapter, is not uncommon in post-1989 writing and culture), is characterized as a chummy club: "Theodore Sorensen swam with the dolphins. Robert McNamara expressed surprise that CINCSAC had sent out the DEFCON 2 alert instructions uncoded, in the clear, so that the Soviets would pick them up. Meetings were scheduled to leave afternoon hours for tennis doubles."[83] This country club version of Cold War theater is, of course, complicated by the story that has preceded it, about the relationship between those players unknown to—or perhaps only unacknowledged by—those powerful men swimming with dolphins, but whose decisions would have nonetheless wound their way around to cause Elena McMahon's death.

In reframing her story with this official version of the Cold War, the narrator returns us to the question of assessment and quantitative prediction that characterizes the novel's general critique of the game theory narrative: "I would like to have seen just such a reassessment of . . . certain actions taken in 1984 in the matter of what later became known as the lethal, as opposed to the humanitarian, resupply [in Nicaragua]. Imperfect memories of the certain incident that should not have occurred and could not have been predicted. By any quantitative measurement."[84] This reminds us that the Cold War frame, as inflected by the game theory narrative, renders certain things visible while other things are left invisible—thus the Cuban Missile Crisis remains among the most visible markers of the Cold War, whereas the small incident, the thousand unnamed situations that make up Didion's global Cold War, are what comprise the texture of the period, however frequently they may go unrecorded.

This chapter as a whole has suggested, in fact, that although it has until now been a less visible aspect of the Cold War rhetorical field, the game theory narrative is an important and influential aspect of this culture. It has been overlooked as a narrative precisely because it was so insistent in proclaiming itself engendered of pure mathematics and abstract rationality. Once we attune ourselves to the narrative's cultural functions, we can see how it encouraged the sense that freedom and control were complexly intertwined. If, as I have suggested throughout *No Accident, Comrade*, the concept of freedom during the Cold War was sometimes associated with the concept of chance—insofar as it foregrounds the importance of personal agency, which is in turn marked by openness and possibility—then the game theory narrative ironically sought to preserve freedom by promising to manage chance. Thus when the narrative claimed that its own special logic was a law of the universe, or when it conceptualized the intricate three-world global situation as a poker game, or when it suggested that even chance was subject to its bounded terms, it did so to diminish the threat of possibility itself, and should as such be recognized as significant among the cultural narratives that governed the Cold War experience.

6

Their Country, Our Culture

The Persistence of the Cold War

In November 1989, teenagers with hammers and chisels chipped away at the Berlin Wall bit by bit. As crowds gathered near the Brandenburg Gate, East Germans in backhoes removed huge sections of the wall slab by slab, and Berliners mingled freely for the first time in twenty-eight years. It was only a few months later, in February 1990, when the republics of the Soviet Union held the elections that would lead to their independence and the ultimate collapse of the once-mighty superpower in 1991. As historical moments, these events tell us something about real changes in geopolitics, not the least of which is that America's professed enemy for nearly half a century was if not utterly vanished from the world stage, then certainly transformed into something else. And yet, as suggested by the lingering effects of the game theory narrative, the Cold War is still with us—both as a powerful explanatory framework with which to understand the recent past and as an Ur-influence on American culture post-1989. In popular memory, the epoch known as "Cold War" has been packaged by such kitschy, nostalgia-tinged enterprises as the privately funded International Spy Museum, which opened in 2002 with black-clad "spies" rappelling down its Washington, D.C. edifice; there, for a mere $10,000, a foursome can book the "Ultimate Spy Adventure," which includes meetings with former CIA "chiefs of disguise." Or consider one of the breakout television hits of the mid-2000s, the series *Mad Men*, set in the early 1960s, and featuring historical touchstones such as the Kennedy assassination and the Cuban Missile Crisis. In 2006, the James Bond film franchise was revived once more for the contemporary world, and in the opening movement of *Casino Royale*, Bond's boss, M (Judi Dench), sighs, "Christ, I miss the Cold War," a sentiment that would likely be echoed by Francis McDormand's character in the comedy *Burn After Reading* (2008), in which two witless gym employees try to sell found CIA documents to the Russian embassy—much to the bewilderment of both Russian and American officials.

The list goes on and on, but this version of the Cold War, which contains a twinge of excitement to go with the nostalgia, comes in part from the half-remembered sense of world order brought on by the balance of power between the United States and the Soviet Union. As one wistful character in DeLillo's *Underworld* puts it, the Cold War is "the one constant thing. It's honest, it's dependable.... The cold war is your friend."[1] Writing in the year between the Berlin Wall's fall and the Soviet Union's, John Mearsheimer argued that while "no one will want to revisit the domestic Cold War, with its purges and loyalty oaths, its xenophobia and stifling of dissent.... We may ... wake up one day lamenting the loss of the order that the Cold War gave to the anarchy of international relations."[2] In the post–Cold War world, there has been the sense that despite the domestic scares and threats of nuclear destruction, the Cold War was oddly comforting because it was somehow manageable and known: its two clearly defined antagonists could be counted on to play by certain rules.[3] Part of the work of *No Accident, Comrade* has been to suggest that such a pervasive rhetorical structuring created an atmosphere in which creative engagements could identify the limitations of this bipolar imaginary.[4]

This chapter recognizes the apparent staying power of the Cold War, but does so from the sense explored throughout this book. If the Cold War was a largely rhetorical conflict, and if this conflict had a complex relationship with the literature written during it, then it stands to reason that works written in its wane and aftermath would evince some legacies of this relationship. I hope it is evident, in fact, that the analyses in the preceding chapters encourage us to consider how and why chance is thematized in post–Cold War work that either historicizes the Cold War or concerns some of its key tropes—totalitarianism versus democracy, control versus freedom, the individual and the state, or the status of racial difference and the American status quo. In this chapter, I look at three novels with markedly different scopes and aims, but which all demonstrate the ways the Cold War lingers, an influence that makes sense given that their authors all came of age during it. In discussing Paul Auster's *The Music of Chance* (1990), I suggest that its thematization of chance and narrative control are vestiges of similar concerns discussed throughout this book, and as such, Auster's metafictional interests are at least partly explained by the Cold War frame. From there, I move on to an example of a 1990s identity novel, Chang-rae Lee's *Native Speaker* (1995), which draws on accident to help clarify its plot concerning racial norms in a post–Cold War world. I end with Harry Mathews's playful *My Life in CIA* (2005), which uses Cold War rhetoric as a staging ground for aesthetic questions, a move which underscores not only the way the conflict was understood as a game but also its potential for encouraging aesthetic innovation. Although there are many novels and other cultural artifacts one could potentially discuss when analyzing the persistence of the Cold War frame, these novels represent different instantiations of post–1989 American literature, and demonstrate the potency of both chance and this frame for those interested in exploring narrative and its relationship to American life.

Chance, Destiny, and Paul Auster

In a 1992 interview, Paul Auster remarked that "[t]he very day I finished writing *The Music of Chance*—which is a book about walls and slavery and freedom—the Berlin Wall came down. There's no conclusion to be drawn from this, but every time I think of it, I start to shake."[5] Auster's teasing suggestion that there is no causal connection between his novel about chance and the Cold War—only the coincidence of a day on the calendar—is a quiet echo of his whole body of work, which so often turns on questions of chance and coincidence that "Happy Accidents" seemed a fitting title for one interview with him.[6] From the publication of his memoir *The Invention of Solitude* (1982) and his breakthrough work, three linked novels collectively titled *The New York Trilogy* (1985–86), Auster has demonstrated an interest in staging existential crises through the prism of chance. The lives of his characters are changed by chance events and shaped by surprising coincidences, and readers have puzzled over exactly how and why his books thematize chance so consistently.[7]

Considering the relationship between chance and the Cold War described throughout this book, it becomes clear that its oblique presence and ideological legacies inform Auster's own use of accidents and coincidence. Although Auster has not written a novel about the Cold War per se, its afterglow is visible throughout his work. The novel *In the Country of Last Things* (1987), for example, is set in a postapocalyptic New York City (as in Whitehead's *The Intuitionist*, this city is not named) where social norms have been so distorted that the capricious weather—"the sky . . . ruled by chance"—becomes a metaphor for the unpredictability of day-to-day existence.[8] *Moon Palace* (1989), about a constellation of coincidences that help the main character understand his past, opens with the high-water mark of the space race, the moon landing in the summer of 1969, a time when "[c]ausality was no longer the hidden demiurge that ruled the universe."[9] Another character, a former WWII bomber pilot who turned down the mission to Nagasaki, deals with his own nuclear fallout by imagining that baseball scores broadcast on the radio are actually encoded locations of H-bombs hidden beneath New York City; he raves, "They've got dozens of them stored in underground tunnels, and they keep moving them around so the Russians won't know where they are."[10] In *Invisible* (2009), one character (whom another suspects of being "in the early stages of Alzheimer's or dementia") offers the nostalgic view explained in the preceding pages: "Distasteful as it might have been, the Cold War had held the world together for forty-four years, and now that the simple, black-and-white binary world of us versus them was gone, we had entered a period of instability and chaos similar to the years prior to World War I."[11] One could certainly locate other obvious references, but more relevant for understanding writing at the tail end of the Cold War is the effect the rhetorical conflict had on narrative chance, which informs the tensions between absolute chance and freedom on the one hand, and narrative chance and control on the other.

When Auster has spoken in interviews about his interest in chance and coincidence, he has stressed that he is "in the strictest sense of the word . . . a realist," and that the inclusion of chance is a way for him to represent real life accurately: "When I talk about coincidence, I'm not referring to a desire to manipulate—mechanical plot devices, the urge to tie everything up, the happy endings in which everyone turns out to be related to everyone else—but the presence of the unpredictable, the powers of contingency."[12] To underscore this point, he lists various coincidences that have happened to him throughout his own life, then asks, "Chance? Destiny? Or simple mathematics, an example of probability theory at work? It doesn't matter what you call it. Life is full of such events. As a writer of novels, I feel my job is to keep myself open to these collisions, to watch out for all these mysterious goings-on in the world."[13]

Auster has indeed remained open to the operation of chance, and yet his fiction seems haunted by the basic problem described in chapter 1: the inclusion of chance in a fictional narrative paradoxically signals both contingent "life" and the constructed artifice of fiction. Because narrative chance must always be interpreted as something other than absolute chance, its presence encourages questions about interpretation and meaning in a fictional world created specifically by "Paul Auster." As he told Larry McCaffery and Sinda Gregory, metafictional techniques such as having himself turn up in his plots reflect his "desire to implicate himself in the machinery of the book. I don't mean my autobiographical self, I mean my author self, that mysterious other who lives inside me and puts my name on the covers of books. . . . I wanted to open up the process, to break down walls, expose the plumbing."[14] If Auster is a descendent of the writers discussed throughout this book, it is because chance seems to him a particularly useful concept for demonstrating the artifice of narrative, and the questions such artifice invites.

Auster's most sustained engagement with the role of chance in narrative is, as the title suggests, his novel *The Music of Chance*. The hero, Jim Nashe (a name which is perhaps a nod to John Nash, the game theorist discussed in the previous chapter), has just inherited some money from his father, and so quits his job as a firefighter in Boston and drives around the country without a purpose or plan. The plot gets going when Nashe meets a poker player named Jack Pozzi, who tells Nashe about an extraordinary poker game he had lined up until he was robbed of all his money. He was to play Flower and Stone, an accountant and optometrist who had split a lottery ticket and become multimillionaires. The eccentrics had since moved to a mansion in the Pennsylvanian countryside where they could indulge their odd hobbies. They had invited Pozzi to their mansion for a rematch, and Pozzi figured he could easily beat them for tens of thousands of dollars, if he only had the initial capital. Nashe decides to stake Pozzi with the remainder of his inheritance, hoping to win enough money to move back home and raise his daughter.

When Pozzi finally plays Flower and Stone, chance is against him (Auster spends several pages narrating the chance turns in the poker game), and he loses; Nashe stakes him more money, putting up his last dollar and his year-old Saab. When Pozzi loses this, too, Nashe convinces the millionaires to take one more bet: the car against $10,000. The "blind turn of a card" crushes Nashe and Pozzi once again, and Flower and Stone are left with a problem: if they let the pair leave, they will never get their money. As a solution, someone proposes that Nashe and Pozzi work off the debt by living in a trailer on the property and building an enormous stone wall from the 10,000 blocks Flower had imported from a ruined castle in Ireland. The rest of the plot concerns the building of the wall, Pozzi's attempt to escape and subsequent beating (and probable death), and finally Nashe's death, which occurs on the final page of the novel, when, "feeling in absolute control," he drives a car into an oncoming vehicle at over 85 miles per hour.[15]

True to the apparent tension of the title metaphor—which suggests that chance is somehow orderly and harmonious, even though it is by definition free from order—*The Music of Chance* is about the tensions between chance and design inherent in fictional narratives. Even from the opening paragraph, which explains that Nashe encountered Pozzi by chance, Auster stages this tension: "It was one of those random, accidental encounters that seem to materialize out of thin air—a twig that breaks off in the wind and suddenly lands at your feet" (1). Although the sentence appears to claim that the meeting of Nashe and Pozzi is an instance of absolute chance, it actually betrays a conflicted sense of chance's place in narrative, for it was one of those encounters that "*seem* to materialize out of thin air." It is not of course strictly analogous to a twig shaken loose by the wind—a product of nature—but is rather a *seemingly* random event that has actually been designed by Paul Auster, the ubiquitous presence throughout his own works. The proliferation of chance events that reveal themselves as narrative chance with words like "seems" and "as if" mark Auster's presence as the controlling author.

Thus when Nashe lights out on the road, he ought to have enjoyed the most freedom he had ever felt ("It was a dizzying prospect—to imagine all that freedom" [6]), and yet he feels uneasy, that "he was no longer in control of himself, that he had fallen into the grip of some baffling, overpowering force" (6–7). The reference to falling suggests that the baffling "force" is chance. And yet it is again not absolute chance, but rather narrative chance—it is Auster assuming the form of chance to guide Nashe along. Despite the apparent freedom of the open road and a cushion of money, then, Nashe "could hear the words coming out of his mouth, but even as he spoke them, he felt they were expressing someone else's thoughts, as if he were no more than an actor performing on the stage of some imaginary theater, repeating lines that had been written for him in advance" (36). *The Music of Chance*'s postmodern joke is that Nashe is precisely an actor mouthing the words Auster has written for him, compelled by narrative chance: "It was as if he finally had no part in what was about to happen to him. And if he was no longer involved in his own fate, where was he, then, and what had become of him?" (59). Nashe's feeling of disquietude stems from a dim, unspoken feeling that he is like a character in a book, a feeling which is literally true, and which, despite Auster's claims to be a realist, marks the differences between fiction and real life. In Auster's almost claustrophobically self-aware world, there can be no freedom for Nashe or any other character, only pseudo-freedom, the appearance of freedom, the harmonious coming together of seemingly random events into a music of narrative chance.

Significantly, the way in which Nashe's life is ordered within *The Music of Chance* echoes the way real life was ordered within the Cold War frame—all the things that happened to Nashe "purely by chance" (14) are somehow enfolded into a "strange inevitability" (15). The connection to Cold War norms is clarified during a tour of Flower and Stone's mansion. Nashe and Pozzi are first shown Flower's wing, a "random" collection of objects, "a monument to trivia" as innately interesting as the castle stones (83). Stone, by contrast, spends his days working on a vast model city he calls City of the World. The City is a miniature version of real places and real moments from Stone's and Flower's lives that Nashe finds disturbing because it is so utterly planned and managed that individuals are encouraged to suffer for the civic good. Even the inmates in the prison yard have smiles on their faces because they know they are being rehabilitated for the benefit of the City. As Nashe thinks, it is a "bizarre, totalitarian world" (87).

The phrase returns us to the narrative legacy of the Cold War, when plots themselves were viewed with suspicion because they contained the possibility of human subjugation; in Stone's model world, the "cuteness and intricacy" mask a "hint of violence." Tim Woods, invoking the Althusserian sense of state ideological apparatuses, has suggested that the City of the World "becomes symbolic of a certain ideological world order, a pattern of social life based on the absolute ideological control of its subjects."[16] This ideological order is not present just in the model itself, but has affinities with the ways that Nashe and Pozzi—who are penniless and thus powerless—are treated by Flower and Stone, who fence them in and assign an armed overseer to monitor their work. But I would point out also that an awareness of the Cold War rhetorical background implies that there is also a "hint of violence" in the act of narrative itself—an insight, recall, that likewise informs Pynchon's *V*. The many instances of chance and coincidence in Auster's novels, instances which for him represent the nature of real life, also mark his own authority and control. If chance seems an antidote to such control, its presence in a fictional narrative is nothing if not vexed, and so *The Music of Chance* ends with a deadly car accident that is not an accident because Nashe deliberately accelerates into the oncoming vehicle ("*feeling* in absolute control," he accelerates into a vehicle that "*seemed* to come out of nowhere" [my emphasis] [216]). The novel's final words recount the split second before the literal collision to which Auster says he is committed; it is in this moment—as yet and forever unnarrated—that Nashe is truly free, beyond the control of even of the author's master plan.

Auster's work is a vestige of Cold War attitudes about narrative insofar as it is uneasy about the nature of its own design, an anxiety made visible through its abiding interest in narrative chance. A novel like *The Music of Chance* is about the relationship between individual lives and the stories that govern them, but it removes this concern from explicit discussions of the state to offer a theory about the tensions between freedom and control in any life that is given sense through narrative; read in this way, Auster's body of work, while superficially apolitical, bears in fact the mark of Cold War rhetoric.

Freak Accidents and Junior Encyclopedias

There is also post–Cold War writing that does not necessarily treat chance as a narrative problem as Auster does, but reflects rather how Cold War norms have been so pervasive that we tend not even to notice them as norms. In Chang-rae Lee's *Native Speaker*—a novel that was elevated to star status in the Asian-American canon soon after its publication in 1995—the Cold War functions not merely as history, but as a complex frame that mandated certain relationships between the individual and the state that would still be consequential in the 1990s.[17] In *Native Speaker*, accident disrupts the causal logic of the Cold War and is key to understanding the novel's critique of a cultural logic so pervasive that it seems merely natural.

At first blush, *Native Speaker*'s conceit is compelling for the ways it revisits high Cold War concerns: Henry Park, the Korean-American narrator, is as introspective about the model minority myth as he is about his job as a spy—not for any government agency but for a private boutique firm called Glimmer & Co. As Henry explains, the company's "clients were multinational corporations, bureaus of foreign governments, individuals of resource and connection. We provided them with information about people working against their vested interests. . . . Typically the subject was a well-to-do immigrant supporting some potential insurgency in his old land, or else funding a fledgling trade union or radical student organization. Sometimes he was simply an agitator. Maybe a writer of conscience. An expatriate artist."[18] Henry's boss, Dennis Hoagland, is an old-school Cold Warrior fond of declaring things like "in our time there were only two or three [intrigues] worth talking about, for complexity, fascination, depth of involvement: JFK, Watergate, the attempt on the Pope" (17), and who, the office joke runs, has squirreled away in his desk "[a] first dub of the Zapruder film. . . . [and] Lady Bird Johnson's silk panties, circa 1969" (28). The implication is that Glimmer & Co. is a privatized, 1990s extension of a CIA-style espionage organization that aims to understand and affect the world as though the Cold War binaries still dominated the global imaginary. But as I suggested in the last chapter with my discussion of Didion's writing, non-state actors such as Glimmer & Co. likewise prove the limitations of this frame's conceptualization of the world, limitations *Native Speaker* also explores.

After being recruited into Glimmer & Co., Henry spends his career, like any good spy, acting—being what people need or expect him to be in order to extract information.[19] One part of the plot involves Henry using this ability to infiltrate the offices of a man who seems to embody the American Dream: Korean-American John Kwang, a successful businessman and city councilman who is running for mayor of New York City. Kwang comes to trust Henry and eventually allows him into the inner circle; although readers get the sense that Kwang is basically a decent person who cares about his constituency and does his best to improve their lives, by the end of the novel, his mayoral bid has been derailed by a scandal brought about at least partly by Henry's efforts.

With this part of the plot, *Native Speaker* seems to reinscribe Cold War norms—or at least demonstrate a certain wistfulness about their efficacy. Dennis Hoagland, for one, would certainly share the opinion of those characters in *Underworld* who found the Cold War comforting. Other moments likewise demonstrate the kind of nostalgia found in *The Intuitionist*; at one point, for example, Henry is described as "old-style charming, like back in 1957" (110); at another, Henry and his Caucasian wife, Leila, balk at a "new technothriller" film on television: "Give us *The Third Man*, we decide, give us *The Manchurian Candidate* and *The Spy Who Came in from the Cold*" (227). To the extent that the novel's structure and espionage plot can be read as familiar tropes, it seems at first only to extend them—but it is ultimately in the intersection of *Native Speaker*'s espionage plot with the story of Henry's personal and emotional life that we understand that these tropes are better left historicized and are inadequate for understanding the world beyond the Cold War.[20]

Given that Lee is explicitly interested in Cold War logic, it makes sense, in light of what I have argued throughout this book, that he demonstrates the limits of this logic through attention to accident, which troubles the pat categories of causation underwritten by the Cold War frame. In *Native Speaker*, the Cold War names a world characterized by clear causal relationships, especially between states and individuals. In the novel's present, though some like Hoagland cling to the belief in such identifiable causal links, chance has freer reign and these links are nothing if not muddied. There is for instance the pointed moment when Henry recalls for his wife a childhood class report on the Korean War. After asking his father about his experiences in the war ("he got choked up and left the room"), Henry recalls:

> I read my junior encyclopedia. . . . The entry didn't mention any Koreans except for Syngman Rhee and Kim Il Sung, the Communist leader. Kim was a *bad* Korean. In the volume there was a picture of him wearing a Chinese jacket. He was fat-faced and maniacal. Bayonets were in the frame behind him. He looked like an evil robot. . . . I didn't know what to do. I didn't want to embarrass myself in front of the class. So my report was about the threat of Communism, the Chinese Army, how MacArthur was a visionary, that Truman should have listened to him. How lucky all of us Koreans were. (225)[21]

Here the Cold War provides a usable system of cause-and-effect: align yourself with American democracy and you are a good Korean; align yourself with Communism and you are bad one. Even at a young age, Henry knows that to avoid embarrassment—that is, to fit in, to assimilate—he needs to toe the (American) party line and reiterate the official story, even if he does not quite believe it. So far this idea that the rigid binary logic of the Cold War could turn people into robotic stakes by erasing individual subjectivities is familiar (think of the Vietcong solider in the cartoon discussed in the previous chapter). But *Native Speaker* is not strictly speaking of the Cold War—it is a novel in which the Cold War is past tense, a specific historical era, which nevertheless has important psychological and geopolitical effects (the still-divided Korean peninsula being among the more visible). Despite the lingering nostalgia and efforts by characters like Hoagland simply to extend the past into the present, the novel suggests that the causal system underwritten by Cold War logic is insufficient for understanding both personal relations and the multiethnic political landscape post–1989.

This critique of Cold War causal logic is centered on two life-changing accidents, the death of Henry's son and the car accident that represents the dramatic end to Kwang's political career. The first, which is presented as back-story to the Kwang espionage plot, concerns Henry's young son, Mitt, who dies accidentally: roughhousing at a birthday party, some friends dog-pile him and stay on long enough to suffocate him. In the novel's present, as Henry grows increasingly adept at manipulating those connected to the Kwang campaign, he loses control of his relationship with his wife Leila, from whom he has become estranged because of their son's death. Their conversation often circles around deciphering and naming the accident:

[Leila said,] "we haven't really come right out together and said it, really named what happened for what it was."

"What was it?" I said softly, hearing the sudden quiver in her voice.

"It was the worst thing that ever happened to us," she said, her fist knuckling down on the bed with each word. . . .

"It was a terrible accident."

"An accident?" she cried, nearly hollering. She covered her mouth. Her voice was breaking. "How can you say it was an accident? We haven't treated it like one. Not for a second. Look at us. Sweetie, can't you see, when your baby dies it's never an accident. I don't care if a truck hit him or he crawled out a window or he put a live wire in his mouth, it was not an accident. And that's a word you and I have no business using. Sometimes I think it's more like some long-turning karma that finally came back for us. Or that we didn't love each other. We thought our life was good enough. Maybe it's that Mitt wasn't all white or all yellow. I go crazy thinking about it. Don't you? Maybe the world wasn't ready for him. God. Maybe it's that he was so damn happy." (120)

In the progressive naming of Mitt's death—the transformation from "it" to "thing" to "terrible accident" to "never an accident"—we see that the source of tension is Leila's and Henry's divergent interpretations of the event. For Henry, the death is merely a chance event, and thus paradoxically explicable as such: if the death is truly a "terrible accident," then it can be understood as uncaused, which in turn means that no further investigation is warranted. For Leila, on the other hand, the accident is symbolic of some other system of causes not yet comprehensible—she is willing to see in Mitt's accidental death evidence of a kind of meaning that neither she nor Henry fully understand. For a logical and methodical mind such as Henry's, naming the death "accident" is sufficient explanation; for the intuitive and emotional Leila, "accident" could name another sort of cause. Mitt's death thus introduces the idea that there are multiple kinds of causal systems at work in *Native Speaker*: although the death is clearly an accident—insofar as it was unplanned and unintended by anyone—it also (perhaps less clearly) constitutes another kind of meaning that makes it not merely accidental (that is, as not *only* a significant cause of Henry's and Leila's suffering and disillusionment), but also an *effect* of something ineffable that Leila makes it her mission to attend.

This disagreement is emblematic of the novel's general sensibility, which is willing to allow for differing causal systems at play in the world. Henry in fact complicates such discussions of cause-and-effect by explaining that race also inflects one's attitude about what is considered "chance" and what is not. Just as Henry is haunted by the death of his son, so too is he haunted by the specter of his father, who became a Korean-American success story by "leaving absolutely nothing to luck or chance or someone else" (45). The idea that the self-reliant immigrant can succeed by banishing chance through discipline and hard work suggests that chance has no place in certain versions of the American Dream. Indeed, Henry later sets a Korean attitude about chance against a Chinese one: "Luck, like most everything else, must be a Chinese invention. We Koreans have reinvented the idea of luck as mostly bad, and try to do everything we can to prevent it. We fear leaving anything to chance" (304). If the Chinese rely on luck to help them in life, according to Henry, Korean success depends on figuring chance as threatening. Thus Henry, who like his father attempts to leave nothing to chance in his professional life, interprets that which is beyond his control (Mitt's death) as a terrible accident so it can become for him ironically comprehensible: an example of the statistically freak occurrences that do happen in real life (think again of the thrown tire in *The Recognitions*). It is terrible because it should not have been left to chance, and this is how Henry understands it—despite his best efforts to calculate and manage the events in his life, he laments that the most important ones seem to come down to "dumb chance" (147).

Leila, by contrast, is adamant about claiming Mitt's death as not accidental, even going so far as to name a few obviously accidental scenarios and interpreting them as potentially meaningful and caused. For her, the death demands interpretation of a broader sort—as evidence (or not) of their love; of the sad fruits of American racism; of unverifiable causal theories like karma. Because Leila allows the accident to remain available for interpretation, it represents the varying kinds of causal potentialities that exist in *Native Speaker*—such connections proliferate, and yet, unlike Cold War causal norms, they do not exclude one another, but rather stand, together, as potentially plausible. These plausible causal systems in the novel mean that it is false to suppose that Mitt's accidental death can ever be completely or utterly accounted for—whether by understanding it only as a terrible accident, as Henry does, or as evidence of some larger, unseen causal system at work, as Leila does. There is instead the sense that causes and effects are infinitely more complex than the one-to-one correspondences demanded by the cultural logic represented by Henry's junior encyclopedia.

By the end of the novel, John Kwang's life is unraveling: there is a firebombing in his office that has killed his favorite assistant, and the media is reporting evidence of his sponsorship of a Korean money-lending system that will look to white America like bribery. The final accident occurs while Kwang crashes his car while driving drunk with a Korean hospitality girl, whom the papers will label a prostitute. Together with the other revelations, this car accident spells the end of his political career, an event certainly unplanned, but which is also an apt conclusion to the narrative arc that Henry has given us of Kwang's life. Kwang did not of course intend to crash his car, and yet readers also know that it is the result of the protracted machinations of those non-state actors in Glimmer & Co., and so it thus becomes an accident that is not an accident. The twinned accidents of Mitt's death and Kwang's crash, then, demonstrate that chance events are significant, and yet their status as accidental is always in question—or, perhaps, a matter of interpretation.[22]

Harry Mathews's Ridiculous Spy Game

As Auster's work internalizes the Cold War sense that chance disrupts narrative control, and as Lee himself disrupts such control by showing how accident challenges causal systems underwritten by Cold War logic, Harry Mathews's fictionalized memoir, *My Life in CIA: A Chronicle of 1973*, contains a plot that simultaneously lampoons and takes seriously ideas about chance and narrative control we have seen throughout this book. Born in New York City, Mathews left the United States in 1952 at least partly because, as he explained to his friend John Ashbery, that time was "a very bad moment" when America was "extremely hostile to the poetic and artistic enthusiasms that I felt were most important."[23] Since that time he has lived predominately in France. From his first novel, *The Conversions* (1962)—an erudite and intricate book whose unresolved central riddle has made it seem to some readers an ancestor to Pynchon's *The Crying of Lot 49*—Mathews has demonstrated an interest in experimentation and aesthetic game playing.[24] This interest has been informed by his membership in the French literary group Oulipo, whose other members have included Italo Calvino, Georges Perec, and Marcel Duchamp, and whose purpose, as Mathews puts it in *My Life in CIA*, is "to explore the *potentialities* mathematics might contribute to literature."[25] In these explorations, the Oulipo tends to stress the idea of play and aesthetic innovation by implementing various kinds of constraints on their writing (producing novels without the letter "e," for example).[26] Such apparent capriciousness has led some to criticize the group (Gérard Genette famously dismissed Oulipo aesthetics as "a game of roulette"); but, as Mathews demonstrates in *My Life in CIA*, such a commitment to game playing is in fact a perfect way to demonstrate the fraught relationship between individuals and Cold War rhetoric.[27]

I began *No Accident, Comrade* with Jerzy Kosinski's worry that totalitarianism is sustained by creating massive fictions and his sense that the use of chance in his own work could rescue it from a similar charge. I end with Mathews because he too emphasizes the connection between the Cold War and fiction making. With the benefit of thirty-two years of hindsight, he uses an Oulipian sensibility to figure the conflict as a lexical playfield, an aesthetic staging ground that actually encourages innovation, but that nevertheless has profound consequences that Mathews cannot completely control.

My Life in CIA is autobiographical to the extent that it concerns a character named Harry Mathews who lives where the real-life Mathews lived, wrote the books he wrote, and knew the people he knew. This Mathews is a suave man of letters who seems acquainted with anybody worth knowing in the postwar Paris arts scene. Mathews opens the book by explaining that many of these acquaintances had the vague suspicion that he was connected in some way to the CIA. Rather than continue to deny these suggestions to no avail—after all, denying such involvement only deepens one's suspicions—Mathews decides in the summer of 1973 to play the role of CIA operative. As a friend advises, the Cold War is itself a game, and Mathews can become a player if he learns its rules: "Make the role your very own. It's a winner. Believe me, respectable men will flatter and pursue you for information you haven't got. . . . Harry, it's only a game. You feel sorry for yourself because you found yourself stranded in the middle of it. . . . Set yourself a few simple rules" (22–23). As the Oulipian would when setting the rules for a particular written composition, Mathews painstakingly creates his CIA persona, which he repeatedly calls "the game I'd chosen to play" (30) or "my ridiculous spy game" (59). As he gets deeper into this persona, in fact, he associates his game/persona with his literary past, as, for example, when he names his front travel agency Locus Solus, the title of a literary journal he had founded with Ashbery and others in the early 1960s (32); or when a shadowy agent of one government or another—who will end up saving Mathews's life in the novel's climactic send-up of an Alpine shoot-out—calls herself names from his other books (168).[28] The Cold War world of spying, in other words, provides Mathews the ideal context for animating a remark he made in 1997: "Playing a game is no less complete than any other kind of human activity."[29]

The event that brings Mathews to the attention of the intelligence community is taken directly from the Oulipian spirit of game playing. He hatches a scheme in which he will lecture on "travel-stress dyslexia," an invented condition in which the anxiety of departure renders one incapable of even reading a timetable. After explaining to the reader how he was once introduced to a fellow Oulipian's predilection for "palindromes, lipograms, salacious spoonerisms," Mathews writes, "I wasn't much impressed . . . until it occurred to me that numerical palindromes might solve travel-stress dyslexia. Numbers were not merely bi- but multilingual; and any number could be read backwards. Once I was home it didn't take me long to formulate the principles of what I was going to tell the AARO audience" (40). It is this Oulipian-inspired lecture that rouses the interest of the Soviet embassy and that propels Mathews into the underworld of espionage. By associating his own fictional entry into this world so closely with his literary self as refracted through Oulipo, Mathews suggests that the Cold War not only encouraged fiction making, but that its special circumstances meant that even seemingly apolitical aesthetic exercises like Oulipian cleverness could in fact be drawn into the ever-expanding frame of political rhetoric.[30]

During this lecture on travel-stress dyslexia, for example, he begins in poetry but ends in politics by explaining how to travel by train through, of all places, the Siberian interior, even going so far as to detail the train schedule to Perm II, site of a super-secret Soviet nuclear facility. As the ultimate plan is to get the attention of the local intelligence community, it seems almost on cue when he receives a summons to the Soviet embassy. There the slightly baffled official of the USSR Tourist Department (which was "in reality the KGB's 2nd Directorate, specializing in counterintelligence work among Americans and Brits visiting the Soviet Union" [99]), is unsure what to make of Mathews and his recent movements. "[Y]our activity does not conform to familiar patterns," he says in a caricature of a Soviet functionary. "This is the point: advocating the journey you described cannot have been due to chance" (103).

Beyond this winking appearance of a Soviet official who is suspicious of anything that appears to be chance, *My Life in CIA* is telling because it explicitly figures the Cold War as a rhetorical frame that dictates how and when events are interpreted as products of chance or design—a frame which, for all the book's tongue-in-cheek nods to the global game of one-upsmanship, turns out to have consequences for Mathews himself. As is expected, the Soviet official is confused because Mathews's behavior does not fit a recognizable pattern—not only has he been lecturing about Siberian rail travel, but he has been attending both anticommunist and French Communist Party meetings. Such apparent intimacy with rival political factions does not fit the bipolar logic of the Cold War, and by so doing Mathews first thinks he can confound—and thereby exploit—the political landscape.

As has been the case with so many works discussed in this book, Mathews uses chance as a site to experiment with the differences between—and continuities among—fictional narratives and objective reality demanded by the Cold War rhetorical frame. Throughout *My Life in CIA*, Mathews contextualizes his idiosyncratic game in the wider world of political events such as Watergate and the unrest in Chile that would lead to Salvador Allende's overthrow in September 1973.[31] But one event is closer to home for him: "On Sunday, June 3, a supersonic Tupolev-144 flown in for the Le Bourget air show crashed in Goussainville, killing six people besides its crew" (96). The Tupolev-144 was the Soviet answer to the supersonic Concorde—a joint effort of the British and French—and its spectacular crash at the Paris Air Show seriously hamstrung Soviet efforts to move the aircraft into more widespread use. As part of its extensive coverage on June 4, 1973, the *New York Times* pointedly noted that "The Soviet radio and television network kept the news from listeners and viewers tonight, in line with an official information policy that seeks to play down Soviet disasters of all kinds. The Kremlin evidently fears that such events reflect unfavorably on the Communist political system, which is generally presented as superior in all respects to Western democracy."[32] With the symbolic importance of the accident immediately clear, Mathews does not figure the disaster as an example of the ineffable texture of objective reality as others might have, but sees it rather as an opportunity to enter further into the Cold War game.

In fact, Mathews decides that by manipulating the plane accident, he can likewise manipulate the Cold War frame that is guiding the creation of his CIA persona. Reading *Le Monde*, Mathews learns "that the police were reinforcing their protection of the Tupolev-144 that had crashed on June 3. That could only mean that pieces of the wreckage had been stolen—CIA work, perhaps? There was an opening for me here, a chance to try my hand peddling an intelligence item.... And I knew where to find what I needed" (111). Mathews proceeds to hire a sculptor to fabricate the twisted remains of the Tupolev's compression chamber out of scrap titanium. By designing tangible evidence of the accident, Mathews generates an "intelligence item" that will, he thinks, give him an edge in the "game [he's] enjoying" (112). When he successfully sells the faked part to an unknown party, he thinks he is completely in control, that he is exploiting the game for his own benefit and amusement.

Thus far, the game still seems "ridiculous" and even light-hearted—Mathews details his endearing attempts at perfecting his role as a CIA agent: "I kept embellishing my new persona. I carried a piece of pink chalk in my pocket and I'd sometimes stop in out-of-the-way streets to scribble a cryptic sign on a wall. I spent forty francs ... on an aluminum suitcase pasted with labels not just from Gstaad and Amalfi but Bucarest and Leningrad" (36). Although such moments are tongue-in-cheek, in the first part of the book, there is still a sense that the Cold War can be brought under the sign of Mathews's own game; in a reversal of the classic thriller plot, it is the individual exploiting state-sponsored rhetoric—not the other way around—and at first he enjoys his calculated parody of a real-life espionage agent.

But despite this initial success with the travel lecture and the faked Tupolev-144 part, in the second half of *My Life in CIA*, Mathews's CIA persona spins out of his control, and the Cold War becomes figured as a meta-game that begins to play *him*. This is illustrated with the idea that chance itself is actually beyond Mathews's control as accidents wind up implicating him in intrigue in ways he had not intended. The counterpoint to his manipulation of the plane accident, for example, comes when he finds himself "by sheer accident" (162) at a dinner party hosted by Ferdinand Zendol, "a notorious right-wing activist" whose presence on various international watch-lists makes Mathews suspicious by association. At the end of the book, after Mathews has fled Paris for fear of his own safety, it is the paranoid Zendol who tries to hunt him down on a remote hiking trail in the Alps (only to be killed himself by the nameless agent mentioned above).

As Mathews becomes increasingly aware of both his lack of control and of the "real" stakes of his game, he seeks the counsel of his friend Patrick Burton-Cheyne. Patrick is introduced earlier in the book, after he attended the travel lecture and then "ran into" Mathews again in the lobby of the Salle Gaveau. Patrick works for Zapata Petroleum, but as he explains to Mathews, he had also been "a graduate student at Duke and written a controversial doctorate on 'Traded Craft in the Work of Eliot and Ashbery'" (49). Impressed as he is by Patrick's evident erudition, Mathews chats with him at various points in the book and even accepts his invitation to attend an opera production in Milan.

It is not until late in the book, after Mathews has been tracked and contacted by real CIA agents who want to question him about his associations (including his presence in Milan, where he was "warmly greeted" by a man later implicated in a bombing [161]), it dawns on him that all along Patrick has been an authentic undercover agent who had been positioning Mathews in strategic locations for some unknown end. It turns out that all the significant associations Mathews had had—while he thought he was controlling the terms of the game—were actually orchestrated by Patrick: "It may have been a coincidence," writes Mathews of "getting involved" with Zendol, "but I soon found out it was no accident" (174). With the realization that Patrick is an undercover agent, there is a turn in the book, and Mathews finds himself subject to the kind of worry discussed in chapter 1, that there are invisible plots capable of manipulating him, so that even what he first interpreted as merely accidental has taken on a more sinister resonance. After the revelation that Patrick was gaming *him* the whole time, for example, his advice to Mathews takes on more significance: "When I met Patrick on Friday, I told him about my Sunday adventures [at Zendol's] and asked for his interpretation of them. He couldn't be absolutely sure, of course, but it sounded to him as if they were due to pure chance" (136). As in Kosinski's *The Future Is Ours, Comrade*, here the question of whether an event may or may not be interpreted as chance stands for a range of questions pertaining to how fiction can come to cloud objective reality. In this case, Patrick wants to convince Mathews that this encounter was "pure chance" only to distract him from the real design to which he is being subjected. The Cold War frame has once again conscripted chance, and as Mathews retroactively realizes Patrick's identity, he feels drained of all agency—a feeling figured, significantly, in terms of language. Upon seeing an armed Zendol on that remote hiking trail, for example, he writes, "I didn't decide what to do. What happened happened as if it was programmed and I'd become a word in someone else's grammar" (175).

The "someone" in this case may be Patrick, but even he is only a proxy for the more pervasive grammar of the Cold War. Mathews's simile is indeed apt as it returns us once again to the conflict's narrative quality, to the idea that the Cold War depended on and created its own logic and grammar in order to nourish and sustain itself. This Mathews recognizes and uses as an occasion for an aesthetic exercise that cannot help but carry the point that within the Cold War frame, acts of narration are inherently political, a truth he so profoundly discovers when he tries to write himself into—and then out of—the game. And yet, there is the final irony that all the espionage-related events in *My Life in CIA* are probably utter fiction. But "probably" is the best we can say, for part of the book's point is to recreate that odd space—somewhere between what we know to be fiction and what we are certain is real—that characterized so much literature trying to grapple with the strange realities of the Cold War.

In the book's coda, in fact, set in Berlin in 1991, Mathews overhears fellow café patrons gossiping about the events he has just related; they conclude that, like Colonel Kurtz in *Apocalypse Now*, Mathews had been "'terminated with extreme prejudice'—the wet solution" (203). Mathews is pleased about the news of his own political assassination and ends the book with the line: "There was not the slightest doubt that this man was telling the truth." This statement once again reverses what has come before—despite what has happened in the world of the book, claims to objective truth are as compromised by the Cold War frame as they are by a fiction writer as playful as Mathews, and he ironically regains his lost control by choosing to write a book about this frame. *My Life in CIA*'s various reversals of control, focalized as they are through the manipulation of accident, demonstrate both the aesthetic character of the Cold War—made visible by its ability to shape language in unusual ways—and a writer's power to confront and indeed affect such language.

Coda: Cold War Meaning

If, like me, you happened to have been walking through the quad of one of a hundred American colleges and universities in the fall of 2009, you might have been treated to a free copy of Charles Darwin's *On the Origin of Species* (1859). In that sesquicentennial year, over 100,000 editions were made for distribution, and volunteers stood in high-traffic campus areas to hand them out to passersby. At the end of the first decade of the twenty-first century, it was not the dissemination of evolutionary theory that soon stirred controversy, but that particular edition's 54-page "special introduction," which claimed to frame Darwin's argument in the spirit of open, critical debate. This introduction, written by one of the most prolific proponents of intelligent design, aims to discredit the ensuing theory by showing that it is more rational to believe that the universe is the product of design rather than chance—there is more "likelihood," this argument goes, that something so complex as human life would have arisen due to outside intention rather than "sheer chance." Given the foregoing discussion of how questions of chance and design can be conceptualized in narrative terms, it is perhaps unsurprising that the critique is illustrated by comparing real life to a book, both of which must have a designer if they are capable of being interpreted:

> Aside from the immense volume of information that your DNA contains, consider the likelihood of all the intricate, interrelated parts of this "book" coming together by sheer chance. Critics claim that would be comparable to believing that this publication happened by accident. Imagine that there was nothing. Then paper appeared, and ink fell from nowhere onto the flat sheets and shaped itself into perfectly formed letters of the English alphabet. Initially, the letters said something like this: *"fgsn&k cn1clxc dumbh cckvkduh vstupidm ncncx."* As you can see, random letters rarely produce words that make sense. But in time, mindless chance formed them into the order of meaningful words with

spaces between them. Periods, commas, capitals, italics, quotes, paragraphs, margins, etc., also came into being in the correct placements. The sentences then grouped themselves to relate to each other, giving them coherence.[1]

In this view, the metaphorical becomes literal: the universe is authored, and therefore absolute chance cannot exist in it. For the author of the introduction, absolute chance is illegible, and so when retrospectively admiring the complexity of human life, he cannot see it as part of this complexity since the total design has arisen from divine intention. Chance, in other words, has no meaning—"mindless chance" and "meaningful words" are mutually exclusive. This idea is most vividly illustrated by the sample of "random letters" which are not random at all: the inclusion of those legible words "dumb," "duh," "stupid"—presumably directed at those who find Darwinian theory intelligent—announce themselves as the best evidence of narrative design. Ironically, were readers to believe that the italicized nonsense words are really comprised of random letters, it would mean that such randomness produces sensible meaning, in English, not "rarely," but a startling fifty percent of the time. These letters, "something like" absolute chance, betray actually the author's own desire for total order that expels chance even from a sample of randomness, which becomes instead a sample of his design. The logic of the argument thus mirrors the logic of a designed universe in that both, when construed in narrative terms, must convert absolute chance into narrative chance.[2]

Although *No Accident, Comrade* has looked at American literature and culture through the Cold War, this confusion of metaphor (the book of life) with scientific reality (the universe is not designed and therefore subject to chance) suggests the staying power that chance has to disrupt coherent frames of meaning beyond the Cold War—whether those generated by literary and cultural narratives or, in this case, Christian worldviews. The issue of legibility raised by the related phenomena of viewing the universe as a book and embedding words in supposedly random letters is likewise important to any narrative in which readers must determine how (and whether) to construe meaning, and is often most visible in those experimental works that bend, dispense with, or otherwise create new formal structures. I have said throughout this book that the concept of chance can be especially disruptive to narrative convention, a function that, when read in the Cold War rhetorical frame, can also carry with it questions about freedom, control, and representation. When held against narrative prose like the special introduction, we might begin to see how many literary narratives (of the type generally discussed in this book) are not merely hospitable to the operation of chance but are indeed interested in lingering over chance because it suggests a profusion of meaning.

One hallmark of literary narrative is that it contains a profuse meaning that cannot be as easily fixed as the sample of not-so-random letters, an idea well illustrated by the later work of David Markson, which reads as a compendium of this kind of profusion. Markson's *This Is Not a Novel* (2001) is with *Reader's Block* (1996) and *Vanishing Point* (2004) an assemblage of absorbing and often surprising facts from literary and cultural history. It is a book, as he writes, "with no *sequence of events*. Which is to say, no indicated *passage of time*"; "A novel with no *setting*"; "a book without characters"; and, "[c]ategorically, with no politics."[3] The emphatic denial of conventional generic markers suggests that the book's meaning must inhere elsewhere. Here is one brief example of the book's collage-like structure:

Leslie Howard died in a plane shot down by the Germans in World War II.
William Gaddis died of prostate cancer.[4]

The death of Leslie Howard, the movie actor of the 1930s, seems worthy of inclusion because of its unusual nature (rumor has it he was involved with British intelligence). This tidbit is juxtaposed with William Gaddis's death, and the ravages of cancer seem doubly poignant in the context of all the other anecdotes about the deaths of great artists in *This Is Not a Novel*. But what else? Are we to suppose that there is any other meaning in this pairing, especially given a remark seven pages later that the book is "Obstinately cross-referential and of cryptic interconnective syntax?"[5] As Markson returns sometimes to the same figures and themes (lines from Gaddis's *The Recognitions* are quoted, for example), the cross-referential aspect of the book is apparent enough, but what of the "cryptic interconnective syntax"? What is the nature of such syntactic meaning in this instance, and in the work as a whole? To put the question in terms used throughout *No Accident, Comrade*: are such sequences products of chance, insofar as Markson could have shuffled them in any order and achieved the same overall effect, or is the ordering itself, the syntax, part of the book's design? Staying within the book itself, this question is perhaps impossible to answer; but the elliptical nature of *This Is Not a Novel* radiates outward, its fragments allude to complex biographies and aesthetic objects that contain meaning that might then be read back onto Markson's book. To read in this way is to think about potential connections in the web of literary and cultural meanings *implied* by the book's anecdotes and facts, not made as explicit as the deployment of narrative chance in the special introduction.

In reading *This Is Not a Novel* for meaning that is largely implied, one logically investigates the various references to see how or whether meaning accrues over the course of the book. At one point, for example, we are reminded of Jack Kerouac's origins: "Lowell, Massachusetts, Jack Kerouac was born in," which, like a hypertext link, sends us to Kerouac's work, which could in turn help us uncover whether there is meaning in placing Gaddis's death after Howard's.[6] In *The Subterraneans* (written 1953), Kerouac writes: "in this manner more or less arriving at the Mask where a kid called Harold Sand came in, a chance acquaintance of Mardou's from a year ago, a young novelist looking like Leslie Howard who'd just had a manuscript accepted and so acquired a strange grace in my eyes I wanted to devour."[7] The "chance acquaintance" of the narrator's love interest, Mardou Fox (a fictionalized Alene Lee) is William Gaddis; the manuscript is what would become *The Recognitions*.[8] What if a reader happens to remember that in *The Subterraneans* Kerouac describes a barely disguised Gaddis as looking like Leslie Howard, and in *This Is Not a Novel* Markson pairs Howard with Gaddis? Or that Markson knew both Kerouac and Gaddis, that he spent time with Kerouac in the very Greenwich Village bars described in *The Subterraneans,* and that he was acquainted with Gaddis from the 1960s on?[9] With all this in mind, the juxtaposition of the two deaths confirms a "cryptic interconnective syntax," and suggests that the pairing is hardly a product of chance. And yet the meaning of this design is not exactly clear—it is not a causal relationship, but rather a subterranean association whose meaning is largely implied. The pairing certainly delivers us to the avant-garde literary circle of bohemian New York in the 1950s and beyond, directs us to Markson's other books (which are filled with references to Gaddis and Kerouac), and causes us to wonder, if nothing else, about the oddness of mentioning Leslie Howard, William Gaddis, and Jack Kerouac in one breath. It also plays with the way meaning tends to be construed in literary narrative—normally it is the depths, not the surfaces, which are most meaningful, and yet here a physical resemblance apparently has relevance to the book's interconnective syntax because it directs readers to implied meaning. Perhaps the most significant function such a realization could have is to announce that meaning in *This Is Not a Novel* is never as final as the faked randomness discussed above—even the *Subterraneans* connection is only reasonable, not definitive.

Despite the claim that there are categorically "no politics" in *This is Not a Novel*, it would hardly be a reach to say that the Cold War has encouraged literary critics to see a politics at work in the sort of implied meaning the novel exemplifies. Indeed, it almost seems that invoking the Cold War frame at all when analyzing a given literary text means that scholars view it as valuable if it exhibits implied meaning, which in turn means it can be seen as evincing a kind of submerged politics. It is worth noting, by way of illustration, that as literary critics began to take Kerouac seriously after the initial dismissals of his work (largely for its perceived anti-intellectualism and adolescent bent), the first task was to show that his work was indeed complex enough to contain a range of meanings not obviously apparent, and then, later, to show that his work—along with the work of other seemingly apolitical Beat writers—was actually political.[10]

Such politics are made visible by the Cold War frame, even when the explicit aim of a given analysis is not to show that Kerouac was really political. Consider, for instance, Ann Douglas's claim that "Kerouac's style is the most important innovation in American prose since Hemingway's . . . [it] reflected the realities of . . . WWII and the Cold War that quickly succeeded it."[11] Defending Kerouac against earlier charges of formlessness and stylistic recklessness, Douglas writes:

> The apparent formlessness that attends Kerouac's narratives, the absence of conventional plotting . . . was in part a response to a world in which there seemed to be too many reasons for things to happen as they did, in which events felt predetermined and overdetermined, in which cues to the unexpected were no longer heard. Drama means that something doesn't happen because something else does. In its crudest form, the girl tied to the railroad tracks isn't run over by the train *because* her lover arrives just in time to cut her free; drama presupposes alternatives and a choice between them. Whether the agent is represented as God or human resourcefulness or happenstance, one side wins and the other loses. Drama is about control threatened and regained; it's part of the special effects of power. Kerouac, however, meant to slip the leash of the preconditioned and overcontrolled. As Mardou Fox asks in *The Subterraneans*, "what's in store for me in the direction I *don't* take?" . . . a question that refuses the distinction between offstage and onstage on which drama depends.[12]

The idea is that the notion of agency, whether stylistic or personal, amounts to a kind of legible politics not immediately visible. Kerouac can be understood as political insofar as his writing reflected the Cold War conceptualization of the world as a drama or fiction, which is why Douglas describes drama in terms of "power," "control," and the possibility of individual "choice"—all preoccupations of the Cold War rhetorical frame. If Kerouac in his writing indulges in possibilities and alternatives, he is being political because he slips "the leash of the preconditioned and overcontrolled," features, again, thought to be of a piece with the Cold War frame. Douglas cites the bluesy, frenetic *The Subterraneans* because it is an example of Kerouac's "spontaneous prose" at its most compelling, a prose that, if nothing else, evades the prescribed meanings of a Cold War environment in favor of the personal, subjective sense of the world that Douglas so admires.[13]

But what interests me is the ways and reasons one might name this political—although Douglas says Kerouac's writing has "more to do with alchemy than politics," the implication is that there is a kind of political work performed in this type of writing, otherwise there is no reason to invoke the Cold War frame in the first place.[14] This line of reasoning, that a foregrounding of individual agency itself suggests political engagement, only makes sense if one accepts the logic inherited from the Cold War, that to bridle against these norms is to be political. In this view, the Cold War becomes something against which the individual—and the individual artist—struggles. This is what I take Andrew Hammond to mean when he writes "The Cold War struggle for the control of political belief was grounded in a Manichean opposition between self and other, good and evil, democracy and tyranny.... This dichotomizing framework was particularly forcible in the United States, where the denigration of the Eastern bloc pervaded all areas of national life."[15] Given such overdetermined frameworks, the argument goes, writers either deliberately responded in kind to such "control of political belief," or, more compellingly, the form and content of their work can be said to reflect or embody such historical realities. Andrew Hoberek has written a whole book showing that, as he puts it, "The fiction of the 1950s ... is characterized by its increasingly tenuous efforts to create via style a preserve of autonomy that would distinguish the artist from the organization man."[16] Although he does not discuss Kerouac at length, Hoberek cites the Douglas essay quoted above and, reading through an economic lens, makes a similar point about how his chosen writers see "autonomy" itself as helping artists evade the conformist norms of the organization man—an act, in the context of the Cold War, that could seem political.

Writing on Cold War literature and culture in 2005—the same year Hoberek's book appeared—Leerom Medovoi noted that his own argument "implies that the various social movements and critiques of race, gender, and sexuality that have come to be associated with the broad term 'identity politics,' all appealed, more or less explicitly, to a rhetoric of the Cold War era that represented political agency itself as a struggle within the regulatory norms of postwar suburbia."[17] Following from this observation, we might say that in literary criticism, whenever the Cold War is conceptualized as pertaining to some manner of "regulatory norms" (as it almost always is), it creates a scenario in which individuality itself amounts to political action. Such a focus on the Cold War frame helps account for a phenomenon described by Sean McCann and Michael Szalay in their critique of postwar "literary thinking" and its failure to engage in what they call "formal politics." In that essay, they lament a "widely shared retreat away from public debate and civic engagement and toward a commitment to personal freedom.... [in postwar writing there are] a range of theories that invoke the singular, the individual, and the inassimilable against the basic elements (norms, institutions, deliberation) of the public realm."[18] Although McCann and Szalay do not emphasize the Cold War frame, it seems to me that, given what I have described throughout *No Accident, Comrade*, this frame goes far in explaining why the singular, the individual, or the inassimilable could seem political in the first place.[19]

One effect of this sense of politics is that in order for a given literary work to seem good or interesting or worthy of study—or, indeed, "literary"—it needs to be shown to embody or exemplify politics in some way, however hidden or elliptical such politics may be. Thus scholars of Cold War literature have taken notice of the implied politics that must be teased out of the texts under consideration. As Christina Klein explains in the introduction to her book, *Cold War Orientalism*, "The texts that I explore do not exist in a cause-and-effect relationship with the Cold War foreign policies pursued by Washington: they did not simply reflect those policies, nor did they determine them. Rather, they served as a cultural space in which the ideologies undergirding those policies could be, at various moments, articulated, endorsed, questioned, softened, and mystified. Nor were the texts I examine unambiguous or internally coherent ideological broadsides. Instead, they provided an arena in which the multiple voices of allied, but still distinct, social groups could be heard."[20] Klein's method, then, is to notice that certain texts, while not "ideological broadsides," are, when read in light of the Cold War, nonetheless politically engaged precisely *because* they are not explicitly political in the way, say, a socialist pamphlet is.

This notion of political is thus simultaneously hidden and made visible by the Cold War frame—a duality that makes it possible to ask questions such as "why innovative fiction has often been misconstrued as a self-indulgent formalism rather than as a meaningful response to a historical and literary crisis."[21] Here again, we might wonder about the nature of this adjective "meaningful"—in what sense is it meaningful? It seems an ironic extension of Cold War logic that a meaningful response to contemporaneous cultural and political norms names that which is precisely not an "ideological broadside," but rather that which operates in what Adam Piette calls "the hazy borders between aesthetic project and political allegory."[22] Not being an ideological broadside, in other words, is what makes a Cold War text political—the more subtle and idiosyncratic the better, the more playful, complex, and replete the better, since repleteness itself can be read as evidence of political engagement, given cultural narratives that sustain themselves by not being replete.[23] Thus for Piette, the "literary Cold War" amounts to "the secret, obsessive and paranoid story of the mind under the compulsions of the Cold War."[24] And likewise for Jodi Kim, writing about Asian-American work and the Cold War, "Asian American critique unsettles and disrupts the dominant Manichaean lens through which the Cold War is made sense of and in turn generates meaning."[25] In these representative views, the "compulsions of the Cold War," its "dominant Manichaean lens," is reductive and constrictive, whereas the complex texts under consideration are not, a fact that seems to make them political.

It is in fact a basic premise of most literary criticism that literature is not reducible to the information it conveys; when this notion is read in light of the Cold War, this very irreducibility—Kerouac's idiosyncratic style, for example—becomes a political stance. Thus to claim the Cold War as an organizing principle when looking at literary production is to claim that there must be a politics embedded in the literature, a move that reinscribes the Cold War idea that all things are tainted by an all-pervasive politics, and that given this fact, texts, especially literary ones, are more than what they seem. This claim is not necessarily bad—I make it at various times throughout this book—but it certainly does merit further reflection about how contemporary readings of postwar literature have been informed by Cold War meaning. As a way to periodize literary and cultural production in the second half of the twentieth century, "Cold War literature" is useful if it becomes shorthand for a particular way of seeing politics in the nonpolitical. If we take this notion as a starting point, then we can further theorize how the term "Cold War literature" itself implies a specific conceptualization of what politics and aesthetics can mean, insofar as it creates rules of legibility that obscures or renders irrelevant other things.

Notes

Chapter 1

1. James Park Sloan, *Jerzy Kosinski: A Biography* (New York: Dutton, 1996), 98–172.
2. *The Future Is Ours, Comrade* was published under a pseudonym, Joseph Novak, purportedly to protect members of Kosinski's family back in Poland. He published another, less successful study of Soviet life two years later: *No Third Path* (Garden City, N.Y.: Double Day, 1962).
3. Eleanor Roosevelt, "My Day" (December 20, 1957), archived at: <http://www.gwu.edu/~erpapers/myday/displaydoc.cfm?_y=1957&_f=md003991>.
4. William Jorden, "Russians Report 10% Output Rise during Overhaul," *New York Times* (December 20, 1957): 1; William Jorden, "Soviet Science Aide Says Country Still Does Not Lead U.S.," *New York Times* (December 20, 1957): 1; Jack Raymond, "Pentagon Seeks an Extra Billion to Spur Weapons," *New York Times* (December 20, 1957): 1.
5. Sloan, *Jerzy Kosinski*, 11–112. For more on the U.S. Information Agency, see Nicholas J. Cull, *The Cold War and the United States Information Agency: American Propaganda and Public Diplomacy, 1945–1989* (Cambridge: Cambridge University Press, 2008), and Frances Stonor Saunders, *The Cultural Cold War* (New York: New Press, 2000). Neither book mentions Kosinski.
6. Sloan, *Jerzy Kosinski*, 129.
7. For a review that emphasizes these aspects, see Richard Hottelet, "From Collective to Kremlin, It's One Big State of Nerves," *New York Times* (May 22, 1960): BR3.
8. For a discussion of the authenticity of Kosinski's Soviet books, see Ray Taras, "Kosinski as Kremlinologist: Soviet Studies or Spoof?" *Polish Review* 49.1 (2004): 621–640.
9. Joseph Novak, *The Future Is Ours, Comrade* (1960. New York: Dutton, 1964), 105.
10. Ibid., 110.
11. In another example, a group of young people attempt to incite the election of new management of their collective farm, claiming "abuse" on the part of the current authorities. Before the movement takes off, "the two principal leaders of the group drowned 'accidentally' during a swimming party in the lake." Kosinski's interlocutor remarks, "A convenient accident, wasn't it? The old management remains unchanged" (150).
12. Novak, *The Future Is Ours, Comrade*, 190; 227.
13. Geoffrey Movius, "A Conversation with Jerzy Kosinski," *New Boston Review* (Winter 1975): 6.
14. Richard Evans, *In Defense of History* (New York: Norton, 2000), 111.
15. Friedrich Engels, "Ludwig Feuerbach and the End of Classical German Philosophy," in *Karl Marx and Friedrich Engels on Religion* (New York: Schocken Books, 1964), 213–268; quotation on 255. For a discussion of Marx's considerably more complex conception of history, see G. A. Cohen, *Karl Marx's Theory of History: A Defence* (1978. Princeton, N.J.: Princeton

Notes to Pages 6–10

University Press, 2000). Although there is, of course, a great body of work on Marxist thought, *No Accident, Comrade* is about Cold War American perceptions of this thought, and as such does not engage the complexities and controversies within Marxist theory.

16. Nikolai Bukharin, *Historical Materialism: A System of Sociology*, intro. Alfred G. Meyer (1925. Ann Arbor: University of Michigan Press, 1969), 44.
17. For a contemporary explanation of chance's role in Marxist dialectics, see Mario Bunge's "What Is Chance?" *Science and Society* (Winter 1951): 209–231. Writing for a Marxist-oriented journal, Bunge argues that "dialectical materialism . . . instead of dogmatically denying chance, adds that the contingent is as real as the necessary, that chance is something more than a word to disguise our ignorance, being in return an object, ontological as well as epistemological, worthy of examination" (219).
18. Daniel Cahill, "An Interview with Jerzy Kosinski on *Blind Date*," *Contemporary Literature* 19.2 (Spring 1978): 133–142; quotation on 135.
19. Randall Jarrell, *Pictures from an Institution* (New York: Farrar, Straus and Giroux, 1954), 40.
20. Dwight Macdonald, "The Now-Non-Conservatism, or Notes on a Career," in his *Memoirs of a Revolutionist: Essays in Political Criticism* (1952. New York: Farrar, Straus and Cudahy, 1957), 319–326; quotation on 325.
21. Vivian Gornick, *The Romance of American Communism* (New York: Basic Books, 1977), 255. The speaker is Carl Marzani, given the pseudonym Eric Lanzetti in the book.
22. Jacques Monod, *Chance and Necessity: An Essay on the Natural Philosophy of Modern Biology*, trans. Austryn Wainhouse (New York: Knopf, 1971), 112. The original French version, *Le Hasard et la Necessite*, was published in 1970.
23. Monod, *Chance and Necessity*, 118–119.
24. Ibid., 145–146.
25. Ibid., 169.
26. Ibid., 41.
27. Ibid., 179.
28. Jerzy Kosinski, *Blind Date* (Boston: Houghton Mifflin Company, 1977), 36.
29. Ibid., 79.
30. *Blind Date*, like many of Kosinski's later books, is unsettlingly plotless as a way to emphasize the "drama of each unique instance of . . . existence"—in a repudiation of Soviet logic that focuses on destiny and design, his books relish the operation of chance. Levanter prefers to "rely on chance encounters" (168) and even publishes an article on "the role of chance in creative investment" (189), which received numerous responses, including a letter from Mary-Jane Kirkland, a fabulously wealthy widow of much-older industrialist (in real life, *The Future Is Ours, Comrade* attracted the attention of Mary Hayward Weir, the widow of fabulously wealthy steel magnate, to whom Kosinski was married in 1962). Whether associated with romance (as when Levanter randomly encounters beautiful women), or tragedy (as when a luggage mix-up causes him to miss an appointment at Sharon Tate's Los Angeles home, where she and others were to be murdered by the followers of Charles Manson, who seemed to be "following a script prepared by an invisible agency" [162]), chance in Kosinski's work represents objective reality. With this interplay of real life and fiction, turning so often on questions of chance, a novel like *Blind Date* attempts to distinguish itself from the mistakes made by both "pulp novels" and manifestations of Marxist ideology by celebrating and thematizing such moments of chance.
31. For a discussion of the Cold War as a "rhetorical state of mind," see Lynn Boyd Hinds and Theodore Otto Windt, Jr., *The Cold War as Rhetoric: The Beginnings, 1945–1950* (New York: Praeger, 1991), 5. *No Accident, Comrade* shares with Hinds and Windt the sense that language generally (and rhetoric more specifically) is intimately connected to the way that reality is understood: "in the postwar period a single all-encompassing reality about the international world arose that, when it took hold, admitted no exceptions to its basic premises. Soon it was transferred to domestic political life. It was the cold war reality and it was an ideological reality" (23). See also Martin Medhurst et al., *Cold War Rhetoric: Strategy, Metaphor, and Ideology* (East Lansing: Michigan State University Press, 1997).

32. See Steven Belletto, "Inventing Other Realities: What the Cold War Means for Literary Studies," in *Uncertain Empire: American History and the Idea of the Cold War*, ed. Joel Isaac and Duncan Bell (Oxford: Oxford University Press, forthcoming).
33. See, for example, Matthew Frye Jacobson and Gaspar González, *What Have They Built You to Do? The Manchurian Candidate and Cold War America* (Minneapolis: University of Minnesota Press, 2006); Arthur Redding, *Turncoats, Traitors, and Fellow Travelers: Culture and Politics of the Early Cold War* (Jackson: University Press of Mississippi, 2008); and David Caute, *Politics and the Novel during the Cold War* (Piscataway, N.J.: Transactions Publishers, Rutgers, 2009), which, as Redding puts it with respect to his own book, focus on "key thinkers and writers who understood their work to be politically and socially engaged" (4).
34. Kristin L. Matthews, "The ABCs of *Mad* Magazine: Reading, Citizenship, and Cold War America," *International Journal of Comic Art* 8.2 (Fall 2006): 248–268; Leerom Medovoi, *Rebels: Youth and the Cold War Origins of Identity* (Durham, N.C.: Duke University Press, 2005); Adam Piette, *The Literary Cold War: 1945 to Vietnam* (Edinburgh: Edinburgh University Press, 2009); Kevin Wetmore, "1954: Selling Kabuki to the West," *Asian Theatre Journal* 26.1 (Spring 2009): 78–93; Redding, *Turncoats, Traitors, and Fellow Travelers*; Fiona Paton, "Beyond Bakhtin: Towards a Cultural Stylistics," *College English* 63.2 (November 2000): 166–193; Virginia Osborne, "'Let's Go to the Woods, Boys': Reading *Deliverance* as a Cold War Novel," *James Dickey Newsletter* 24.2 (Spring 2008): 1–20; and Kenneth Payne, "McCarthyism and Cold War America in Patricia Highsmith's *The Blunderer*," *McNeese Review* 41 (2003): 76–84.
35. See Donald Pease, *Visionary Compacts: American Renaissance Writings in Cultural Context* (Madison: University of Wisconsin Press, 1987) and William Spanos, *The Errant Art of Moby-Dick: The Canon, the Cold War, and the Struggle for American Studies* (Durham, N.C.: Duke University Press, 1995) (Spanos offers a critique of Pease). Elaine Tyler May's *Homeward Bound: American Families in the Cold War Era* (New York: Basic Books, 1988) has been influential for literary critics for demonstrating a relationship between government policies and domestic life. Alan Nadel's *Containment Culture: American Narratives, Postmodernism, and the Atomic Age* (Durham, N.C.: Duke University Press, 1995) is the best and most wide-ranging discussion of the cultural logic of containment (and its failures) in Cold War American culture.
36. Nadel, *Containment Culture*, 3.
37. For a critique of the containment thesis, see Morris Dickstein, *Leopards in the Temple: The Transformation of American Fiction, 1945–1970* (Cambridge, Mass.: Harvard University Press, 2002), 7–10.
38. See Amy Kaplan, "'Left Alone with America': The Absence of Empire in the Study of American Culture," in *Cultures of United States Imperialism*, ed. Amy Kaplan and Donald Pease (Durham, N.C.: Duke University Press, 1993). See also Christian Appy, ed., *Cold War Constructions: The Political Culture of United States Imperialism, 1945–1966* (Amherst: University of Massachusetts Press, 2000); and Odd Arne Westad, *The Global Cold War: Third World Interventions and the Making of Our Times* (Cambridge: Cambridge University Press, 2005).
39. Medovoi, *Rebels*. See also Christina Klein, *Cold War Orientalism: Asia in the Middlebrow Imagination, 1945–1961* (Berkeley: University of California Press, 2003); Uta Poiger, *Jazz, Rock, and Rebels: Cold War Politics and American Culture in a Divided Germany* (Berkeley: University of California Press, 2000); Andrew Hammond, ed., *Cold War Literature: Writing the Global Conflict* (New York: Routledge, 2005); Rebecca M. Schreiber, *Cold War Exiles in Mexico: U.S. Dissidents and the Culture of Critical Resistance* (Minneapolis: University of Minnesota Press, 2008); Ann Sherif, *Japan's Cold War: Media, Literature, and the Law* (New York: Columbia University Press, 2009); Eric Keenaghan, *Queering Cold War Poetry: Ethics of Vulnerability in Cuba and the United States* (Columbus: Ohio State University Press, 2009); Jodi Kim, *Ends of Empire: Asian American Critique and the Cold War* (Minneapolis: University of Minnesota Press, 2010); and Andrew Hammond, ed., *Cold War Literature*, vol. 2, *Western, Eastern and Postcolonial Perspectives*, forthcoming.
40. Nadel, *Containment Culture*, 4.

41. Identifying the years that bracket the Cold War is tricky, especially if one considers its rhetorical dimensions. For the purposes of this book, I will say that the first phase of the Cold War roughly coincides with the long 1950s, beginning perhaps with the 1947 Truman Doctrine (which affirmed that the United States would support "free peoples" around the world in resisting "totalitarian regimes"), and culminating in the tensions of the Cuban Missile Crisis in 1962, but these bookends are somewhat arbitrary. For a discussion of the naming of the Cold War and a consideration of its potential beginnings, see Susan L. Carruthers, *Cold War Captives: Imprisonment, Escape, and Brainwashing* (Berkeley: University of California Press, 2009), 1–22.

42. See Ann Douglas, "Periodizing the American Century: Modernism, Postmodernism, and Postcolonialism in the Cold War Context," *Modernism/Modernity* 5.3 (September 1998): 71–98.

43. The most thorough discussion of chance's role in Western culture in Ross Hamilton's *Accident: A Philosophical and Literary History* (Chicago: University of Chicago Press, 2007). See also the first chapter of Leland Monk's *Standard Deviations: Chance and the Modern British Novel* (Stanford, Calif.: Stanford University Press, 1993), which provides an argument against the neglect chance has suffered in literary studies (15–45). David Bell has written on chance and the French realist novel by exploring the connections between the "device of chance encounters" and conceptions of chance in scientific thought; see Bell, *Circumstances: Chance in the Literary Text* (Lincoln: University of Nebraska Press, 1993). In 1994, *Michigan Romance Studies* published a special number on "Chance, Culture and the Literary Text"—all the contributions except one concern continental writers. Gerald Vizenor has linked chance in narrative to freedom in a completely different context; see Vizenor, ed., *Narrative Chance: Postmodern Discourse on Native American Indian Literatures* (Norman: University of Oklahoma Press, 1993). For another discussion of chance and literature (focalized through the work of experimental French writer Georges Perec), see Alison James, *Constraining Chance: Georges Perec and the* Oulipo (Evanston, Ill.: Northwestern University Press, 2009).

44. Lucretius, *The Nature of Things*, trans. Frank O. Copley (New York: Norton, 1977), lines 217–220.

45. Ian Hacking, *The Taming of Chance* (Cambridge: Cambridge University Press, 1990), 1. See also Gerd Gigerenzer et al., *The Empire of Chance: How Probability Changed Science and Everyday Life* (Cambridge: Cambridge University Press, 1989).

46. Charles S. Peirce, *Selected Writings (Values in a Universe of Chance)*, ed. with intro. and notes by Philip P. Wiener (New York: Dover, 1966), 170. See also John Kaag, "Chance and Creativity: The Nature of Contingency in Classical American Philosophy," *Transactions of the Charles S. Peirce Society* 44.3 (Summer 2008): 393–411.

47. Karl Popper, *The Open Universe: An Argument for Indeterminism* (1956. Totowa, N.J.: Rowman and Littlefield, 1982), 125.

48. Throughout *No Accident, Comrade*, the terms "chance" and "accident" are used more or less interchangeably, although there are fine distinctions. See, for example, D. W. Theobald, "Accident and Chance," *Philosophy* (April 1970): 106–113, "The expressions 'by accident' or 'accidentally' are used when something unforeseen *occurs despite* the fact that what we were trying to do at the time we were trying to do to the best of our ability. The expression 'by chance' is used when something unforeseen *arises from* what we are doing at the time" (108). In this book, an accident means a chance event.

49. Karl Popper, *The Poverty of Historicism* (1957. New York: Routledge, 2002), ix.

50. A broader cultural and social interest in chance during the Cold War is reflected in the range of titles exploring the concept: there are books on aesthetics such as Richard Hertz's *Chance and Symbol* (Chicago: University of Chicago Press, 1948); and books about history and historiography such as Walter Blumenthal's *Rendezvous with Chance* (New York: Exposition Press, 1954) and Oscar Handlin's *Chance or Destiny: Turning Points in American History* (Boston: Little, Brown, 1955). William Pollard's *Chance and Providence* (New York: Scribner, 1958) and John Harrington's "The Concept of Chance and Divine Providence" (*Proceedings of the American Catholic Philosophical Association* 28 [1954]) are examples of how religious thinkers grappled with the place of chance in a world governed by providential design.

Harold Sampson's doctoral dissertation, "An Investigation of the Relationship of Chance-Taking Behavior to Authoritarianism and Impulsivity" (Ph.D. Diss., University of California, 1953), assumed a connection between the absence of chance-taking and the authoritarian personality so that the absence of "[c]hance-taking behavior . . . is conceptualized by the writer as an expression of intolerance of ambiguity, and is predicted to be most characteristic of authoritarian persons" (3).

51. The most exhaustive history of Cold War–era Soviet studies is David Engerman's *Know Your Enemy: The Rise and Fall of America's Soviet Experts* (Oxford: Oxford University Press, 2009).

52. A version of this chapter first appeared as Daniel Bell, "Ten Theories in Search of Reality: The Prediction of Soviet Behavior in the Social Sciences," *World Politics* (April 1958): 327–365.

53. Daniel Bell, *The End of Ideology: On the Exhaustion of Political Ideas in the Fifties* (New York: Free Press, 1960), 327.

54. "Deplorable but not Political," *New York Times* (November 30, 1946): 12. *Pravda*'s interpretation was summarized in Irving Spiegel, "Facts on Shooting Sought by Byrnes," *New York Times* (November 25, 1946): 11.

55. Paul Virilio, *The Original Accident*, trans. Julie Rose (Cambridge: Polity Press, 2007), 27.

56. Another example of this phenomenon was the opposing interpretations of the Korean Airlines Disaster, when Korean Airlines flight 007 from New York City was shot down by Soviet fighters after it had strayed into Soviet airspace in September 1983. American authorities claimed that the flight had accidentally crossed over into restricted airspace, whereas Soviet officials claimed the flight, laden with civilian passengers, was an elaborate spy mission. As Richard Klein and William Warner have shown, one specific point of contention was whether the coincidence of the flight number 007 being the same number as the most famous Cold War spy was mere chance (as the Americans maintained), or whether it could be read meaningfully, as evidence of covert planning (as the Soviets claimed): "The US statement dismissed the Russian insinuation concerning 007 as 'ridiculous'; the flight number could have been nothing else than a trivial coincidence. What spy, they must have asked, would broadcast his motives by adopting the signature of Bond? We know the SU's reaction. Entirely consistent with their initial responses . . . they were persuaded that the US intelligence forces specifically chose that flight number in order to send them a signal. In their minds that choice is perfectly congruent with the fact that from the beginning the US had wanted the spy plane to be shot down, in order to mobilize world opinion against the SU, at a crucial moment when cruise and Pershing missiles were being installed on the soil of Europe" (Richard Klein and William B. Warner, "Nuclear Coincidence and the Korean Airline Disaster," *Diacritics* 16.1 [Spring 1986]: 2–21, quotation on 7).

57. Bell, *The End of Ideology*, 311.

58. Nathan Leites, *A Study of Bolshevism* (Glencoe, Ill.: Free Press, 1953), 15.

59. Ibid., 67. The opening section of this first chapter contains a useful compendium of ideas about chance and accident that Leites has compiled from a variety of thinkers, including Lenin and Stalin (67–73).

60. Ibid., 67–68.

61. Margaret Mead, *Soviet Attitudes toward Authority: An Interdisciplinary Approach to Problems of Soviet Character* (1951. New York: William Morrow & Co., Inc., 1955), 68.

62. For another angle on such observations, see Raymond Bauer, Alex Inkeles, and Clyde Kluckhohn, *How the Soviet System Works: Cultural, Psychological, and Social Themes* (Cambridge, Mass.: Harvard University Press, 1959), which, while taking pains to show that the Soviet Union was a modern industrial society, told its readers that for the "small group of men" who run the Soviet Union, "everything must be planned and rationally calculated. Nothing can be left to chance or to the natural tendency in healthy societies for varied strands of activities to fit reasonably together" (36). Daniel Bell was critical of *How the Soviet System Works* because for him the authors did not focus enough on the idea that "the Soviet system is characterized, essentially, by the central control of political power"

(quoted in Engerman, *Know Your Enemy*, 186). According to Sovietologist Merle Fainsod, author of what David Engerman calls a "field-defining" textbook (210), *How Russia is Ruled* (Cambridge, Mass.: Harvard University Press, 1953), "the plan" is the guiding characteristic of Soviet life: "The plan plays a central role in Soviet life. Its discipline regulates the tempo and activity of every Soviet administrator" (339).

63. For reviews of Brill, see Claude F. Baxter, "Review of *The Chance Character of Human Existence*," *Quarterly Review of Biology*, 31.4 (December 1956): 289–290; Rollo Handy, "Rev. of *The Chance Character of Human Existence*," *Philosophy and Phenomenological Research* (March 1957): 421–422; and V. C. Chappell, "Rev. of *The Chance Character of Human Existence*," *Review of Metaphysics* (September 1956): 173.
64. John Brill, *The Chance Character of Human Existence* (New York: Philosophical Library, 1956), 41.
65. Ibid., 76.
66. Herbert Marcuse, "Dialectic and Logic since the War," in *Continuity and Change in Russian and Soviet Thought*, ed. and intro. Ernest J. Simmons (Cambridge, Mass.: Harvard University Press, 1955), 347–358; quotation on 353.
67. Ibid., 354.
68. In his later book, *Soviet Marxism: A Critical Analysis* (New York: Columbia University Press, 1958), Marcuse expanded on this analysis to argue that after 1848, a "socialism defined in terms of human aspirations and potentialities gave way to a 'scientific socialism governed by inexorable objective laws'" (147). (Marcuse is quoting from Leonard Krieger, "Marx and Engels as Historians," *Journal of the History of Ideas* [June 1953]: 396). For an engagement with Marcuse's contribution to *Continuity and Change in Russian and Soviet Thought*, see George Tanquary Robinson's review in that volume (372–376).
69. Jackson Lears, *Something for Nothing: Luck in America* (New York: Viking, 2003), 310.
70. See also Spencer Weart, *Nuclear Fear: A History of Images* (Cambridge, Mass.: Harvard University Press, 1988), especially the section "Advertising the Maximum Accident" (288–294).
71. Tony Jackson, "Postmodernism, Narrative, and the Cold War Sense of an Ending," *Narrative* 8 (October 2000): 332. See also Frank Kermode, *The Sense of an Ending: Studies in the Theory of Fiction with a New Epilogue* (Oxford: Oxford University Press, 2000), especially the chapter "Literary Fiction and Reality."
72. Daniel Belgrad's work on the "culture of spontaneity" at mid-century offers a corollary to this argument; he shows that during WWII and after, a range of artists, writers, and musicians turned to the use of spontaneity in their work. Insofar as "spontaneity privileges the unpremeditated act," it has some conceptual affinities with the sense of chance as that which is unplanned. Belgrad argues that spontaneity could have a political dimension: "the culture of spontaneity developed to replace the organized Left of the thirties as a challenge to the American political center" (Daniel Belgrad, *The Culture of Spontaneity: Improvisation and the Arts in Postwar America* [Chicago: University of Chicago Press, 1998], quotations on 6 and 21).
73. Arthur Schlesinger, Jr., *The Vital Center: The Politics of Freedom* (Boston: Houghton Mifflin, 1949), 83.
74. Sidney Hook, "Introduction," in *Determinism and Freedom in the Age of Modern Science*, ed. Hook (New York: New York University Press, 1958), xiv. In *The Hero in History: A Study in Limitation and Possibility* (New York: John Day, 1943), Hook takes up the question of the Marxist "logic of history." In working through a historiographical method, Hook explores the role of accident in history and criticizes the determinism implied by "orthodox Marxism," which leaves little room for chance. In discussing the work of George Plechanov, whom he calls "the best oriented philosophical intelligence among the orthodox Marxists of his generation" (82), Hook finds fault with the orthodox Marxist's dismissal of chance: "A historical accident, as Plechanov had the merit of seeing, is not an uncaused event. . . . it is the point of intersection between two or more series of events which are themselves determined. The point of intersection cannot be predicted from the laws determining any or all of the series. It is clear that whoever takes the role

of accident in history seriously cannot be a monist. But orthodox Marxists are monists" (92–93).

75. See Schaub, *American Fiction in the Cold War*, 3–49. For a sample of Hook's numerous writings on Marxism and freedom, see: *Towards the Understanding of Karl Marx: A Revolutionary Interpretation* (1933); *The Meaning of Marx* (edited collection, 1934); *From Hegel to Marx* (1936); *The Hero in History* (1943); *Heresy, Yes; Conspiracy, No* (1953); *Marx and the Marxists: The Ambiguous Legacy* (1955); *Political Power and Personal Freedom* (1959); *The Paradoxes of Freedom* (1963); *The Place of Religion in a Free Society* (1968).

76. For more on the potential menace of social planning, see Daniel Belgrad, "Democracy, Decentralization, and Feedback," in *American Literature and Culture in an Age of Cold War*, ed. Steven Belletto and Daniel Grausam (Iowa City: University of Iowa Press, forthcoming).

77. William Barrett, "Determinism and Novelty," in Hook, ed., *Determinism and Freedom*, 38.

78. Ibid., 38–39.

79. Although chance has some conceptual affinities with the study of chaos and literature, *No Accident, Comrade* is only tangentially concerned with chaos theory. There is, for example, a large body of work using chaos theory to help understand what N. Katherine Hayles has called "orderly disorder," which names the complex, often unstable relationship between order and disorder in scientific thinking, and in literature and critical theory. See N. Katherine Hayles, *Chaos Bound: Orderly Disorder in Contemporary Literature and Science* (Ithaca, N.Y.: Cornell University Press, 1990); N. Katherine Hayles, ed., *Chaos and Order: Complex Dynamics in Literature and Science* (Chicago: University of Chicago Press, 1991); and Joseph M. Conte, *Design and Debris: A Chaotics of Postmodern American Fiction* (Tuscaloosa: University of Alabama Press, 2002).

80. For a summary of Aristotle's argument about substance and accident, see Hamilton, *Accident*, 11–20; note also, as Hamilton puts it, "To distinguish an unexpected event that occurs in nature, Aristotle employed a second and wider term, 'spontaneity,' (*to automaton*). Like chance causes, spontaneous ones require analysis of intent" (18).

81. Ibid., 17–18.

82. Ibid., 21.

83. Ibid., 22.

84. William Paulson, "Chance, Complexity, and Narrative Explanation," *SubStance* 74 (1994): 5–21; 12.

85. Monk, *Standard Deviations*, 8.

86. Ibid., 9. See also Thomas Kavanagh, "Introduction," *Chance, Culture and the Literary Text*, *Michigan Romance Studies* 14 (1994): v–vi: "Chance is culture's Other" (v); and Brian Richardson, *Unlikely Stories: Causality and the Nature of Modern Narrative* (Newark: University of Delaware Press, 1997), which begins by claiming the "systematic official suppression of the notion of chance for most of Western history" (20). See also Rémy Lestienne, *The Creative Power of Chance*, trans. E. C. Neher (Urbana: University of Illinois Press, 1998), which contributes to our understanding of how "chance brings us closer to a general problem of epistemology: what is the limit of the knowable?" (139); and Christopher Butler, *After the Wake: An Essay on the Contemporary Avant-Garde* (Oxford: Clarendon Press, 1980), 102–108. For a meticulous study of what chance means within the fictional realm, see Werner Wolf, "Chance in Fiction as a Privileged Index of Implied World-views: A Contribution to the Study of the World Modelling Functions of Narrative Fiction," in *Theorizing Narrativity*, ed. John Pier and José Ángel García Landa (Berlin: Walter de Gruyter, 2008), 165–210.

87. Some writers have attempted to include absolute chance in a fictional narrative. B. S. Johnson's novel, *The Unfortunates* (1969), was issued in a box containing 27 stapled booklets, only the first and last of which had a fixed order. The remaining 25 sections could be shuffled "into any other random order before reading." Johnson was known for experimentation, but his book in a box is no mere gimmick. It is narrated by a sports writer thinking about his close friend who has died of cancer, and the shuffled booklets, each containing a brief memory, are meant to reflect the random nature of memory and the

random effects of cancer on the body. To the extent that the narrative order is disrupted while the emotional arc remains intact, a generous reader could say that *The Unfortunates* succeeds in representing chance and in being absolute chance—at least on the higher-order structural level. See also Marc Saporta, *Composition No. 1*, trans. Richard Howard (New York: Simon and Schuster, 1963); and Julio Cortázar, *Hopscotch*, trans. Gregory Rabasa (1963. New York: Pantheon, 1987) (Saporta's book, like Johnson's, was issued on loose pages placed in a cardboard box).

88. Gary Saul Morson, *Narrative and Freedom: The Shadows of Time* (New Haven, Conn.: Yale University Press, 1994), 43.
89. Ibid., 6.
90. Ibid., 78.
91. The problem with this difference between real life and fictional narrative is that it calls into question narrative's very ability to accurately represent objective reality. Significantly, when describing various ways that structures are imposed on objective reality as "people sometimes imagine that life is more or less like novels," Morson pauses over Marxist conceptions of history: "Some philosophies of history that purport to know its laws and to discern the inevitable future allow its proponents to read current events as signs foreshadowing events to come. The doctrine of types in nineteenth-century Russian radical criticism and its Soviet inheritor ostensibly shows how the future may be read in the same way as novels. As readers of fiction can often guess what is to come through advance familiarity with works of a given sort, so social critics armed with the right theory can discern patterns in the making" (Morson, *Narrative and Freedom*, 7). Given the various problems Morson associates with foreshadowing, his mention of Marxist historiography implies that such theories are dismissible because they are artificial.
92. A cursory history of the most memorable attempts would include *Tristram Shandy*, written when the novel as a genre was still finding its legs. Laurence Sterne toys with the disruptive effect chance can have on narrative; after Tristram's father remarks "what a long chapter of chances do the events of this world lay open to us," Tristram realizes that the unforeseen threatens to defer endlessly the forward progression of a narrative. "By my grandfather's whiskers," he writes, "I shall never get half of 'em [chapters] through this year" (Laurence Sterne, *The Life and Opinions of Tristram Shandy, Gentleman* [Ed. Ian Watt. Boston: Houghton Mifflin, 1965], 210). Sterne's attempt to represent the chance events of "this world" results in *Tristram Shandy*'s famously digressive structure, which indulges, to use Morson's words, "incidental causes that need not have happened." There is a likewise famous moment in Henry James's *The Ambassadors* when Lambert Strether, who has spent much of the novel trying to figure out why his young charge Chad Newsome refuses to return to America, takes a day trip to the French countryside, having selected a train station "almost at random" (Henry James, *The Ambassadors* [1903. Ed. and Intro. Leon Edel. Boston: Houghton Mifflin, 1960], 318). Walking around the countryside, Strether happens upon Chad and his unexpected lover, Madame de Vionnet, an encounter that retroactively explains Chad's behavior, and that Strether thinks is "too prodigious, a chance in a million" (326). David Lodge argues that this scene stages the "trade-off in the writing of fiction between the achievement of structure, pattern and closure on the one hand, and the imitation of life's randomness, inconsequentiality and openness on the other" (*The Art of Fiction* [London: Secker & Warburg, 1992], 150). For a writer as thoughtful about the craft of narrative as James, the revelatory scene in *The Ambassadors* occurs "almost at random" because in a novel occurrences are always almost—but not quite—random; they are examples of narrative chance. James's response to the problem of narrative chance is to have this encounter occur just as Strether feels that walking around in the countryside is like walking inside a painting. The moment of narrative chance, in other words, is the moment that is simultaneously the most faithful to real life (since chance encounters do happen) and the most obviously artificial (since the encounter happens in an aesthetically stylized realm).
93. In his analysis of the relationship between form and political critique during the 1950s, for example, Sean McCann, *A Pinnacle of Feeling* (Princeton, N.J.: Princeton University Press, 2008), writes in passing of Holden Caulfield's "mature acceptance of accident" (102)

and the "accidental entanglements in *Lolita*" (122), but he does not make chance the focus of systematic inquiry. For a slightly more sustained discussion of accident's relationship to historical re-creation in postwar fiction, see Stacey Olster, *Reminiscence and Re-Creation in Contemporary American Fiction* (New York: Cambridge University Press, 1989).

94. Flannery O'Connor, *Mystery and Manners*, ed. Sally and Robert Fitzgerald (New York: Farrar, Straus and Giroux, 1962), 175.
95. Flannery O'Connor, *The Complete Stories* (New York: Farrar, Straus and Giroux, 1971), 117.
96. Ibid., 118.
97. Ibid., 125.
98. For an explanation of the ways that O'Connor's Catholic faith informed her writing, see O'Connor, *Mystery and Manners*, 109–114. In 1954, O'Connor's contemporary, historian John Harrington, explained a Christian view of history like this: "What seems to be an accident to one going along a road not seeing far in front or in back of him is not an accident to one who is looking down from above, can see what is happening, and to One, above all, who is causing it. What is termed by some chance or fortune or fate is used by providence in its designs" ("Concept of Chance and Divine Providence," 178).
99. O'Connor's relationship to the Cold War has been explored most extensively by Jon Lance Bacon in *Flannery O'Connor and Cold War Culture* (New York: Cambridge University Press, 1993) and by Schaub in *American Fiction in the Cold War*, 116–136. For a critique of Schaub and Bacon that frames O'Connor's Cold War dissent in terms of a "broader opposition to secular modernity," see Jason W. Stevens, *God-Fearing and Free: A Spiritual History of America's Cold War* (Cambridge, Mass.: Harvard University Press, 2010), 255–262; quotation on 256.
100. O'Connor, *Mystery and Manners*, 175.
101. Studies about chance and providence point to how chance has been historically conceived, that from God's perspective, there is no such thing as chance. Lorraine Daston has suggested, for example, how in the eighteenth century, chance "was merely apparent, the figment of human ignorance" (*Classical Probability in the Enlightenment* [Princeton, N.J.: Princeton University Press, 1988]), 10. See also Hacking, *The Taming of Chance*.
102. See, for example, James Agee's *A Death in the Family* (1957) and John Hawkes's *Travesty* (1976).
103. Vladimir Nabokov, *The Annotated Lolita* (Revised and Updated) (1955. Ed. Alfred Appel, Jr.; New York: Vintage, 1991), 98.
104. Ibid., 84.
105. Ibid., 105.
106. Ibid., 102.
107. Nicholas Mosley, *Accident* (1965. Elmwood Park, Ill.: Dalkey Archive Press, 1985), 103.
108. Stephen Weisenburger, "An Afterword," in Mosley, *Accident*, 193–198; quotation on 195. For more examples of chance in the modern British novel, see Monk, *Standard Deviations*.
109. Tony Tanner, *City of Words: American Fiction, 1950–1970* (New York: Harper, 1971), 15.
110. Timothy Melley, *Empire of Conspiracy: The Culture of Paranoia in Postwar America* (Ithaca, N.Y.: Cornell University Press, 2000).
111. William S. Burroughs, "On Coincidence," in his *The Adding Machine: Selected Essays* (New York: Arcade, 1986), 99–105; quotation on 102.
112. William S. Burroughs, "Deposition: Testimony Concerning a Sickness," in his *Naked Lunch* (1959. New York: Grove Press, 1990), xiii.
113. William S. Burroughs, *Naked Lunch* (1959. New York: Grove Press, 1990), 200.
114. Ibid., 203. Speaking in 1976 on the cut-up method, Burroughs said, "How random is random? We know so much that we don't consciously know that perhaps the cut-in was not random," "Origin and Theory of the Tape Cut-Ups," track from the CD *Break Through in Grey Room* (Sub Rosa CD006-8).
115. Frank Kermode thinks that Burroughs's use of chance can only have meaning if his accidents are "skillfully contrived": "we shall find such accidents happy only when we see in them some allusion, direct or ironical, to our inherited notions of linguistic and narrative structure" (Kermode, *The Sense of an Ending*, 118).

Notes to Pages 30-38

116. See Anna Dezeuze, "Origins of the Fluxus Score: From Indeterminacy to 'Do-It-Yourself' Artwork," in *Chance*, ed. Margaret Iversen (Cambridge, Mass.: MIT Press, 2010), 73–85.
117. Ellen Zweig, "Jackson Mac Low: The Limits of Formalism," *Poetics Today* 3.3 (Summer 1982): 79–86; quotation on 85.
118. La Monte Young and Jackson Mac Low, ed., *An Anthology of Chance Operations* (New York: La Monte Young and Jackson Mac Low, 1963), no page number.
119. Konrad Boehmer, "Chance as Ideology," trans. Ian Pepper, *October* (Fall 1997): 62–77; quotation on 67. See also N. Katherine Hayles, "Chance Operations: Cagean Paradox and Contemporary Science," in *John Cage: Composed in America*, ed. Marjorie Perloff and Charles Junkerman (Chicago: University of Chicago Press, 1994).
120. For a discussion of chance's role in twentieth century visual arts, see Margaret Iversen, "The Aesthetics of Chance," in *Chance*, ed. Iversen, 12–27.

Chapter 2

1. William Gaddis, *The Recognitions* (1955. New York: Penguin, 1993), 566. For Kathleen Lathrop, this passage suggests that "Gaddis sees modern science as a cause of, not a cure for, a diseased society." "Comic-Ironic Parallels in William Gaddis's *The Recognitions*," *Review of Contemporary Fiction* 2 (Summer 1982): 32–40; quotation on 35.
2. Hacking, *The Taming of Chance*, 1–2.
3. If chance is an example of Jean-François Lyotard's notion of the "unpresentable," then thematizing chance seems suited to a postmodern sensibility. Whatever else postmodernism means, it signals also an interest in what theorists have termed the aleatory—accident, randomness, contingency, indeterminacy. See, for example, theorizations of the postmodern such as Linda Hutcheon, "Beginning to Theorize the Postmodern," in *A Postmodern Reader*, ed. Joseph Natoli and Linda Hutcheon (1987. Albany: SUNY Press, 1993), 243–272, and Ihab Hassan, *The Postmodern Turn: Essays in Postmodern Theory and Culture* (Columbus: Ohio State University Press, 1987); or introductions to postmodern fiction for students such as Barry Lewis, "Postmodernism and Fiction," in *The Routledge Companion to Postmodernism*, ed. Stuart Sim (London: Routledge, 2005), 111–121: "Another means by which many postmodern writers disrupted the smooth production and reception of texts was by welcoming chance into the compositional process" (117). See also John Johnston, *Carnival of Repetition: Gaddis's* The Recognitions *and Postmodern Theory* (Philadelphia: University of Pennsylvania Press, 1990), which argues that *The Recognitions* is the first postmodern novel partly because it wrestles with the notion of the unpresentable (183–196).
4. Thomas Pynchon, *V.* (1963. New York: Harper Perennial, 2005), 450. Hereinafter cited parenthetically.
5. Note also the following: "There's no magic words. Not even I love you is magic enough. Can you see Eisenhower telling Malenkov or Khrushchev that? Ho-ho" (Pynchon, *V.*, 406).
6. No critic, to my knowledge, has written an extended analysis of *V.* that focuses on chance as such, although nearly all critics register the importance or presence of chance and accident in Pynchon's work. See, for example, works as different as Theodore Kharpertian, *A Hand to Turn the Time: The Menippean Satires of Thomas Pynchon* (Madison, N.J.: Fairleigh Dickinson University Press, 1990), 60, and Tony Tanner, *Thomas Pynchon* (New York: Methuen, 1982), 47.
7. In George Plimpton's *New York Times* review, for example, he notes that Profane is a new type of picaro who bounces around "buffeted by circumstance and not caring to do much about it" ("The Whole Sick Crew," *New York Times* [April 21, 1963]: BR3). See also—to cite divergent approaches—Raymond Olderman, *Beyond the Waste Land: A Study of the American Novel in the 1960s* (New Haven, Conn.: Yale University Press, 1972), 123–144; and Marcel Cornis-Pope, *Narrative Innovation and Cultural Rewriting in the Cold War Era and After* (New York: Palgrave, 2001), 111–117.
8. Tanner, *Thomas Pynchon*, 47.

9. See Marc Redfield, "Pynchon's Postmodern Sublime," *PMLA* 104.2 (March 1989): 152–162.
10. Paul Celmer, "Pynchon's *V.* and the Rhetoric of the Cold War," *Pynchon Notes* 32–33 (Spring–Fall 1993): 5–32; quotation on 6.
11. Ibid., 26. For more on paranoia and conspiracy as hallmarks of Cold War culture, see Melley, *Empire of Conspiracy*.
12. Larry Langman, *Encyclopedia of American Film Comedy* (New York: Garland, 1987), 548.
13. Max Horkheimer and Theodor Adorno, *Dialectic of Enlightenment*, ed. Gunzelin Schmid Noerr and trans. Edmund Jephcott (Stanford, Calif.: Stanford University Press, 2002), 110.
14. Robert Holton, "In the Rathouse of History with Thomas Pynchon: Rereading *V.*," *Textual Practice* 2.3 (Winter 1988): 324–344, sees slapstick as closing off a reader's interaction with Pynchon's characters: "Much of the book is written in a slapstick tone which encourages at best a limited identification with the characters" (337).
15. For an alternative reading of this passage, see Stephan Mattessich, *Lines of Flight: Discursive Time and Countercultural Desire in the Work of Thomas Pynchon* (Durham, N.C.: Duke University Press, 2002), 31–32.
16. Hamilton, *Accident*, 284–285.
17. David Foster Wallace, *Infinite Jest* (New York: Back Bay Books, 1996), 139.
18. Ibid., 140.
19. See the "Barrel of Bricks" entry in Jan Harold Brunvand, *Encyclopedia of Urban Legends* (New York: Norton, 2002), 31. The television program *Mythbusters*, which as its name suggests debunks urban legends, tested the physical possibility of the barrel of bricks story in its first season and found that the unfortunate bricklayer would not have lived to write the report (original air date October 10, 2003).
20. For a discussion of the role of accident in early film, see James Leo Cahill, "How It Feels to be Run Over: Early Film Accidents," *Discourse* 30.3 (Fall 2008): 289–316. Cahill's essay is part of a special number of *Discourse* on "Cinema and Accident," which contains many useful essays, including Greg Siegel's "The Accident is Uncontainable/The Accident Must Be Contained: High-Speed Cinematography and the Development of Scientific Crash Testing," which is particularly suggestive for the scenes in *V.* in which Profane works at a crash test dummy facility.
21. Virilio, *The Original Accident*, 5.
22. Ibid., 70.
23. Ibid., 12.
24. See, for example, Paul Boyer, *By the Bomb's Early Light: American Thought and Culture at the Dawn of the Atomic Age* (New York: Pantheon, 1985); and Weart, *Nuclear Fear*.
25. Edmund C. Berkeley, "We Are Safer Than We Think," *New York Times* (July 29, 1951): 11; 20, quotation on 20.
26. Virilio, *The Original Accident*, 76.
27. Thomas H. Pynchon [sic], "Togetherness," *Aerospace Safety* (December 1960): 6–8; quotation on 6. See also Adrian Wisnicki, "A Trove of New Works by Thomas Pynchon?: Bomarc Service News Rediscovered," *Pynchon Notes* 46–49 (Spring–Fall 2000–2001), 9–34.
28. Just as Horkheimer and Adorno in *Dialectic of Enlightenment* single out examples from popular culture that make American culture seem eerily like totalitarian regimes—from the aesthetics of slapstick comedy, which makes cruelty tolerable, to television game shows, which presuppose such a degree of faith in chance's working that "Chance itself is planned" (117)—Pynchon offers some examples of American culture in 1956 that echo what is happening in German Southwest Africa. I discuss some examples at the end of the chapter.
29. Laurent Milesi, "Postmodern Ana-Apocalyptics: Pynchon's V-Effect and the End (of Our Century)," *Pynchon Notes* 42–43 (1998): 213–243; quotation on 221.
30. Virilio, *The Original Accident*, 41.
31. Writing against a tendency to regard Pynchon as apolitical, Holton argues that "perhaps the most critically neglected aspect of *V.* is its political use of epistemological and

historiographical problems as a means to break down the wall of objective realism, a wall that has protected the hegemonic culture of Western society" (330). Ronald Cooley, "The Hothouse or the Street: Imperialism and Narrative in Pynchon's *V.*" *Modern Fiction Studies* 39.2 (Summer 1993): 307–325, advances a more detailed argument about the novel's "critique of imperialism" (315).

32. For a discussion of the evolution of "Mondaugen's Story," based on comparisons of the published novel to the typescripts at the University of Texas at Austin's Harry Ransom Center and elsewhere, see Luc Herman and John M. Krafft, "From the Ground Up: The Evolution of the South-West Africa Chapter in Pynchon's *V.*," *Contemporary Literature* 47.2 (2006): 261–288.
33. See, for example, Cooley, "Hothouse," 308–311.
34. For more on the influence of *The Origins of Totalitarianism*, see Dana Villa, "Genealogies of Total Domination: Arendt, Adorno, and Auschwitz," *New German Critique* (Winter 2007): 1–45; Elisabeth Young-Bruehl, *Why Arendt Matters* (New Haven, Conn.: Yale University Press, 2006); and Steven Aschheim, "Nazism, Culture, and *The Origins of Totalitarianism*: Hannah Arendt and the Discourse of Evil," *New German Critique* (Winter 1997): 117–139. See also Slavoj Žižek, *Did Somebody Say Totalitarianism? Five Interventions in the (Mis)use of a Notion* (London: Verso, 2001).
35. Hannah Arendt, *The Origins of Totalitarianism* (New Edition with Added Prefaces) (1951. New York: Harcourt Brace Jovanovich, 1979), 352–353.
36. For more on Pynchon's uses of *Heart of Darkness*, see Cooley, "Hothouse," 313–315.
37. For a discussion of Pynchon's use of Arendt's *The Origins of Totalitarianism*, see Cooley, "Hothouse," 308–311.
38. Arendt, *Origins*, 345.
39. This passage also prefigures *Gravity Rainbow*'s "Oven-state" (102) a sadomasochistic game, engineered by Weissmann himself (as Captain Blicero) that reflects the aestheticized politics of the Nazi state (see Thomas Pynchon, *Gravity's Rainbow* [1973. New York: Penguin, 2006]). For an elaboration of this connection in the context of Pynchon's political critique, see Denis Crowley, "'Before the Oven': Aesthetics and Politics in *Gravity's Rainbow*," *Pynchon Notes* 42–43 (1998): 181–198; especially 185.
40. To find out what Mondaugen has been up to later in life, see Pynchon, *Gravity's Rainbow*, 408–430.
41. Arendt, *Origins*, 395.
42. In "Togetherness," Pynchon relates how one engineer subjected the transported missiles to "nit-picking inspection."
43. Thomas Schaub, *Pynchon: The Voice of Ambiguity* (Urbana: University of Illinois Press, 1981), 122.
44. Cooley, "Hothouse," 310.
45. Although it is clear that Pynchon wants readers to notice some echoes and continuities among the historical and present-day chapters, I am not, of course, claiming that things like Esther's nose job or Mafia Winsome's anti-Semitism ("'I don't hate the Jewish people,' Mafia was explaining, 'only the things they do'" [313]) are the equivalents of acts like the ones committed in "Mondaugen's Story." See Holton (quoting Molly Hite): "There can be no question . . . of reversing the genocidal atrocities carried out against the Hereros, and to suggest an equivalence to 'Mafia Winsome's intellectual racism' is clearly as disproportionate as is her equivalence of Foppl's siege party (with its racist torture, murder, rape, and depravity) and the . . . bohemianism of the Whole Sick Crew" (336). See also Molly Hite, *Ideas of Order in the Novels of Thomas Pynchon* (Columbus: Ohio State University Press, 1983), 64–65.
46. There is an echo of the engineer's world in Bloody Chiclitz's empire, "an interlocking kingdom responsible for systems management, airframes, propulsion, command systems, ground support equipment" (245).
47. See Alfred G. Meyer, *Leninism* (Cambridge, Mass.: Harvard University Press, 1957), 157.
48. Michiko Kakutani, "Pynchon Hits the Road with Mason and Dixon," *New York Times* (April 29, 1997): C11.

Notes to Pages 57-62   167

49. Thomas Pynchon, *The Crying of Lot 49* (1966. New York: Harper Perennial, 2006), 150.
50. Ibid., 36. For a discussion of how paranoid thinking amounts to reading the world like a book, see Peter Knight, "Everything is Connected: *Underworld*'s Secret History of Paranoia," *Modern Fiction Studies* 45.3 (Fall 1999): 811–836.
51. Pynchon, *The Crying of Lot 49*, 63. See also Daniel Grausam, *On Endings: American Postmodern Fiction and the Cold War* (Charlottesville: University of Virginia Press, 2011).
52. Thomas Pynchon, *Against the Day* (New York: Penguin, 2006), 123.
53. See, for instance, Lance Olsen, "Stand by to Crash! Avant-pop, Hypertextuality, and Postmodern Comic Vision in Coover's *The Public Burning*," *Critique* 42.1 (Fall 2000): 52; Frank Lentricchia, "*Libra* as Postmodern Critique," *South Atlantic Quarterly* 89 (Spring 1990): 431–453 and a response to Lentricchia, Stuart Hutchinson, "DeLillo's *Libra* and the Real," *Cambridge Quarterly* 30.2 (2001): 117–131; and Mark McGurl, *The Program Era* (Cambridge, Mass.: Harvard University Press, 2009), which groups Powers, along with Pynchon, DeLillo, and others, as examples of "technomodernism," his term for what many people call postmodernism.
54. Robert Coover, *The Public Burning* (New York: Viking, 1977), 362.
55. Don DeLillo, *Libra* (New York: Viking, 1988), 441.
56. Ibid., 50 and 78.
57. Ibid., 440.
58. Ibid., 147.
59. Richard Powers, *The Gold Bug Variations* (1991. New York: Harper Perennial, 1992), 331.
60. Ibid., 333.
61. Stephen J. Burn, "An Interview with Richard Powers," *Contemporary Literature* 49.2 (Summer 2008): 172–173.

Chapter 3

1. Vladimir Nabokov, *Speak, Memory: An Autobiography Revisited* (New York: Putnam, 1966), 257. In *Speak, Memory*, Nabokov gives his father's birthday as July 20, 1870 (173), but some Nabokov specialists disagree about the exact date. Alexey Sklyarenko thinks the correct date is 21 July ("Addendum to '*Ada* as a Triple Dream,'" *The Nabokovian* 53 [Fall 2004]: 23).
2. Nabokov, *Speak, Memory*, 257–258.
3. See, for example, Nabokov, *Strong Opinions* (1973. New York: Vintage, 1990), 94, 118. Understanding *Pale Fire*—and Nabokov in general—as chiefly (or only) an aesthetic exercise has been a common critical assessment since the novel's publication. For the best examples of this sort of reading, see the early reviews from 1962, including Mary McCarthy, "A Bolt from the Blue," in her *The Writing on the Wall and Other Literary Essays* (New York: Harcourt, 1970), 15–34; Frank Kermode, "Zemblances," *New Statesman* (November 9, 1962): 671–672; and Dwight Macdonald, "Virtuosity Rewarded, or Dr. Kinbote's Revenge," *Partisan Review* 29 (Summer 1962): 437–442. See also Andrew Field, *Nabokov, His Life in Art* (Boston: Little, Brown, 1967); Tanner, *City of Words*; David Walker, "'The Viewer of the View': Chance and Choice in *Pale Fire*,'" *Studies in American Fiction* 4 (1976): 203–222; and Priscilla Meyer, *Find What the Sailor Has Hidden: Vladimir Nabokov's* Pale Fire (Middletown, Conn.: Wesleyan University Press, 1988). Recently, however, there has been renewed interest in the ways that Nabokov's aesthetics reflect a political or moral sense; examples of such readings include Leland de la Durantaye, *Style is Matter: The Moral Art of Vladimir Nabokov* (Ithaca, NY: Cornell University Press, 2007); Nina L. Khruscheva, *Imagining Nabokov: Russia between Art and Politics* (New Haven, Conn.: Yale University Press, 2008); Piette, *The Literary Cold War*; and Steven Belletto, "Of Pickaninnies and Nymphets: Race in *Lolita*," *Nabokov Studies* 9 (2005): 1–17.
4. In this chapter, when I write of the homophobic narrative doing something, I am treating it metonymically, as a way of referring to Cold War psychologists, social critics, clergy, government officials, and others who were active proponents of the homophobic narrative.

5. Jonathan Culler, "The Call of the Phoneme: Introduction," in *On Puns: The Foundation of Letters*, ed. Culler (Oxford: Basil Blackwell, 1988), 16.
6. In light of the critical recurrence of so-called single-author theories, let me say here that, for the purposes of this book, I assume that Shade and Kinbote are two distinct characters in the world of the novel, and that each character has written the part attributed to him. One of the principal debates about *Pale Fire* over the years has been whether Kinbote and Shade "really" wrote the sections of the work attributed to them by Nabokov. In order to propose solutions to some of the novel's most urgent problems (for example, why there are so many subtle correspondences between the poem and the commentary), some critics have suggested that either Kinbote or Shade has really written both poem and commentary. Page Stegner in his *Escape into Aesthetics: The Art of Vladimir Nabokov* (New York: Dial, 1966) was the first to propose Kinbote as the sole author (116–132); Field argued that Shade was the sole author (291–322). Amplifications of both theories have found their way into Nabokov studies since then, a debate helpfully summarized in Brian Boyd, *Nabokov's* Pale Fire: *The Magic of Artistic Discovery* (Princeton, N.J.: Princeton University Press, 1999), 114–126. Boyd concludes that there are two authors (see note 7).
7. The most elaborate and ingenious theory that accounts for *Pale Fire*'s coincidences is Boyd's *Nabokov's* Pale Fire. Boyd modifies an earlier argument of his to suggest that the spirits of both Hazel and John Shade influenced Kinbote from beyond the grave; he offers compelling evidence for this argument, and it is hard to deny his carefully argued insistence not only that the supernatural plays an important role in *Pale Fire* but also that Aunt Maud communicated with Hazel in "The Haunted Barn" scene, and that after her suicide Hazel herself has transformed from an ugly girl to a beautiful butterfly that flutters around Shade in the moment before his murder.
8. Nabokov, *Pale Fire* (1962. New York: Knopf, 1992), 294. Hereinafter cited parenthetically.
9. The parenthetical next to New Wye is meant to suggest that although in *Pale Fire* even the real locale of New Wye takes place in the non-state of Appalachia rather than New York, this non-state can only be evaluated by us relative to our real world. Even so, there is something of a fictional worlds theory to Nabokov's novels—if his characters' narratives are mimetic, they must be said to be faithful not to our real world, but to the real fictional world of the novel, an idea elaborated in Thomas Pavel, *Fictional Worlds* (Cambridge, Mass.: Harvard University Press, 1986). See also Richard Walsh, "Fictionality and Mimesis: Between Narrativity and Fictional Worlds," *Narrative* 11 (January 2003): 110–121. Walsh offers an able amendment to the fictional worlds theory: "Readers cannot be content merely to construct fictional worlds, as if this in itself were endlessly satisfying; they must also be concerned to evaluate them, to bring them into relation with the larger context of their own experience and understanding" (114). It is this "relation" between New Wye and New York that Nabokov often exploits in *Pale Fire* and upon which my argument partly rests.
10. I borrow the term "narrativize" from Hayden White and invoke it in the sense that he explains in "The Value of Narrativity in the Representation of Reality" (*Critical Inquiry* 7 [1980]), a pithy version of which is the well-known rhetorical question he uses to close the essay: "Could we ever narrativize *without* moralizing?" (27). Shade's death is the cause of the Zembla narrative because Kinbote generates the story based on the text of "Pale Fire" and is spurred by the inexplicability of the murder; it is also the effect because through this very Zembla narrative Kinbote hopes to provide a causal explanation for the accidental death.
11. This argument does not presume that Nabokov the man was wholly comfortable with homosexuality, but rather that the construction of homosexuality specific to Cold War America was as ridiculous to him as Kinbote's Zembla. Nabokov's personal attitude toward homosexuality is a complicated matter that shifted over time and I will not engage the question at length in this book. Lev Grossman argues that despite his love for his brother Sergey, Nabokov "was a confirmed homophobe" ("The Gay Nabokov," *Salon.com*, May 17, 2000, <http://archive.salon.com/books/feature/2000/05/17/nabokov/index.html>). As I alluded to above, it is true Nabokov had a troubled relationship with Sergey. Steven Bruhm ("Queer, Queer Vladimir," *American Imago* 53 [1996]: 281–306) cites a 1932 letter quoted

by Boyd, *Vladimir Nabokov: The Russian Years* (Princeton, N.J.: Princeton University Press, 1990): "[Sergey's] husband, I must admit, is very pleasant, quiet, not at all the pederast type, attractive in face and manner" (Boyd, *The Russian Years*, 396). Of this letter Bruhm writes: "What we have here is the epistemology of a closet that is both homophobic and queer, one that sees the gay man as a 'type' yet that ostentatiously dissociates him from that typology" (295). While a case can be made for Nabokov's vacillation between these two poles, what Bruhm leaves out of this mix is Nabokov's conclusion to the transgression of his brother's privacy in *Speak, Memory*; after relating that Sergey later died in a Nazi concentration camp (his first confinement to which was because of his sexuality), Nabokov strikes a plaintive note: "It is one of those lives that hopelessly claim a belated something—compassion, understanding, no matter what—which the mere recognition of such a want can neither replace or redeem" (258). This reads to me like a man who—with the benefit of a half-century's reflection—is publicly resisting the homosexual "type" he dropped in a private letter. That this resistance comes ironically in public silence—since one would never know from reading *Speak, Memory* that Sergey's "oddities" amounted to homosexuality—is indeed a problem worth thinking about. Although Brian Boyd does not make too much of homosexuality in *Pale Fire*, he does offer the following comment in a note to a passage explaining how Kinbote often turns away from women rather than toward men: "This, I suspect, happens to reflect Nabokov's attitude to homosexuality. For all his prodigious imagination, he appears not to have been able to imagine in any detail sexual pleasure between men, but he *could* imagine vividly—and only feel as wonderfully absurd—a man's turning away from the beauties of women" (*Nabokov's* Pale Fire, 279 n. 10). Stacy Shiff, *Véra (Mrs. Vladimir Nabokov)* (New York: Random House, 1999), concurs that Sergey's homosexuality was something "his brother could not easily abide" (99). On the representation of homosexuality in Nabokov's work, including *Pale Fire*, see Dana Dragunoiu, "Vladimir Nabokov's *Ada*: Art, Deception, Ethics," *Contemporary Literature* 46 (Summer 2005): 311–339, especially 335–336.

12. See also Jean Walton, "Dissenting in an Age of Frenzied Heterosexualism: Kinbote's Transparent Closet in Nabokov's *Pale Fire*," *College Literature* 21.2 (June 1994): 89–105, especially 101.

13. See D. A. Miller, "Secret Subjects, Open Secrets," in his *The Novel and the Police* (Berkeley: University of California Press, 1988), 192–220. My use of "pathological" plays on the fact that Cold War dissidence—treasonous, sexual, or otherwise—was often equated with germs and pathogens; see, for instance, David Raney, "Culture of Contagion: Germs, Aliens, and American Identity," *Popular Culture Review* 14 (February 2003): 55–66; and Michael Rogin, "Kiss Me Deadly: Communism, Motherhood, and Cold War Movies," *Representations* 6 (1984): 1–36.

14. Norman Mailer, "The Homosexual Villain," in his *Advertisements for Myself* (1959. Cambridge, Mass.: Harvard University Press, 1992), 223, 227.

15. For another example of an apparently uncritical pairing of homosexuality with political subversion, see the novel from which this chapter takes its title: John LeCarré, *The Spy Who Came in from the Cold* (New York: Dell, 1963). When Alec Leamas—the titular British spy—is tapped as a potential defector by Ashe, a Soviet agent, Leamas thinks: "a little bit petulant, a little bit of a pansy" (46). Later, when describing Ashe to his superiors, Leamas labels him thus: "'A man called Ashe. . . . A pansy.'" (50). LeCarré has Leamas insist on Ashe's visible homosexuality, but, after these initial impressions, the subject is dropped, so it seems the conflation of Communism and homosexuality has little function in the book other than its being symbolically just to LeCarré's readership. See also Chester Himes, *Lonely Crusade* (1947. New York: Thunder's Mouth Press, 1997), in which a racist cop asks an African-American union organizer: "[I]s there any truth in the Communists making you boys turn pansy after you become members of the Party?" (218).

16. For discussions of Nabokov's attitude toward Freud, see J. P. Shute, "Nabokov and Freud: The Play of Power," *Modern Fiction Studies* 30 (1984): 637–650; Geoffrey Green, *Freud and Nabokov* (Lincoln: University of Nebraska Press, 1988); and Leland de le Durantaye, "Vladimir Nabokov and Sigmund Freud, or a Particular Problem," *American Imago* 62.1

(Spring 2005): 59–73. For remarks pertaining directly to Freud, see Nabokov, *Strong Opinions*, 66; and *Pale Fire*, 271, 109. See also Peter Welsen, "Kinbote's Psychosis—A Key to Vladimir Nabokov's *Pale Fire*," in *Russian Literature and Psychoanalysis*, ed. Daniel Rancour-Laferriere (Amsterdam: John Benjamins Publishing Co., 1989), 382–400; and Phyllis Roth, "The Psychology of the Double in Nabokov's *Pale Fire*," *Essays in Literature* 2 (1975): 209–229.

17. Edmund Bergler, *Homosexuality: Disease or Way of Life?* (New York: Hill and Wang, 1956), 49. See also: Gordon Westwood, *Society and the Homosexual* (New York: Dutton, 1953); Clifford Allen, *Homosexuality: Its Nature, Causation and Treatment* (London: Staples Press, 1958); Jess Stearn, *The Sixth Man* (New York: Doubleday, 1961); and Alfred Gross, *Strangers in Our Midst: Problems of the Homosexual in American Society* (Washington, D.C.: Public Affairs Press, 1962).
18. Westwood, *Society and the Homosexual*, 145.
19. Stearn, *Sixth Man*, 22.
20. See David K. Johnson, *The Lavender Scare: The Cold War Persecution of Gays and Lesbians in the Federal Government* (Chicago: University of Chicago Press, 2004); the first chapter of Suzanne Clark, *Cold Warriors: Manliness on Trial in the Rhetoric of the West* (Carbondale: Southern Illinois University Press, 2000); the introduction to Robert J. Corber, *Homosexuality in Cold War America: Resistance and the Crisis of Masculinity* (Durham, N.C.: Duke University Press, 1997); Lee Edelman, "Tearooms and Sympathy, or, The Epistemology of the Water Closet," in his *Homographesis: Essays in Gay Literary and Cultural Theory* (New York: Routledge, 1994); David Savran, *Communists, Cowboys, and Queers: The Politics of Masculinity in the Work of Arthur Miller and Tennessee Williams* (Minneapolis: University of Minnesota Press, 1992); and Andrea Friedman, "The Smearing of Joe McCarthy: The Lavender Scare, Gossip, and Cold War Politics," *American Quarterly* 57 (December 2005): 1105–1129.
21. This document is included in Donald Webster Cory, *The Homosexual in America: A Subjective Approach* (New York: Greenberg, 1957), 274–275, which had been through seven printings by 1957. As the subtitle implies, Cory's study offers a homosexual perspective on the various misunderstandings and prejudices homosexual people faced during the 1950s; "Employment of Homosexuals and Other Sex Perverts in Government" is included in an appendix as evidence of the officially sanctioned discrimination against homosexuals. In "The Homosexual Villain," Mailer names Cory's book as the work that changed his attitude toward homosexuality (224–227); the book was also the object of special attack by Bergler, *Homosexuality*, 173, 298–300.
22. Writing with particular reference to Hazel Shade, Walton remarks that despite Nabokov's treatment of male homosexuality in *Pale Fire*, female homosexuality is scarcely conceivable: "Lesbianism, in the world of New Wye, in the world of *Pale Fire* (and doubtless in the world of 1950s middle America) is invisible—not even on the map of erotic possibilities" (94). If there is one thing *Pale Fire* does, however, it indulges in possibility, even the lesbianism of Shade's unmarried Aunt Maud and friends; according to Kinbote: "Aunt Maud was far from spinsterish, and the extravagant and sardonic turn of her mind must have shocked sometimes the genteel dames of New Wye" (*Pale Fire*, 113). When, moreover, Shade has a birthday party, Kinbote sees "ensconced in their tiny Pulex, manned by her boy-handsome tousle-haired girl friend, the patroness of the arts who had sponsored Aunt Maud's last exhibition" (*Pale Fire*, 160). Granted these observations are coming from Kinbote, and whether or not Aunt Maud or the patroness with which she is associated are actually lesbians seems less important than the fact that Nabokov lets such relationships stand on the "map of erotic possibilities."
23. Vladimir Nabokov, *Pnin* (1957. New York: Vintage, 1989), 114.
24. Nabokov, *Strong Opinions*, 67–68. Nabokov also once remarked that he "derive[d] no pleasure from . . . the artificial coincidences" in Tolstoy's *War and Peace* (*Strong Opinions*, 148).
25. Boyd, *Nabokov's Pale Fire*, 87.
26. Yet by the end of his tale, Kinbote himself is guilty of punning on an institution's acronym: Shade's murderer "gave his name as Jack Grey, no fixed abode, except the Institute for the Criminal Insane, *ici*, good dog" (*Pale Fire*, 295). Shade later equates the I.P.H. with other

institutions, including Communism: "Among our auditors [at the I.P.H.] were a young priest / And an old Communist. Iph could at least / Compete with churches and the party line" (*Pale Fire*, 56).
27. Jackson, "Postmodernism, Narrative, and the Cold War Sense of an Ending," 328.
28. We deduce over the course of the novel that Kinbote's actual name is Botkin, and that if he is not the deposed king of Zembla, then he is a scholar from Russia (*Pale Fire*, 267).
29. McCarthy, "Bolt," 20–21.
30. McCarthy does, however, intimate a political context: "[T]here is in fact a 'Zembla,' behind the Iron Curtain" ("Bolt," 18). With one recent exception, the handful of short studies that focus on the sources for Zembla do not mention the political importance of Novaya Zemlya in 1959. See, for instance: Gavrilo Shapiro, "Nova Zembla Revisited Once Again," *The Nabokovian* 26 (Spring 1991): 49–51; and John Rea, "And a Nearctic Zembla," *The Nabokovian* 42 (Spring 1999): 9–10. Kinbote insists that "the name Zembla is a corruption not of the Russian *zemlya*, but of Semblerland, a land of reflections" (Nabokov, *Pale Fire*, 265); in *Speak, Memory*, Nabokov calls Novaya Zemlya "Nova Zembla" (52, 126).
31. *New York Times* (March 9, 1958): 41.
32. "New Soviet Tests of Atom Weapons Disclosed by U.S.," *New York Times* (November 8, 1958): 1. In a 1959 book on the development of Soviet nuclear technology, one discovers that despite initial talks of a test ban, the Soviets stayed their course: "Resume the tests they did, in the fall of 1958, at their Novaya Zemlya test locale just before serious test suspension talks were to begin" (Arnold Kramish, *Atomic Energy in the Soviet Union* [Stanford, Calif.: Stanford Univ. Press, 1959], 131). See also Hanson W. Baldwin, "Decision in Moscow: Khrushchev Is Seen Starting a New Phase of Power Politics," *New York Times* (September 3, 1961): E3.
33. For further information on Nabokov's understanding of the real Zembla, see Andrea Pitzer, "Memory Speaks: History and Witnessing in Nabokov's *Pale Fire*," *Nabokov Studies* (forthcoming). Pitzer has recovered some important information showing that in addition to being the site where the Soviets tested a large number of atomic weapons, Novaya Zemlya was also the site of a notorious concentration camp. Given this information, Pitzer argues that Kinbote could be a refugee of the Soviet Gulag system, which helps explain his psychosis and coy allusions, and why the sympathetic Shade would treat him with such humanity.
34. Boyd, *Nabokov's* Pale Fire, 81.
35. Although more recent readers tend to ignore or downplay the resemblance of Communism to Zemblan Extremism, the similarity was obvious to the novel's first reviewers. As mentioned earlier, McCarthy notes Zembla exists behind the iron curtain (18), and Kermode draws attention to Nabokov's "loathing of Marxism" (671). Macdonald wrote his cantankerous review for the *Partisan Review*, a cultural arbiter that had become staunch in its anti-Stalinism after WWII. In the course of disparaging *Pale Fire* and extolling Mailer's "The Man Who Studied Yoga" as one of the "best things" from one of the "best novelists of the middle generation" (438), Macdonald reads the Zemblan Revolution as a version of its Russian counterpart by conflating real and imaginary worlds: Kinbote "escapes his Extremist (Communist) assasins [sic]" (440).
36. Werner Wiskari, "Khrushchev Calls Off Plan for a Visit to Scandinavia; KHRUSHCHEV TRIP TO NORTH PUT OFF," *New York Times* (July 21, 1959): 1–2.
37. When Kinbote remarks he is trying to "coordinate" his notes, he alludes to the strange design Shade sees at work in the universe: "Coordinating these / Events and objects with remote events / And vanished objects. Making ornaments / Of accidents and possibilities" (*Pale Fire*, 63). But this coordinate mastery is again undercut by Nabokov, as the very presence of absolute chance in real life, from the minor demon radio to the major accident of Shade's death, tells us that for all Kinbote's apparent mastery, he is capable of manipulating only text and never texture.
38. A pertinent line from *Ada* (1969) may clarify Nabokov's view of a patterned universe. During a discussion of the movies, the sometime-actress Ada tells Van: "In 'real' life we are

creatures of chance in an absolute void—unless we be artists ourselves, naturally; but in a good play I feel authored, I feel passed by the board of censors, I feel secure" (Nabokov, *Ada; or Ardor: A Family Chronicle* [New York: McGraw-Hill, 1969], 426). Prefiguring Ada, Shade's great epiphany as an artist is that the universe is for him akin to a good play, and he feels as though accidents and other chance events are actually "ornaments" designed by unknown game players.

39. Nabokov, "On a Book Entitled Lolita" (1956), in *The Annotated Lolita*, 314.

Chapter 4

1. See Michael Bérubé, "Race and Modernity in Colson Whitehead's *The Intuitionist*," in *The Holodeck in the Garden: Science and Technology in Contemporary American Fiction*, ed. Peter Freese and Charles Harris (Normal, Ill.: Dalkey Archive, 2004), 163–178; Saundra Liggins, "The Urban Gothic Vision of Colson Whitehead's *The Intuitionist*," *African American Review* 40.2 (Summer 2006): 358–369; and Alison Russell, "Recalibrating the Past: Colson Whitehead's *The Intuitionist*," *Critique* 49.1 (Fall 2007): 46–60.
2. Colson Whitehead, *The Intuitionist* (New York: Anchor, 1999), 58. Hereinafter cited parenthetically.
3. Historical discussions of the relationship between the Cold War and the African-American experience more broadly include Gerald Horne, *Black and Red: W. E. B. Du Bois and the Afro-American Response to the Cold War, 1944–1963* (Albany: SUNY Press, 1986); Brenda Gayle Plummer, *Rising Wind: Black Americans and U.S. Foreign Affairs, 1935–1960* (Chapel Hill: University of North Carolina Press, 1996); Penny Von Eschen, *Race against Empire: Black Americans and Anticolonialism, 1937–1957* (Ithaca, N.Y.: Cornell University Press, 1997); Mary L. Dudziak, *Cold War Civil Rights: Race and the Image of American Democracy* (Princeton, N.J.: Princeton University Press, 2000); Kate Baldwin, *Beyond the Color Line and the Iron Curtain: Reading Encounters between Black and Red, 1922–1963* (Durham, N.C.: Duke University Press, 2002); and Nikhil Pal Singh, *Black is a Country: Race and the Unfinished Struggle for Democracy* (Cambridge, Mass.: Harvard University Press, 2004). For a discussion of African Americans and the Cold War that brings together rhetoric about the atomic bomb with rhetoric about race, see Abby Kinchy, "African Americans in the Atomic Age: Postwar Perspectives on Race and the Bomb, 1945–1967," *Technology and Culture* 50.2 (April 2009): 291–315. See also the chapter on "the Cold War and the geopolitics of race" in Redding, *Turncoats, Traitors, and Fellow Travelers*, 57–78.
4. For an alternative reading of the novel's ending, see Russell, "Recalibrating the Past," 57–59.
5. See, for example, Anthony Dawahare, *Nationalism, Marxism, and African American Literature between the Wars* (Jackson: University of Mississippi Press, 2003). Dawahare argues for a recovery of Marxism's influence on African-American writing that he thinks has been elided in influential accounts such as the *Norton Anthology of African American Literature* (135).
6. For a discussion of how Wright's representation of Communism differed in various versions of "I Tried to Be a Communist" (from the original publication in *The Atlantic Monthly* to the version published in the seminal anti-Communist volume *The God That Failed* to the lengthier material found in *American Hunger*), see Christopher Z. Hobson, "Richard Wright's Communisms: Textual Variance, Intentionality, and Socialization in *American Hunger*, 'I Tried to Be a Communist,' and *The God That Failed*," *Text* 6 (1994): 307–344.
7. William A. Nolan, *Communism versus the Negro* (Chicago: Henry Regnery Company, 1951), 206.
8. William Maxwell, *New Negro, Old Left: African-American Writing and Communism between the Wars* (New York: Columbia University Press, 1999), 4–5.
9. Ibid., 5.
10. E. Franklin Frazier, *Black Bourgeoisie* (1957. New York: Free Press, 1997), 210. For more on Frazier, see Kevin Gaines, "E. Franklin Frazier's Revenge: Anticolonialism, Nonalignment, and Black Intellectuals' Critiques of Western Culture," *American Literary*

History 17.3 (Fall 2005): 506–529; and Anthony Platt, *E. Franklin Frazier Reconsidered* (New Brunswick, N.J.: Rutgers University Press, 1991).
11. Richard Wright, *Native Son* (1940. New York: Harper Perennial, 1996), 461.
12. Wright, *Native Son*, 469.
13. See George Grinnell, "Exchanging Ghosts: Haunting, History, and Communism in *Native Son*," *English Studies in Canada* 30.3 (September 2004): 145–174.
14. Robert Bone, *The Negro Novel in America* (New Haven, Conn.: Yale University Press, 1958), 157–166.
15. Wright, *Native Son*, 7.
16. William Demby, *Beetlecreek* (1950. Jackson: Banner Books/University Press of Mississippi, 1998), 201.
17. Ann Petry, *The Narrows* (1953. New York: Dafina Books, 2008), 237. For a discussion of Petry's "social criticism" as functioning in the "tradition of naturalism," see Theodore L. Gross, "Ann Petry: The Novelist as Social Critic," in *Black Fiction: New Studies in the Afro-American Novel Since 1945*, ed. A. Robert Lee (London: Vision, 1980), 41–53; 41.
18. Willard Motley, *Knock on Any Door* (New York: Appleton-Century, 1947), 5.
19. For a discussion of the ways that *Native Son* has been ironized and revised by later African-American writers and critics, see David Ikard, *Breaking the Silence: Toward a Black Male Feminist Criticism* (Baton Rouge: Louisiana State University Press, 2007), 1–27.
20. For a discussion of Max's theories with respect to Bigger's agency, see Michael Szalay, *New Deal Modernism: American Literature and the Invention of the Welfare State* (Durham, N.C.: Duke University Press, 2000), 217–220.
21. Gwendolyn Brooks, *Maud Martha* (1953. Chicago: Third World Press, 1993), 70. Valerie Frazier, "Domestic Epic Warfare in *Maud Martha*," *African American Review* 39.1–2 (Spring–Summer 2005): 133–141; quotation on 137.
22. Brooks, *Maud Martha*, 71. See also Mary Helen Washington, "'Taming All That Anger Down': Rage and Silence in Gwendolyn Brooks' *Maud Martha*," *Massachusetts Review* 24.2 (Summer 1983): 453–466; and Malin LaVon Walther, "Re-Wrighting Native: Gwendolyn Brooks's Domestic Aesthetic in *Maud Martha*," *Tulsa Studies in Women's Literature* 13.1 (Spring 1994): 143–145.
23. Ralph Ellison, *Invisible Man* (1952. New York: Vintage, 1995), 153. Hereinafter cited parenthetically. For a discussion that notes Ellison's use of games, especially poker, in the context of an argument about the politics of risk, see Jason Puskar, "Risking Ralph Ellison," *Daedalus* 138.2 (Spring 2009): 83–93.
24. Lears, *Something for Nothing*, 312.
25. Ibid., 318.
26. The accident of birth also marks absolute chance—so that when James Baldwin writes: "I don't like people who like me because I'm a Negro; neither do I like people who find in the same accident grounds for contempt," he, like Ellison, conceptualizes race both as an Aristotelian accident and as an instance of absolute chance. James Baldwin, *Collected Essays of James Baldwin* (New York: Library of America, 1998), 9. See also Heather's Neff's novel *Accident of Birth* (New York: Harlem Moon/Broadway Books, 2004).
27. In 1957, Japanese-American writer John Okada, conceptualizing race beyond the opposition between black and white, had a sense of race as a great biological lottery in which the merest apostrophe, the "little scale on which hinged the fortunes of the universe," separates a vilified Ohara from the already-assimilated O'Hara. John Okada, *No-No Boy* (1957. Seattle: University of Washington Press, 1978), 228–229.
28. Henry Louis Gates, Jr., *The Signifying Monkey: A Theory of African-American Literary Criticism* (New York: Oxford University Press, 1988), 28. See also 31–32.
29. For a discussion of the relationship between such plans and the structure of the novel, see Alan Nadel, *Invisible Criticism: Ralph Ellison and the American Canon* (Iowa City: University of Iowa Press, 1988), 80–84.
30. Barbara Foley, "From Communism to Brotherhood: The Drafts of *Invisible Man*," in *Left of the Color Line: Race, Radicalism, and Twentieth-Century Literature of the United States*, ed. Bill V. Mullen and James Smethurst (Chapel Hill: University of North Carolina Press, 2003), 165.

For more on Ellison's earlier sympathies with Communism, see Foley, "Ralph Ellison, Intertextuality, and Biographical Criticism: An Answer to Brian Roberts," *JNT: Journal of Narrative Theory* 34.2 (Summer 2004): 229–257, and Schaub, *American Fiction in the Cold War*, 93–98.
31. Foley, "Drafts," 166.
32. Barbara Foley, "The Rhetoric of Anticommunism in *Invisible Man*," *College English* 59.5 (September 1997): 531.
33. For a discussion of how the Brotherhood views the Invisible Man only in terms of their scientific plan, see Jesse Wolfe, "'Ambivalent Man': Ellison's Rejection of Communism," *African American Review* 34.4 (Winter 2000): 621–637, especially 627–628.
34. Alfred Chester and Vilma Howard, "The Art of Fiction: An Interview," *Paris Review* (Spring 1955) reprinted in Maryemma Graham and Amritjit Singh, *Conversations with Ralph Ellison* (Jackson: University of Mississippi Press, 1995), 18.
35. See Lawrence Jackson, *Ralph Ellison: Emergence of a Genius* (Athens: University of Georgia Press, 2007), especially the chapter "Cold War and Inauthentic Blacks: 1950."
36. Richard Wright, "I Tried to Be a Communist," in *The God That Failed*, ed. Richard Crossman (New York: Bantam, 1950), 151; 157.
37. Richard Wright, *The Outsider* (New York: Harper & Brothers, 1953), 299. Hereinafter cited parenthetically. According to Wright's biographer, Hazel Rowley, Wright had not read *Invisible Man* until after he completed *The Outsider*; see Hazel Rowley, *Richard Wright: The Life and Times* (New York: Henry Holt, 2001), 406.
38. See John O. Killens, *Youngblood* (1954. New York: Trident Books, 1966), 287.
39. See, for example, reviews such as Phoebe Adams, "The Wrong Road," *Atlantic Monthly* (May 1953): 77–78; and Stephen Marcus, "The American Negro in Search of an Identity," *Commentary* 56 (November 1953): 456–463. See also Michel Fabre, *The Unfinished Quest of Richard Wright* (New York: Morrow, 1973), 369–374; and Chidi Maduka, "Irony and Vision in Richard Wright's *The Outsider*," *Western Humanities Review* 38.2 (Summer 1984): 161–169. For a more sympathetic contemporary review, see Arthur Davis, "*The Outsider* as a Novel of Race," *Midwest Journal* 7 (1955): 320–326.
40. Kingsley Widmer, "The Existential Darkness: Richard Wright's *The Outsider*," *Wisconsin Studies in Contemporary Literature* 3 (Fall 1960): 13–21; quotation on 15.
41. Sarah Relyea, "The Vanguard of Modernity: Richard Wright's *The Outsider*," *Texas Studies in Literature and Language* 48.3 (Fall 2006): 187–219; quotation on 212. See also Relyea's *Outsider Citizens: The Remaking of Postwar Identity in Wright, Beauvoir, and Baldwin* (New York: Routledge, 2006).
42. Some of this plot material, especially Cross's terrorizing his wife, is found (with differences) in Wright's first novel *Lawd Today!* (written in the 1930s but not published until 1963). For more on the changes in Wright's fiction, see Gillian Johns, "Reading for the Comic and the Tragic in Modern Black Fiction; or, Reflections on Richard Wright's Change of Heart from *Lawd Today!* to *Native Son*," *CLA Journal* 49.3 (March 2006): 249–282.
43. *Silk Stockings*, DVD, directed by Rouben Mamoulian (1957. Warner Home Video, 2003).
44. For a discussion of how Wright's "uncompromising challenge to the universal and positivistic pretensions of Stalin's dialectical materialism" relate to his theory of modernity, see Paul Gilroy, *The Black Atlantic: Modernity and Double Consciousness* (Cambridge, Mass.: Harvard University Press, 1993), 164–173; quotation on 166. For an argument about Wright's use of chance and the rise of the welfare state, see Szalay, *New Deal Modernism*.
45. Raymond Barthes, "Interview" (radio broadcast on ORTF, Paris, 1956), trans. Michel Fabre reprinted in Keneth Kinnamon and Michel Fabre, eds., *Conversations with Richard Wright* (Jackson: University of Mississippi Press, 1993), 167.
46. Another important novel about an African-American relationship to the CPUSA is Chester Himes's *Lonely Crusade* (1947). As in *Invisible Man*, when protagonist Lee Gordon encounters Communist characters, they often stress that "Communism is the acceptance of reality" (152), which for them is rooted in the scientific theories of Marx and his descendents: "They ask me," says Lee, "what I know of the Marxian Scientific Formula and want to know sarcastically if I am not aware of a great class struggle going on of which I am a part and parcel" (85). The plot begins when Lee is hired as the first African-American labor organizer

at a large airplane manufacturing facility in wartime Los Angeles. Lee is warned that Communists will try to conscript him into their organization (which is something of a rival to the labor union); soon enough, true to form, they dispatch both a white woman who seduces Lee, and a black man, Luther—whom his girlfriend describes as "my dark, designing commissar" (80)—and who eventually murders a police officer in Lee's presence. In fact, when Lee accompanies Luther to this police officer's house to accept a bribe from the aircraft company's vice president, Luther brutally stabs him to death as Lee watches, and he too feels drained of his personal agency: "Lee had ceased to have a will, and when Luther moved, he moved as though he were a puppet controlled by Luther's will" (321). As he later admits to the Union lawyer: "I don't always understand myself" (354). Although not quite an example of the Wright-inspired naturalism discussed above, *Lonely Crusade* nonetheless suggests that in his contact with Communists, Lee becomes like a puppet; it is only in his final act, when on bail after having been arrested for the murder Luther committed, he breaks the police lines in a tense labor standoff, an action that will surely lead to his death. See also Himes's *If He Hollers Let Him Go* (1945), in which protagonist Bob Jones is something of an intellectual Bigger Thomas: like his fictional forebearer, he also murders a white woman, but he does so with an awareness that he is subject to larger forces at work, an idea signaled by his repeated complaint that he has never had a "chance" in the world, which dictates the range of his possible experience. Chester Himes, *If He Hollers Let Him Go* (1945. New York: Thunder's Mouth Press, 1986), 99, 132, 168, 187, 193.
47. John A. Williams, *The Man Who Cried I Am* (1967. New York: Thunder's Mouth Press, 1985), 120. Hereinafter cited parenthetically.
48. See Matthew Calihman, "Black Power beyond Black Nationalism: John A. Williams, Cultural Pluralism, and the Popular Front," *MELUS* 34.1 (Spring 2009): 139–162; and John Reilly, "Thinking History in *The Man Who Cried I Am*," *Black American Literature Forum* 21.1-2 (Spring–Summer 1987): 25–42. For a discussion of *The Man Who Cried I Am* in the context of containment, see Nadel, *Containment Culture*, 236–239. William Burke frames his discussion of the novel specifically in terms of chance: "The real determiners of the quality of human life are the accidents of history that put first one group then another into power" ("The Resistance of John A. Williams: *The Man Who Cried I Am*," *Critique* 15.3 (1973): 5–14; quotation on 10.
49. This idea is echoed by James Baldwin in his essay "Notes on the House of Bondage" (1980), in which he remarks of African Americans dying: "This is not by chance, and it is not an act of God. It is a result of the action of the American institutions, all of which are racist: it is revelatory of the real and helpless impulse of most white Americans toward black people" (*Collected Essays*, 803).
50. For a historical account of African-American perspectives on Africa, including the Mau Mau rebellion, see James Meriwether, *Proudly We Can Be Africans: Black Americans and Africa, 1935–1961* (Chapel Hill: University of North Carolina Press, 2002).

Chapter 5

1. Don DeLillo, *Underworld* (New York: Scribner, 1997), 421. Obama is quoted in David Mendell, "Obama Would Consider Missile Strikes on Iran," *Chicago Tribune* (September 25, 2004); Richard Powers quotation from *The Gold Bug Variations*, 420.
2. See Melley, *Empire of Conspiracy*.
3. For an explanation of the atomic bomb's cultural reception that includes a discussion of American scientists, see Boyer, *By the Bomb's Early Light*.
4. *A Beautiful Mind*, DVD, directed by Ron Howard (2001; Universal City, Calif.: Universal, 2002).
5. Herbert De Ley has noted that "Game theory, for some reason, seems to lend itself to popularization, whether for 'hard' scientists, social scientists, economists, military people, or laymen" (Herbert De Ley, "The Name of the Game: Applying Game Theory in Literature," *SubStance* 17.1 [1988]: 33–46; 45 n. 2).
6. John McDonald, "Secret Weapon: Theory of Games," *Science Digest* (December 1950): 7.

7. Thus, this chapter does not attempt to "apply" game theory to literature, as others have done. It is rather my aim to outline the salient features of a historically specific cultural narrative and suggest how this narrative was engaged, amplified, and challenged by some fiction and film of the era. For examples of how one might use the hermeneutic power of game theory to read a literary text, see the special number of *Yale French Studies* devoted to "Game, Play, Literature" (1968), particularly Ehrmann, "Homo Ludens Revisited," 31–57; Steven Brams, *Biblical Games: A Strategic Analysis of Stories in the Old Testament* (Cambridge, Mass.: MIT Press, 1980); Robert Rawdon Wilson, "In Palamedes' Shadow: Game and Play Concepts Today," *Canadian Review of Literature* (June 1985): 177–199; Ronald E. Foust, "The Rules of the Game: A Para-Theory of Literary Theories," *South Central Review* 3.4 (Winter 1986): 5–14; De Ley, "The Name of the Game: Applying Game Theory in Literature"; Diane Long Hoeveler, "Game Theory and Ellison's King of the Bingo Game," *Journal of American Culture* 15.2 (Summer 1992): 39–42; Peter Swirski, "Game Theory in the Third Pentagon: A Study in Strategy and Rationality," *Criticism* (1996): 303–330; Peter Swirski, "The Role of Game Theory in Literary Studies," in *Empirical Approaches to Literature*, ed. Gebhard Rusch (Siegen: LUMIS-Publications, 1994), 37–43; Paula K. Kamenish, "New Applications of Game Theory: Genet's 'Prisoner's Dilemma,'" *Cincinnati Romance Review* 15 (1996): 184–191; and Brian Cooper and Margueritte Murphy, "Taking Chances: Speculation and Games of Detection in Dashiell Hammett's *Red Harvest*," *Mosaic* 33.1 (March 2000): 145–160.

8. Clark, *Cold Warriors*, 3. Clark argues that Cold War "hypermasculinity" meant "a male gendering elevated above all questions of marked gender. That is, far from advocating openly a manliness that might have been contested, they took their own whiteness and maleness, together with American authenticity, as unmarked, neutral positions of superior reason" (3). As is implied throughout this chapter, the "superior reason" promised by the game theory narrative is likewise marked by these assumptions, and so is likewise an extension of the hypermasculine sensibility Clark describes. See also Corber, *Homosexuality in Cold War America*; and Savran, *Communists, Cowboys, and Queers*.

9. Philip Mirowski, "When Games Grow Deadly Serious: The Military Influence on the Evolution of Game Theory," in *Economics and National Security: A History of Their Interaction*, ed. Craufurd D. W. Goodwin (Durham, N.C.: Duke University Press, 1991), 229.

10. For more on these specifics, see Robert J. Leonard, "Creating a Context for Game Theory," in *Toward a History of Game Theory*, ed. E. Roy Weintraub (Durham, N.C.: Duke University Press, 1992), 29–76; Angela O'Rand, "Mathematizing Social Science in the 1950s: The Early Development and Diffusion of Game Theory," in *Toward a History of Game Theory*, ed. E. Roy Weintraub (Durham, N.C.: Duke University Press, 1992), 178–204. For the early development of game theory, see Robert Leonard, *Von Neumann, Morgenstern, and the Creation of Game Theory: From Chess to Social Science, 1900–1960* (Cambridge: Cambridge University Press, 2010).

11. This should not mitigate the fact that professionals considered *Theory of Games and Economic Behavior* a landmark achievement; while the various theoretical engagements with its ideas are far too numerous to detail here, many people would have agreed with an assessment made by A. H. Copeland in the *Bulletin of the American Mathematical Society* in 1945: "[P]osterity may regard this book as one of the major scientific achievements of the first half of the twentieth century" (quoted in H. W. Kuhn and A. W. Tucker, "Preface," *Contributions to the Theory of Games*, vol. 2 [Princeton, N.J.: Princeton University Press, 1953], v).

12. Will Lissner, "Mathematical Theory of Poker is Applied to Business Problems," *New York Times* (March 10, 1946).

13. John McDonald, *Strategy in Poker, Business, and War* (New York: Dutton, 1950). This book was issued in paperback in 1963 and reissued in 1989 and 1996. Initial reviewers tended to be interested in McDonald's book for the way it articulated game theory's promise; the *Washington Post* reviewer, for example, wrote: "The theory, if properly established, would have immense importance for all of us, and I don't mean poker" ("Theory of Games," *Washington Post* [September 3, 1950]). See also Rex Lardner, "How to Make a Sucker Out of Your Opponent," *New York Times* (August 27, 1950); and the brief *New Yorker* review (September 9, 1950): 121.

14. John McDonald, "A Theory of Strategy," *Fortune* (June 1949): 100.
15. See Richard Bellman and David Blackwell, "Red Dog, Blackjack and Poker," *Scientific American* (January 1951): 44–47; "Planned Chance," *Newsweek* (May 21, 1951): 58; J. D. Williams, *The Compleat Strategyst: Being a Primer on the Theory of Games of Strategy* (New York: McGraw Hill, 1954); and Leonid Hurwicz, "Game Theory and Decisions," *Scientific American* (February 1955): 78–83. For introductions aimed at more advanced readers, see: J. C. C. McKinsey, *Introduction to the Theory of Games* (New York: McGraw-Hill, 1952); Duncan R. Luce and Howard Raïffa, *Games and Decisions: Introduction and Critical Survey* (New York: John Wiley & Sons, Inc., 1957). See also Oskar Morgenstern's *The Question of National Defense*, 2d rev. ed. (New York: Vintage Books, 1961).
16. See Fred Kaplan, *The Wizards of Armageddon* (Stanford, Calif.: Stanford University Press, 1991), 67. For an explanation of how an interest in game theory led RAND to bring on social scientists who could analyze "the actual behavior and values of various nations," see Kaplan, 67–73.
17. "Games of Survival," *Newsweek* (May 18, 1953), 75.
18. Bill Becker, "RAND Corporation Furnishes Brain Power for the Air Force," *New York Times* (May 22, 1960). See also: John McDonald, "War of Wits," *Fortune* (March 1951): 99–157; W. K., "Poker in the Interest of Science," *New York Times* (February 1, 1953); "Games of Survival"; "Valuable Batch of Brains," *Life* (May 11, 1959); Joseph Kraft, "RAND: Arsenal for Ideas," *Harpers*, July 1960; Saul Friedman, "The RAND Corporation and our Policy Makers," *Atlantic Monthly* (September 1963); and Bruce Smith, *The RAND Corporation: Case Study of a Nonprofit Advisory Corporation* (Cambridge, Mass.: Harvard University Press, 1966). For a contemporary critique of RAND-generated theories of "political gaming," see Herbert Goldhammer and Hans Speier, "Some Observations on Political Gaming," *World Politics* 12.1 (October 1959): 71–83. At one point, Goldhammer and Speier note how RAND attempted to "devise a 'cold war game,'" 72.
19. McDonald, *Strategy*, 126.
20. Ibid.
21. Ibid., 81.
22. William S. Burroughs, "The Cut Up Method of Brion Gysin," in *A Casebook on the Beat*, ed. Thomas Parkinson (New York: Thomas Crowell, 1961), 106.
23. Kurt Vonnegut, *Player Piano* (1952. New York: Dial Press, 1999).
24. The *Steve Canyon* strip is discussed in Sharon Ghamari-Tabrizi, *The Worlds of Herman Kahn: The Intuitive Science of Thermonuclear War* (Cambridge, Mass.: Harvard University Press, 2005), 160. Ghamari-Tabrizi writes that the *Steve Canyon* strip of June 9, 1963 "leaked" the story that the Pentagon was engaged in war games. See also Edward Brunner, "'How Can I Tell My Grandchildren What I Did in the Cold War?': Militarizing the Funny Pages and Milton Caniff's *Steve Canyon*," in *Pressing the Fight: Print, Propaganda, and the Cold War*, ed. Greg Barnhisel and Catherine Turner (Amherst: University of Massachusetts Press, 2010), 169–192.
25. John W. Campbell, Jr., "Game Theory," *Astounding Science Fiction* (September 1955), 5–7; 160–162, quotation on 7.
26. Philip K. Dick, *Solar Lottery* (New York: Ace Book, 1955), 5. Hereinafter cited parenthetically.
27. For an introduction to *Solar Lottery*, see Thomas M. Disch, "Toward the Transcendent: An Introduction to *Solar Lottery* and Other Works," in *Philip K. Dick*, ed. Martin Harry Greenberg and Joseph Olander (New York: Taplinger Publishing Company, 1983), 13–25. Jackson Lears briefly mentions how game theory "acquired special resonance as a means of planning moves and countermoves against the Soviet Union" and with this context gestures toward the potential interest of *Solar Lottery* (Lears, *Something for Nothing*, 241, 357, n. 29).
28. See "Appointment for a Gamesman," *Time* (November 1, 1954), which reports that von Neumann, "a cheerful, portly professor with a passion for cookies and ionospheric mathematical problems," is "eminently qualified to sit across the atomic table from the Russians in the greatest game in the world" (20).

29. For a kind of update to *Solar Lottery*, see Jonathan Lethem's novel *Amnesia Moon* (New York: Harvest, 1995), which is set after what seems at first a full-scale nuclear war, and in which characters regularly have their luck measured.
30. Robert Coover, "The Second Son," *Evergreen Review* 31 (October–November 1963): 72–88.
31. Robert Coover, *The Universal Baseball Association, Inc., J. Henry Waugh, Prop.*, (New York: Plume, 1968), 40. Hereinafter cited parenthetically.
32. See Larry McCaffery, *The Metafictional Muse: The Works of Robert Coover, Donald Barthelme, and William H. Gass* (Pittsburgh: University of Pittsburgh Press, 1982). For an argument about the connection between *The Universal Baseball Association* and Heisenberg's Uncertainty Principle, see Arlen Hansen, "The Dice of God: Einstein, Heisenberg, and Robert Coover," *Novel* 10.1 (Autumn 1976): 49–58. For an argument about the novel and Cold War game playing, see the chapter "Unthinking the Thinkability of the Unthinkable," in Grausam, *On Endings*.
33. Another significant engagement with this aspect of the game theory narrative is Don DeLillo's second novel, *End Zone*, which draws comparisons between the game of football and the game of the Cold War. Toward the end of the novel, the narrator and a major play war games in a hotel room, the description of which implies the critique seen elsewhere in this chapter: "The gaming environment, as he [the major] called it, could never elicit the kind of emotions generated in times of actual stress; therefore gaming was probably just a second-rate guide (hopefully not too misleading) to what might be expected from governments when armies were poised and lithe missiles were rising from their silos. . . . 'Now this scenario is premised on futuribles,' he [the major] said. 'The basic situation as I've set it up for us is definitely in the area of what we know to be projected crisis situations. It could happen. Tensions. Possible accidents. Unrelated hostilities.'" (Don DeLillo, *End Zone* [Boston: Houghton Mifflin, 1972], 219–220).
34. Luce and Raïffa, *Games*, 57.
35. According to David Hounshell: "Under Kahn, who brought to RAND expertise in Monte Carlo methods and also contributed to RAND's work in game theory and war simulation, the study of bomb effects became the basis for his belief that nuclear war was not only survivable but also in some sense winnable" (David Hounshell, "The Cold War, RAND, and the Generation of Knowledge, 1946–1962," *Historical Studies in the Physical and Biological Sciences* 27.2 [1997]: 249).
36. Sherman Rigby, "Tit for Tat," *New York Times* (January 3, 1965): SM 2.
37. Stephen Whitfield, *The Culture of the Cold War* (Baltimore, MD: The Johns Hopkins University Press, 1991), 218–225; Margot Henriksen, *Dr. Strangelove's America: Society and Culture in the Atomic Age* (Berkeley: University of California Press, 1997), 318–331; Stephen E. Kercher, *Revel with a Cause: Liberal Satire in Postwar America* (Chicago: University of Chicago Press, 2006), 330–342. Fred Kaplan also emphasized the connection between Kahn and Dr. Strangelove on the occasion of the release of the DVD special edition; see Fred Kaplan, "Truth Stranger than 'Strangelove,'" *New York Times* (October 10, 2004). For more on the connection between Kahn and Kubrick (emphasizing the latter), see Ghamari-Tabrizi, *Worlds*, 274–280.
38. Quoted in Whitfield, *Culture*, 220.
39. Herman Kahn, *On Thermonuclear War*, 2d ed. (Princeton, N.J.: Princeton University Press, 1961), 71.
40. Ibid., 34.
41. James R. Newman, "Two Discussions of Thermonuclear War," *Scientific American* (March 1961): 197. Excerpts from Newman's *Scientific American* review were reprinted, for a wider audience, in *The Washington Post* (James R. Newman, "A Moral Tract on Mass Murder," *Washington Post* [February 26, 1961]).
42. See Ghamari-Tabrizi, *Worlds*, 19–21; 284–292. Ghamari-Tabrizi suggests that part of *On Thermonuclear War*'s reception was "repugnance for Kahn's grotesque style" (292).
43. See also the 1962 novel on which the film *Fail-Safe* was based: Eugene Burdick and Harvey Wheeler, *Fail-Safe* (New York: Harper Perennial, 1999): "for years there has been a fellow named Fred Ilké, who has been working with the Rand Corporation and the Air Force on

Notes to Pages 113-121   179

how to reduce war by accident. He had found flaw after flaw in the system, at just the same time that the newspapers were saying it was perfect" (207).
44. *Dr. Strangelove, or: How I Stopped Worrying and Learned to Love the Bomb*, DVD, directed by Stanley Kubrick (1964; Sony Pictures, 2001).
45. See, for example, J. C. Furnas, "The Fight over Fluoridation," *Saturday Evening Post* (May 19, 1956); and Donald R. McNeil, *The Fight for Fluoridation* (New York: Oxford University Press, 1957).
46. "Inside the Making of *Dr. Strangelove*," in *Dr. Strangelove, or: How I Stopped Worrying and Learned to Love the Bomb*, DVD, directed by Stanley Kubrick (1964; Sony Pictures, 2001).
47. See Clark, *Cold Warriors*, 1–42.
48. For Kahn's thoughts on what he calls the "Doomsday Machine" and the "Doomsday-in-a-Hurry Machine," see *On Thermonuclear War*, 144–154 (he agrees with Strangelove that a Doomsday Machine is "not acceptable," 149).
49. For a discussion of what he calls *Dr. Strangelove*'s "often ecstatic reviews," see Kercher, *Revel*, 339–342.
50. Mirowski, "When," 227. Mirowski also notes that Oskar Morgenstern, co-author of *Theory of Games and Economic Behavior*, kept a copy of "Game" in his files. In 1991, the story was included in *Economics and National Security: A History of Their Interaction*, edited by Craufurd D. W. Goodwin.
51. Donald Barthelme, "Game," *New Yorker* (July 31, 1965): 29–30, quotation on 29.
52. Ibid.
53. Anatol Rapoport, "The Use and Misuse of Game Theory," *Scientific American* (December 1962): 108–118;" 108.
54. Ibid.
55. Ibid.
56. For a later argument that discusses game theory in light of rationality, see: Michael Hechter, "On the Inadequacy of Game Theory for the Solution of Real-World Collective Action Problems," in *The Limits of Rationality*, ed. Karen Schweers Cook and Margaret Levi (Chicago: University of Chicago Press, 1990), 240–249.
57. See, for example, Anatol Rapoport, *Strategy and Conscience* (New York: Harper & Row, 1964). By 1973, Rapoport was regularly singled-out as the "chief advocate" of the position that, as Morton Kaplan put it, "argued that strategic analysis inevitably produced evil results and corrupted the nature of the political process" (Morton Kaplan, "Introduction," in *Strategic Thinking and Its Moral Implications*, ed. Morton Kaplan [Chicago: University of Chicago Center for Policy Study, 1973], 5). For an earlier statement that is careful to limit what game theory can do, see Luce and Raïffa, *Games and Decisions*: "[W]e have the historical fact that many social sciences have become disillusioned with game theory. Initially there was a naive band-wagon feeling that game theory solved innumerable problems of sociology and economics, or that, at the least, it made their solution a practical matter of a few year's work. This has not turned out to be the case" (10).
58. See Robert Scheer, *With Enough Shovels: Reagan, Bush and Nuclear War* (New York: Random House, 1982). There is a large body of work on the nuclear strategy of the 1980s; for example, see Stephen J. Cimbala, *Nuclear War and Nuclear Strategy: Unfinished Business* (New York: Greenwood, 1987) and David Shepheard, "Nuclear Strategy/Nuclear Politics" *Paragraph* 9 (March 1987): 31–48.
59. Robert Jervis, *The Illogic of American Nuclear Strategy* (Ithaca, N.Y.: Cornell University Press, 1984), 19; 148.
60. Richard Powers, *Prisoner's Dilemma* (1988. New York: Perennial, 2002), 72.
61. Ibid., 69–70.
62. Ibid., 282–283.
63. Ibid., 327.
64. Christina Klein, *Cold War Orientalism*, 23. Leerom Medovoi, "Cold War American Culture as the Age of Three Worlds," *Minnesota Review* 55–27 (2002): 167–186.
65. Medovoi, *Rebels*, 10–11.
66. Gore Vidal, *Dark Green, Bright Red* (New York: Dutton, 1950), 52, 22.

67. Ibid., 289.
68. Ibid., 292–293.
69. See Westad, *Global Cold War*, 146–149.
70. Gore Vidal, "In the Lair of the Octopus," in his *Dreaming War: Blood for Oil and the Cheney-Bush Junta* (New York: Thunder's Mouth Press, 2002), 145.
71. Joan Didion, *A Book of Common Prayer* (1977. New York: Vintage, 1995), 193. In her discussion of the particulars of Boca Grande politics, Grace emphasizes the game metaphor: "There were always these strangers there, third-rate people Gerardo was using in his game, the object of which seemed to be to place his marker in Victor's office in as few moves as possible" (225); "Gerardo only talked about 'the people' that spring as a move in the particular game he was playing" (231).
72. Ibid., 38. Later, readers learn also that on a given day, Leonard would be jetting off "to assist in the sale of four French Mirages from one Caribbean independency to another" (131).
73. Ibid., 95, 243.
74. Ibid., 249. For more on Didion's Cold War story-telling, with particular emphasis on *The Last Thing He Wanted*, see Samuel Cohen, *After the End of History: American Fiction in the 1990s* (Iowa City: University of Iowa Press, 2009), 138–153.
75. Joan Didion, *Democracy* (1984. New York: Vintage, 1995), 36–37.
76. Joan Didion, *The Last Thing He Wanted* (1996. New York: Vintage, 1997), 31.
77. Ibid., 38.
78. Ibid., 6.
79. Ibid., 13.
80. The narrator relates, for example, that she knows the answers to some of the questions that "neither Rand nor the congressional investigators" could discern because there "would have been daunting structural obstacles, entire layers of bureaucracy dedicated to the principle that self-perpetuation depended on the ability not to elucidate but to obscure. 'The cooperation of those individuals and agencies who responded to our numerous requests is appreciated,' the preface to the Rand study noted in this connection. 'Although some other individuals and agencies did not acknowledge or respond to our requests, it is to be hoped that future assessments of this incident will benefit from their assistance and clarification'" (169).
81. Another critique of the game theory narrative's predictive pretensions is the mention of the Delphi Method: "I recall hearing at this embassy [on the unnamed island] a good deal about 'the Del' before I learned that it referred to a formula for predicting events developed by the Rand Corporation and less jauntily known as the Delphi Method (that which should not have happened and could not have been predicted by any quantitative measurement had presumably not been predicted by employment of the Del)" (91). This idea, that one can define events as "that which should not have happened" *because* they do not conform to the Del's predictions, seems of a piece with those criticisms of political fictions that do not allow for chance operations because they do not conform to party ideology. See also Don DeLillo's novel *The Names* (New York: Vintage, 1982), in which James Axton is a risk analyst whose job it is to calculate the relative stability or instability of various third world countries for large companies interested in insuring their executives. By the end of the novel, it turns out that, unbeknownst to him, Axton's work was actually used for "back-channel dialogue with the CIA" (315).
82. Didion, *The Last Thing He Wanted*, 225. The article being referred to is J. Anthony Lukas, "Class Reunion: Kennedy's Men Relive the Cuban Missile Crisis," *New York Times* (August 30, 1987): SM22+. The article ends, portentously, with this dialogue between a reporter and his wife: "'Now that we've finally got a clear day,' says the reporter, 'I wonder if we can see Cuba.' 'On a very clear day,' replies his wife, moving from today's history to tomorrow's, 'we ought to see Nicaragua'" (59).
83. Didion, *The Last Thing He Wanted*, 225.
84. Ibid., 226.

Chapter 6

1. DeLillo, *Underworld*, 170.
2. John Mearsheimer, "Why We Will Soon Miss the Cold War," *Atlantic Monthly* 266.2 (August 1990): 35–50; quotation on 35.
3. See Daniel Grausam, "'It is only a statement of the power of what comes after': Atomic Nostalgia, the 1990s, and the Ends of Postmodernism," in press; Piette, *The Literary Cold War*, 1–17; Cohen, *After the End of History*, 3–29; and Ellen Schrecker, ed., *Cold War Triumphalism: The Misuse of History after the Fall of Communism* (New York: New Press, 2004).
4. In addition to this nostalgic sense found in popular culture, there has been another serious persistence of the Cold War's rhetorical frame in the decades since the collapse of the Soviet Union. As numerous observers were quick to point out, the Cold War offered great explanatory power for the War on Terror. As Anne McClintock writes: "With the collapse of the Soviet Union in December 1991, the grand antagonism of the United States and the USSR evaporated like a quickly fading nightmare. The cold war rhetoric of totalitarianism, Finlandization, present danger, fifth columnist, and infiltration vanished. Where were the enemies now to justify the continuing escalation of the military colossus? . . . The 9/11 attacks came as a dazzling solution, both to the enemy deficit and the problem of legitimacy, offering the Bush administration what they would claim as a political casus belli and the military unimaginable license to expand its reach" (Anne McClintock, "Paranoid Empire: Specters from Guantánamo and Abu Ghraib" *Small Axe* 28, 13.1 [March 2009]: 50–74; quotation on 55). This sort of thinking has been fairly typical of those critical of the Bush administration and its aims, who tend to view the War on Terror as a justification for the renewal of an American empire. See, for example, Carol Winkler, "Parallels in Preemptive War Rhetoric: Reagan on Libya; Bush 43 on Iraq," *Rhetoric & Public Affairs* 10.2 (Summer 2007): 303–334; David Noon, "Operation Enduring Analogy: World War II, the War on Terror, and the Uses of Historical Memory," *Rhetoric and Public Affairs* 7 (Fall 2004): 339–65; and Nikhil Pal Singh, "Cold War Redux: On the 'New Totalitarianism,'" *Radical History Review* 85 (Winter 2003): 171–181.
5. Larry McCaffery and Sinda Gregory, "An Interview with Paul Auster," *Contemporary Literature* 33.1 (Spring 1992): 1–23; quotation on 6.
6. Jesús Ángel González, "'Happy Accidents': An Interview with Paul Auster," *Literature/Film Quarterly* 37.1 (2009): 18–27.
7. See, for example, Steven Alford, "Chance in Contemporary Narrative: The Example of Paul Auster," *LIT: Literature, Interpretation, Theory* 11.1 (July 2000): 59–82; Tim Woods, "The Music of Chance: Aleatorical (Dis)harmonies within 'The City of the World,'" in *Beyond the Red Notebook: Essays on Paul Auster*, ed. Dennis Barone (Philadelphia: University of Pennsylvania Press, 1995): 143–161; Ilana Shiloh, "A Place Both Imaginary and Realistic: Paul Auster's *The Music of Chance*," *Contemporary Literature* 43.3 (Fall 2002): 488–517.
8. Paul Auster, *In the Country of Last Things* (New York: Viking, 1987), 27–28.
9. Paul Auster, *Moon Palace* (New York: Viking, 1989), 62.
10. Ibid., 223.
11. Paul Auster, *Invisible* (New York: Picador, 2009), 298–299.
12. McCaffery and Gregory, "An Interview with Paul Auster," 3.
13. Ibid., 4.
14. Ibid., 14.
15. Paul Auster, *The Music of Chance* (New York: Penguin, 1990), 216. Hereinafter cited parenthetically.
16. Woods, "The Music of Chance: Aleatorical (Dis)harmonies within 'The City of the World,'" 152.
17. One example of the kind of response Lee's novel has received is Hyungji Park's comment that "[i]n any context, *Native Speaker* is a natural choice for an 'essential' Asian American literary text" ("The Immigrant as Spy," *American Book Review* 31.1 [November/December 2009]: 7–8; quotation on 8).

18. Chang-rae Lee, *Native Speaker* (New York: Riverhead, 1995), 16. Hereinafter cited parenthetically.
19. For more on Henry's impersonation skills, see Tina Chen, *Double Agency: Acts of Impersonation in Asian American Literature and Culture* (Stanford, Calif.: Stanford University Press, 2005).
20. Jodi Kim has argued that *Native Speaker* replaces the menace of global Communism with "that of global *capitalism*, seemingly the ultimate realization of the US's Cold War aims" (Jodi Kim, "From *Mee-gook* to Gook: The Cold War and Racialized Undocumented Capital in Chang-rae Lee's *Native Speaker*," *MELUS* 34.1 (Spring 2009): 117–137; quotation on 118). While Kim is certainly correct to draw attention to how what she calls "Cold War capitalist logics" are related to "race, racialized subjectivity, and multiracial politics" (119), my argument focuses more on how Henry's subjective experiences subvert a rigid causal logic encouraged by the Cold War. Other studies that describe *Native Speaker*'s political work include: Betsy Huang, "Citizen Kwang: Chang-rae Lee's *Native Speaker* and the Politics of Consent," *Journal of Asian American Studies* 9.3 (October 2006): 243–269; and Daniel Kim, "Do I, Too, Sing America?: Vernacular Representations and Chang-rae Lee's *Native Speaker*," *Journal of Asian American Studies* 6.3 (October 2003): 231–260.
21. In Susan Choi's novel *The Foreign Student* (New York: Harper Perennial, 1999), Chang (Chuck) Ahn, the titular character, becomes an exchange student at Sewanee in the aftermath of the Korean War, and, when invited to speak about Korea to church groups, offers a similarly purposely reductive version of the conflict (whereas the novel does not).
22. Writing about Zadie Smith's novel *White Teeth* (2000), Jonathan Sell offers another perspective on chance and multicultural identity: "By slipping the bonds of causality, by emancipating herself from historical determinism, and by fixing her eyes on the present, Smith is able to inscribe identities which are no longer hung-up on historical injustices or immersed in sombre, unproductive introspection. As such she forms part of the multicultural generation and offers a more positive model of identity" (Jonathan Sell, "Chance and Gesture in Zadie Smith's *White Teeth* and *The Autograph Man*: A Model for Multicultural Identity?" *Journal of Commonwealth Literature* 41.3 [September 2006]: 27–44; quotation on 33).
23. John Ashbery, "John Ashbery Interviewing Harry Mathews," *Review of Contemporary Fiction* 7.3 (1987): 36–48; quotation on 46.
24. Lytle Shaw, "An Interview with Harry Mathews," *Chicago Review* (Spring 1997): 36–52; 49.
25. Harry Mathews, *My Life in CIA: A Memoir of 1973* (Normal, Ill.: Dalkey Archive Press, 2005), 40. Hereinafter cited parenthetically.
26. For a description of Oulipo, with particular reference to Georges Perec, see James, *Constraining Chance*.
27. Genette quoted in Alison James, "Automatism, Arbitrariness, and the Oulipian Author," *French Forum* 31.2 (Spring 2006): 111–125; 111. In his essay "The Oulipo and Combinational Art," which is used as an introduction to the Oulipo section in *Oulipo Compendium* (ed. Harry Mathews and Alastair Brotchie [Los Angeles, Calif.: Make Now Press, 2005]), Jacques Roubaud dismisses Genette's dismissal: "It is clear . . . that Oulipian procedures are as remote as possible from 'automatic writing' and, more generally, from the notion of any kind of literature whose strategic foundation is chance (considered the indispensable auxiliary of freedom). This is one of the most extraordinary and most durable absurdities proffered . . . about the Oulipo. . . . The misunderstanding has been perpetuated by Gérard Genette, a generally sensible theoretician who one might have expected to be better informed, more thoughtful, and less credulous, and who permitted himself to write a thoroughly mediocre article on the subject" (41).
28. For more on the trope of games in Mathews's work (with special attention to *The Conversions*), see Eric Mottram, "'Eleusions Truths': Harry Mathews's Strategies and Games," *Review of Contemporary Fiction* 7.3 (Fall 1987): 154–172.
29. Shaw, "An Interview with Harry Mathews," 41.
30. Through a series of what the back of the book calls "improbable coincidences," Mathews finds himself swept along by the logic of the Cold War, which converts seemingly chance events into meaningful coincidences; thus, if he was in Laos as "evidently the only tourist

in the country" (11), it must "really" be because he is CIA: "He did not ask me why I was in Laos. He told me. They all knew I was CIA" (15).

31. As one character remarks: "Whatever its true role, most people assume CIA helped overthrow Allende" (163). With the benefit of historical perspective, we know that this is basically true; see Michael Grow, *U.S. Presidents and Latin American Interventions: Pursuing Regime Change in the Cold War* (Lawrence: University of Kansas Press, 2008).

32. "Accident Seen as Major Blow to Soviet Hope for World Sales," *New York Times* (June 4, 1973): 19.

Coda: Cold War Meaning

1. Ray Comfort, intro to Charles Darwin, *The Origin of Species: 150th Anniversary Edition* (Alachua, Fla.: Bridge-Logos Foundation, 2009), 9.
2. It would certainly be fruitful to parse the religious subtext of some of the texts discussed in *No Accident, Comrade* by asking, for example, how questions of belief inflect attitudes toward chance and design; two recent books explore questions of religion in postwar America. Jason Stevens's *God-Fearing and Free* is a cultural history framed in terms of the Cold War, whereas Amy Hungerford's *Postmodern Belief: American Literature and Religion since 1960* (Princeton, N.J.: Princeton University Press, 2010) looks at the belief in meaninglessness in postwar American writing. See also John McClure, *Partial Faiths: Postsecular Fiction in the Age of Pynchon and Morrison* (Athens: University of Georgia Press, 2007).
3. David Markson, *This Is Not a Novel* (Berkeley: Counterpoint, 2001), 4, 5, 12, 7.
4. Ibid., 121.
5. Ibid., 128.
6. Ibid., 102.
7. Jack Kerouac, *The Subterraneans* (New York: Grove, 1958), 83.
8. Paul Maher, *Kerouac: The Definitive Biography* (New York: Taylor Trade, 2004), 488.
9. Ann Charters, *Kerouac: A Biography* (1973. New York: St. Martin's, 1994), 344–346; Steven Moore, *William Gaddis* (New York: Twayne, 1989).
10. I myself have made a variation on this argument; see Steven Belletto, "Kerouac His Own Historian: *Visions of Cody* and the Politics of Historiography," *Clio* 37 (2008): 193–218. For a recent discussion of "Beat politics" more broadly, see Todd Tietchen, *The Cubalogues: Beat Writers in Revolutionary Havana* (Gainesville: University Press of Florida, 2010), 5–9.
11. Ann Douglas, "'Telepathic Shock and Meaning Excitement': Kerouac's Poetics of Intimacy," *College Literature* 27.1 (Winter 2000): 8–21, quotation on 13.
12. Ibid., 14–15.
13. See also Belgrad, *Culture of Spontaneity*, 196–221.
14. Or to say, as she does: "Kerouac's dual language track, the balance he struck between the written text and an earlier oral performance, also had echoes in the wider life of his times. The Cold War era was the period that saw the liberation of the nations of Africa and Asia from colonial rule. . . . Like the native West African dialects, like the Celtic and Breton tongues of his distant forefathers, the joual that haunts and reshapes Kerouac's American English is also in some sense a 'colonial' language; it, too, is the idiom of a people defeated in war, left behind by modernization, a people who claim their identity not on the strength of the battles they have won or the land they rule but solely on the strength of the language they speak" (Douglas, "Telepathic Shock," 16–17).
15. Andrew Hammond, "From Rhetoric to Rollback: Introductory Thoughts on Cold War Writing," in *Cold War Literature*, ed. Hammond, 1–14; quotation on 5.
16. Andrew Hoberek, *The Twilight of the Middle Class: Post-World War II American Fiction and White-Collar Work* (Princeton, N.J.: Princeton University Press, 2005), 116.
17. Medovoi, *Rebels*, 50–51.
18. Sean McCann and Michael Szalay, "Do You Believe in Magic? Literary Thinking after the New Left," *Yale Journal of Criticism* 18.2 (Fall 2005): 435–468; quotation on 459.
19. For a critique of McCann and Szalay's essay, see John A. McClure, "Do They Believe in Magic? Politics and Postmodern Literature," *boundary 2*, 36.2 (Summer 2009): 125–143.

For a response to this critique, see Sean McCann and Michael Szalay, "Eerie Serenity: A Response to John McClure," *boundary 2*, 36.2 (Summer 2009): 145–153.
20. Klein, *Cold War Orientalism*, 8–9.
21. Cornis-Pope, *Narrative Innovation*, 6.
22. Piette, *The Literary Cold War*, 11.
23. In this way, the Cold War frame explains another reason behind a remark Mark McGurl made in his book about postwar literature that is framed by the rise of creative writing programs rather than the Cold War; he writes: "[L]iterary scholars have generally been on the side of excess—not fewer meanings for the literary text but more, always more!" (McGurl, *The Program Era*, 401).
24. Piette, *The Literary Cold War*, 12.
25. Kim, *Ends of Empire*, 5.

Bibliography

"Accident Seen as Major Blow To Soviet Hope for World Sales," *New York Times* (June 4, 1973): 19.
Adams, Phoebe. "The Wrong Road," *Atlantic Monthly* (May 1953): 77–78.
Agee, James. *A Death in the Family*. 1957. New York: Penguin, 2009.
Alford, Steven. "Chance in Contemporary Narrative: The Example of Paul Auster," *LIT: Literature, Interpretation, Theory* 11.1 (July 2000): 59–82.
Allen, Clifford. *Homosexuality: Its Nature, Causation and Treatment*. London: Staples Press, 1958.
"Appointment for a Gamesman," *Time* (November 1, 1954): 20.
Appy, Christian, ed. *Cold War Constructions: The Political Culture of United States Imperialism, 1945–1966*. Amherst: University of Massachusetts Press, 2000.
Arendt, Hannah. *The Origins of Totalitarianism* (New Edition with Added Prefaces). 1951. New York: Harcourt Brace Jovanovich, 1979.
Aschheim, Steven. "Nazism, Culture, and *The Origins of Totalitarianism*: Hannah Arendt and the Discourse of Evil," *New German Critique* (Winter 1997): 117–139.
Ashbery, John. "John Ashbery Interviewing Harry Mathews," *Review of Contemporary Fiction* 7.3 (1987): 36–48.
Auster, Paul. *In the Country of Last Things*. New York: Viking, 1987.
———. *Invisible*. New York: Picador, 2009.
———. *Moon Palace*. New York: Viking, 1989.
———. *The Music of Chance*. New York: Penguin, 1990.
Bacon, Jon Lance. *Flannery O'Connor and Cold War Culture*. New York: Cambridge University Press, 1993.
Baldwin, Hanson W. "Decision in Moscow: Khrushchev Is Seen Starting a New Phase of Power Politics," *New York Times* (September 3, 1961): E3.
Baldwin, James. *Collected Essays of James Baldwin*. New York: Library of America, 1998.
Baldwin, Kate. *Beyond the Color Line and the Iron Curtain: Reading Encounters Between Black and Red, 1922–1963*. Durham, N.C.: Duke University Press, 2002.
Barrett, William. "Determinism and Novelty," in *Determinism and Freedom in the Age of Modern Science*, ed. Sidney Hook. New York: New York University Press, 1958.
Barthelme, Donald. "Game," *New Yorker* (July 31, 1965): 29–30.
Barthes, Raymond. "Interview" (radio broadcast on ORTF, Paris, 1956), trans. Michel Fabre, reprinted in Keneth Kinnamon and Michel Fabre, eds., *Conversations with Richard Wright*. Jackson: University of Mississippi Press, 1993.
Bauer, Raymond, Alex Inkeles, and Clyde Kluckhohn. *How the Soviet System Works: Cultural, Psychological, and Social Themes*. Cambridge, Mass.: Harvard University Press, 1959.
Baxter, Claude F. "Review of *The Chance Character of Human Existence*," *Quarterly Review of Biology* 31.4 (December 1956): 289–290.

A Beautiful Mind, DVD, directed by Ron Howard. 2001. Universal City, Calif.: Universal, 2002.
Becker, Bill. "RAND Corporation Furnishes Brain Power for the Air Force," *New York Times* (May 22, 1960): F1+.
Belgrad, Daniel. *The Culture of Spontaneity: Improvisation and the Arts in Postwar America*. Chicago: University of Chicago Press, 1998.
———. "Democracy, Decentralization, and Feedback," in *American Literature and Culture in an Age of Cold War*, ed. Steven Belletto and Daniel Grausam. Iowa City: University of Iowa Press, forthcoming.
Bell, Daniel. *The End of Ideology: On the Exhaustion of Political Ideas in the Fifties*. New York: Free Press, 1960.
———. "Ten Theories in Search of Reality: The Prediction of Soviet Behavior in the Social Sciences," *World Politics* (April 1958): 327–365.
Bell, David. *Circumstances: Chance in the Literary Text*. Lincoln: University of Nebraska Press, 1993.
Belletto, Steven. "Inventing Other Realities: What the Cold War Means for Literary Studies," in *Uncertain Empire: American History and the Idea of the Cold War*, ed. Joel Isaac and Duncan Bell. Oxford: Oxford University Press, forthcoming.
———. "Kerouac His Own Historian: *Visions of Cody* and the Politics of Historiography," *Clio* 37 (2008): 193–218.
———. "Of Pickaninnies and Nymphets: Race in *Lolita*," *Nabokov Studies* 9 (2005): 1–17.
Bellman, Richard, and David Blackwell, "Red Dog, Blackjack and Poker," *Scientific American* (January 1951): 44–47.
Bergler, Edmund. *Homosexuality: Disease or Way of Life?* New York: Hill and Wang, 1956.
Berkeley, Edmund C. "We Are Safer Than We Think," *New York Times* (July 29, 1951): 11, 20.
Bérubé, Michael. "Race and Modernity in Colson Whitehead's *The Intuitionist*," in *The Holodeck in the Garden: Science and Technology in Contemporary American Fiction*, ed. Peter Freese and Charles Harris. Normal, Ill.: Dalkey Archive, 2004.
Blumenthal, Walter. *Rendezvous with Chance*. New York: Exposition Press, 1954.
Boehmer, Konrad. "Chance as Ideology," trans. Ian Pepper. *October* (Fall 1997): 62–77.
Bone, Robert. *The Negro Novel in America*. New Haven, Conn.: Yale University Press, 1958.
Boyd, Brian. *Nabokov's Pale Fire: The Magic of Artistic Discovery*. Princeton, N.J.: Princeton University Press, 1999.
———. *Vladimir Nabokov: The Russian Years*. Princeton, N.J.: Princeton University Press, 1990.
Boyer, Paul. *By the Bomb's Early Light: American Thought and Culture at the Dawn of the Atomic Age*. New York: Pantheon, 1985.
Brams, Steven. *Biblical Games: A Strategic Analysis of Stories in the Old Testament*. Cambridge, Mass.: MIT Press, 1980.
Brill, John. *The Chance Character of Human Existence*. New York: Philosophical Library, 1956.
Brooks, Gwendolyn. *Maud Martha*. 1953. Chicago: Third World Press, 1993.
Bruhm, Steven. "Queer, Queer Vladimir," *American Imago* 53 (1996): 281–306.
Brunner, Edward. "'How Can I Tell My Grandchildren What I Did in the Cold War?': Militarizing the Funny Pages and Milton Caniff's *Steve Canyon*," in *Pressing the Fight: Print, Propaganda, and the Cold War*, ed. Greg Barnhisel and Catherine Turner. Amherst: University of Massachusetts Press, 2010.
Brunvand, Jan Harold. *Encyclopedia of Urban Legends*. New York: Norton, 2002.
Bukharin, Nikolai. *Historical Materialism: A System of Sociology*, intro. Alfred G. Meyer. 1925. Ann Arbor: University of Michigan Press, 1969.
Bunge, Mario. "What Is Chance?" *Science and Society* (Winter 1951): 209–231.
Burdick, Eugene, and Harvey Wheeler. *Fail-Safe*. 1962. New York: Harper Perennial, 1999.
Burke, William. "The Resistance of John A. Williams: *The Man Who Cried I Am*," *Critique* 15.3 (1973): 5–14.
Burn, Stephen J. "An Interview with Richard Powers," *Contemporary Literature* 49.2 (Summer 2008): 163–179.
Burroughs, William S. "The Cut Up Method of Brion Gysin," in *A Casebook on the Beat*, ed. Thomas Parkinson. New York: Thomas Crowell, 1961.

———. "Deposition: Testimony Concerning a Sickness," in *Naked Lunch*. 1959. New York: Grove Press, 1990.

———. *Naked Lunch*. 1959. New York: Grove Press, 1990.

———. "On Coincidence," *The Adding Machine: Selected Essays*. New York: Arcade, 1986.

———. "Origin and Theory of the Tape Cut-Ups," *Break Through in Grey Room* (Sub Rosa CD006-8).

Butler, Christopher. *After the Wake: An Essay on the Contemporary Avant-Garde*. Oxford: Clarendon Press, 1980.

Cahill, Daniel. "An Interview with Jerzy Kosinski on *Blind Date*," *Contemporary Literature* 19.2 (Spring 1978): 133–142.

Cahill, James Leo. "How It Feels to be Run Over: Early Film Accidents," *Discourse* 30.3 (Fall 2008): 289–316.

Calihman, Matthew. "Black Power beyond Black Nationalism: John A. Williams, Cultural Pluralism, and the Popular Front," *MELUS* 34.1 (Spring 2009): 139–162.

Campbell, Jr., John W. "Game Theory," *Astounding Science Fiction* (September 1955): 5–7; 160–162.

Carruthers, Susan L. *Cold War Captives: Imprisonment, Escape, and Brainwashing*. Berkeley: University of California Press, 2009.

Caute, David. *Politics and the Novel during the Cold War*. Piscataway, N.J.: Transactions Publishers, Rutgers, 2009.

Celmer, Paul. "Pynchon's *V.* and the Rhetoric of the Cold War," *Pynchon Notes* 32–3 (Spring–Fall 1993): 5–32.

Chappell, V. C. "Rev. of *The Chance Character of Human Existence*," *Review of Metaphysics* (September 1956): 173.

Charters, Ann. *Kerouac: A Biography*. 1973. New York: St. Martin's, 1994.

Chen, Tina. *Double Agency: Acts of Impersonation in Asian American Literature and Culture*. Stanford, Calif.: Stanford University Press, 2005.

Chester, Alfred, and Vilma Howard. "The Art of Fiction: An Interview," *Paris Review* (Spring 1955), reprinted in Maryemma Graham and Amritjit Singh, *Conversations with Ralph Ellison*. Jackson: University of Mississippi Press, 1995.

Choi, Susan. *The Foreign Student*. New York: Harper Perennial, 1999.

Cimbala, Stephen J. *Nuclear War and Nuclear Strategy: Unfinished Business*. New York: Greenwood, 1987.

Clark, Suzanne. *Cold Warriors: Manliness on Trial in the Rhetoric of the West*. Carbondale: Southern Illinois University Press, 2000.

Cohen, G. A. *Karl Marx's Theory of History: A Defence*. 1978. Princeton, N.J.: Princeton University Press, 2000.

Cohen, Samuel. *After the End of History: American Fiction in the 1990s*. Iowa City: University of Iowa Press, 2009.

Comfort, Ray. Introduction to Charles Darwin. *The Origin of Species: 150th Anniversary Edition*. Alachua, Fla.: Bridge-Logos Foundation, 2009.

Conte, Joseph M. *Design and Debris: A Chaotics of Postmodern American Fiction*. Tuscaloosa: University of Alabama Press, 2002.

Cooley, Ronald. "The Hothouse or the Street: Imperialism and Narrative in Pynchon's *V.*" *Modern Fiction Studies* 39.2 (Summer 1993): 307–325.

Cooper, Brian, and Margueritte Murphy. "Taking Chances: Speculation and Games of Detection in Dashiell Hammett's *Red Harvest*," *Mosaic* 33.1 (March 2000): 145–160.

Coover, Robert. *The Public Burning*. New York: Viking, 1977.

———. "The Second Son," *Evergreen Review* 31 (October–November 1963): 72–88.

———. *The Universal Baseball Association, Inc., J. Henry Waugh, Prop*. New York: Plume, 1968.

Corber, Robert J. *Homosexuality in Cold War America: Resistance and the Crisis of Masculinity*. Durham, N.C.: Duke University Press, 1997.

Cornis-Pope, Marcel. *Narrative Innovation and Cultural Rewriting in the Cold War Era and After*. New York: Palgrave, 2001.

Cortázar, Julio. *Hopscotch*, trans. Gregory Rabasa. 1963. New York: Pantheon, 1987.

Cory, Donald Webster. *The Homosexual in America: A Subjective Approach*. New York: Greenberg, 1957.
Crowley, Denis. "'Before the Oven': Aesthetics and Politics in *Gravity's Rainbow*," *Pynchon Notes* 42–43 (1998): 181–198.
Cull, Nicholas J. *The Cold War and the United States Information Agency: American Propaganda and Public Diplomacy, 1945–1989*. Cambridge: Cambridge University Press, 2008.
Culler, Jonathan. "The Call of the Phoneme: Introduction," in *On Puns: The Foundation of Letters*, ed. Culler. Oxford: Basil Blackwell, 1988.
Daston, Lorraine. *Classical Probability in the Enlightenment*. Princeton, N.J.: Princeton University Press, 1988.
Davis, Arthur. "*The Outsider* as a Novel of Race," *Midwest Journal* 7 (1955): 320–326.
Dawahare, Anthony. *Nationalism, Marxism, and African American Literature between the Wars: A New Pandora's Box*. Jackson: University of Mississippi Press, 2003.
de la Durantaye, Leland. *Style is Matter: The Moral Art of Vladimir Nabokov*. Ithaca, NY: Cornell University Press, 2007.
———. "Vladimir Nabokov and Sigmund Freud, or a Particular Problem," *American Imago* 62.1 (Spring 2005): 59–73.
De Ley, Herbert. "The Name of the Game: Applying Game Theory in Literature," *SubStance* 17.1 (1988): 33–46.
DeLillo, Don. *End Zone*. Boston: Houghton Mifflin, 1972.
———. *Libra*. New York: Viking, 1988.
———. *The Names*. New York: Vintage, 1982.
———. *Underworld*. New York: Scribner, 1997.
Demby, William. *Beetlecreek*. 1950. Jackson: Banner Books/University Press of Mississippi, 1998.
"Deplorable but not Political," *New York Times* (November 30, 1946): 12.
Dezeuze, Anna. "Origins of the Fluxus Score: From Indeterminacy to 'Do-It-Yourself' Artwork," in *Chance*, ed. Margaret Iversen. Boston, Mass.: MIT Press, 2010.
Dick, Philip K. *Solar Lottery*. New York: Ace Book, 1955.
Dickstein, Morris. *Leopards in the Temple: The Transformation of American Fiction, 1945–1970*. Cambridge, Mass.: Harvard University Press, 2002.
Didion, Joan. *A Book of Common Prayer*. 1977. New York: Vintage, 1995.
———. *Democracy*. 1984. New York: Vintage, 1995.
———. *The Last Thing He Wanted*. 1996. New York: Vintage, 1997.
Disch, Thomas M. "Toward the Transcendent: An Introduction to *Solar Lottery* and Other Works," in *Philip K. Dick*, ed. Martin Harry Greenberg and Joseph Olander. New York: Taplinger Publishing Company, 1983.
Douglas, Ann. "Periodizing the American Century: Modernism, Postmodernism, and Postcolonialism in the Cold War Context," *Modernism/Modernity* 5.3 (September 1998): 71–98.
———. "'Telepathic Shock and Meaning Excitement': Kerouac's Poetics of Intimacy," *College Literature* 27.1 (Winter 2000): 8–21.
Dr. Strangelove, or: How I Stopped Worrying and Learned to Love the Bomb, DVD, directed by Stanley Kubrick. 1964. Sony Pictures, 2001.
Dragunoiu, Dana. "Vladimir Nabokov's *Ada*: Art, Deception, Ethics," *Contemporary Literature* 46.2 (Summer 2005): 311–339.
Dudziak, Mary L. *Cold War Civil Rights: Race and the Image of American Democracy*. Princeton, N.J.: Princeton University Press, 2000.
Edelman, Lee. "Tearooms and Sympathy, or, The Epistemology of the Water Closet," in his *Homographesis: Essays in Gay Literary and Cultural Theory*. New York: Routledge, 1994.
Ehrmann, Jacques. "Homo Ludens Revisited," *Yale French Studies* 41 (1968): 31–57.
Ellison, Ralph. *Invisible Man*. 1952. New York: Vintage, 1995.
Engels, Friedrich. "Ludwig Feuerbach and the End of Classical German Philosophy," in *Karl Marx and Friedrich Engels on Religion*. New York: Schocken Books, 1964.
Engerman, David. *Know Your Enemy: The Rise and Fall of America's Soviet Experts*. Oxford: Oxford University Press, 2009.
Evans, Richard. *In Defense of History*. New York: Norton, 2000.
Fabre, Michel. *The Unfinished Quest of Richard Wright*. New York: Morrow, 1973.

Fail-Safe, DVD, directed by Sidney Lumet. 1964. Sony Pictures, 2000.
Fainsod, Merle. *How Russia is Ruled*. Cambridge, Mass.: Harvard University Press, 1953.
Field, Andrew. *Nabokov, His Life in Art: A Critical Narrative*. Boston: Little, Brown, 1967.
Foley, Barbara. "From Communism to Brotherhood: The Drafts of *Invisible Man*," in *Left of the Color Line: Race, Radicalism, and Twentieth-Century Literature of the United States*, ed. Bill V. Mullen and James Smethurst. Chapel Hill: University of North Carolina Press, 2003.
———. "Ralph Ellison, Intertextuality, and Biographical Criticism: An Answer to Brian Roberts," *JNT: Journal of Narrative Theory* 34.2 (Summer 2004): 229–257.
———. "The Rhetoric of Anticommunism in *Invisible Man*," *College English* 59.5 (September 1997): 530–547.
Foust, Ronald E. "The Rules of the Game: A Para-Theory of Literary Theories," *South Central Review* 3.4 (Winter 1986): 5–14.
Frazier, E. Franklin. *Black Bourgeoisie*. 1957. New York: Free Press, 1997.
Frazier, Valerie. "Domestic Epic Warfare in *Maud Martha*," *African American Review* 39.1–2 (Spring–Summer 2005): 133–141.
Friedman, Andrea. "The Smearing of Joe McCarthy: The Lavender Scare, Gossip, and Cold War Politics," *American Quarterly* 57 (December 2005): 1105–1129.
Friedman, Saul. "The RAND Corporation and our Policy Makers," *Atlantic Monthly* (September 1963): 61–68.
Furnas, J. C. "The Fight Over Fluoridation," *The Saturday Evening Post* (May 19, 1956): 37+.
Gaddis, William. *The Recognitions*. 1955. New York: Penguin, 1993.
Gaines, Kevin. "E. Franklin Frazier's Revenge: Anticolonialism, Nonalignment, and Black Intellectuals' Critiques of Western Culture," *American Literary History* 17.3 (Fall 2005): 506–529.
"Games of Survival," *Newsweek* (May 18, 1953): 75.
Gates, Jr., Henry Louis. *The Signifying Monkey: A Theory of African-American Literary Criticism*. New York: Oxford University Press, 1988.
Ghamari-Tabrizi, Sharon. *The Worlds of Herman Kahn: The Intuitive Science of Thermonuclear War*. Cambridge, Mass.: Harvard University Press, 2005.
Gigerenzer, Gerd, et al. *The Empire of Chance: How Probability Changed Science and Everyday Life*. Cambridge: Cambridge University Press, 1989.
Gilroy, Paul. *The Black Atlantic: Modernity and Double Consciousness*. Cambridge, Mass.: Harvard University Press, 1993.
Goldhammer, Herbert, and Hans Speier, "Some Observations on Political Gaming," *World Politics* 12.1 (October 1959): 71–83.
González, Jesús Ángel. "'Happy Accidents': An Interview with Paul Auster," *Literature/Film Quarterly* 37.1 (2009): 18–27.
Gornick, Vivian. *The Romance of American Communism*. New York: Basic Books, 1977.
Grausam, Daniel. "'It is only a statement of the power of what comes after': Atomic Nostalgia, the 1990s, and the Ends of Postmodernism," in press.
———. *On Endings: American Postmodern Fiction and the Cold War*. Charlottesville: University of Virginia Press, 2011.
Green, Geoffrey. *Freud and Nabokov*. Lincoln: University of Nebraska Press, 1988.
Grinnell, George. "Exchanging Ghosts: Haunting, History, and Communism in *Native Son*," *English Studies in Canada* 30.3 (September 2004): 145–174.
Gross, Alfred. *Strangers in Our Midst: Problems of the Homosexual in American Society*. Washington, D.C.: Public Affairs Press, 1962.
Gross, Theodore L. "Ann Petry: The Novelist as Social Critic," in *Black Fiction: New Studies in the Afro-American Novel since 1945*, ed. A. Robert Lee. London: Vision, 1980.
Grossman, Lev. "The Gay Nabokov," *Salon.com*. May 17, 2000. Accessed December 20, 2010.
Grow, Michael. *U.S. Presidents and Latin American Interventions: Pursuing Regime Change in the Cold War*. Lawrence: University of Kansas Press, 2008.
Hacking, Ian. *The Taming of Chance*. Cambridge: Cambridge University Press, 1990.
Hamilton, Ross. *Accident: A Philosophical and Literary History*. Chicago: University of Chicago Press, 2007.

Hammond, Andrew. "From Rhetoric to Rollback: Introductory Thoughts on Cold War Writing," in *Cold War Literature*, ed. Hammond.

Hammond, Andrew, ed. *Cold War Literature*, vol. 2, *Western, Eastern and Postcolonial Perspectives*. New York: Routledge, forthcoming.

———. *Cold War Literature: Writing the Global Conflict*. New York: Routledge, 2005.

Handlin, Oscar. *Chance or Destiny: Turning Points in American History*. Boston, Mass.: Little, Brown, 1955.

Handy, Rollo. "Rev. of *The Chance Character of Human Existence*," *Philosophy and Phenomenological Research* (March 1957): 421–422.

Hansen, Arlen. "The Dice of God: Einstein, Heisenberg, and Robert Coover," *Novel* 10.1 (Autumn 1976): 49–58.

Harrington, John. "The Concept of Chance and Divine Providence," *Proceedings of the American Catholic Philosophical Association* 28 (1954): 176–183.

Hassan, Ihab. *The Postmodern Turn: Essays in Postmodern Theory and Culture*. Columbus: Ohio State University Press, 1987.

Hawkes, John. *Travesty*. New York: New Directions, 1976.

Hayles, N. Katherine. "Chance Operations: Cagean Paradox and Contemporary Science," in *John Cage: Composed in America*, ed. Marjorie Perloff and Charles Junkerman. Chicago: University of Chicago Press, 1994.

———. *Chaos Bound: Orderly Disorder in Contemporary Literature and Science*. Ithaca, N.Y.: Cornell University Press, 1990.

Hayles, N. Katherine, ed. *Chaos and Order: Complex Dynamics in Literature and Science*. Chicago: University of Chicago Press, 1991.

Hechter, Michael. "On the Inadequacy of Game Theory for the Solution of Real-World Collective Action Problems," in *The Limits of Rationality*, ed. Karen Schweers Cook and Margaret Levi. Chicago: University of Chicago Press, 1990.

Henriksen, Margot. *Dr. Strangelove's America: Society and Culture in the Atomic Age*. Berkeley: University of California Press, 1997.

Herman, Luc, and John M. Krafft, "From the Ground Up: The Evolution of the South-West Africa Chapter in Pynchon's *V.*" *Contemporary Literature* 47.2 (Summer 2006): 261–288.

Hertz, Richard. *Chance and Symbol*. Chicago: University of Chicago Press, 1948.

Himes, Chester. *If He Hollers Let Him Go*. 1945. New York: Thunder's Mouth Press, 1986.

———. *Lonely Crusade*. 1947. New York: Thunder's Mouth Press, 1997.

Hinds, Lynn Boyd, and Theodore Otto Windt, Jr. *The Cold War as Rhetoric: The Beginnings, 1945–1950*. New York: Praeger, 1991.

Hite, Molly. *Ideas of Order in the Novels of Thomas Pynchon*. Columbus: Ohio State University Press, 1983.

Hoberek, Andrew. *The Twilight of the Middle Class: Post-World War II American Fiction and White-Collar Work*. Princeton, N.J.: Princeton University Press, 2005.

Hobson, Christopher Z. "Richard Wright's Communisms: Textual Variance, Intentionality, and Socialization in *American Hunger*, 'I Tried to Be a Communist,' and *The God That Failed*," *Text* 6 (1994): 307–344.

Hoeveler, Diane Long. "Game Theory and Ellison's King of the Bingo Game," *Journal of American Culture* 15.2 (Summer 1992): 39–42.

Holton, Robert. "In the Rathouse of History with Thomas Pynchon: Rereading *V.*" *Textual Practice* 2.3 (Winter 1988): 324–344.

Hook, Sidney. *The Hero in History: A Study in Limitation and Possibility*. New York: John Day, 1943.

———. "Introduction," in *Determinism and Freedom in the Age of Modern Science*, ed. Sidney Hook. New York: New York University Press, 1958.

Horkheimer, Max, and Theodor Adorno. *Dialectic of Enlightenment*, ed. Gunzelin Schmid Noerr and trans. Edmund Jephcott. Stanford, Calif.: Stanford University Press, 2002.

Horne, Gerald. *Black and Red: W. E. B. Du Bois and the Afro-American Response to the Cold War, 1944–1963*. Albany: SUNY Press, 1986.

Hottelet, Richard. "From Collective to Kremlin, It's One Big State of Nerves," *New York Times* (May 22, 1960): BR3.

Hounshell, David. "The Cold War, RAND, and the Generation of Knowledge, 1946–1962," *Historical Studies in the Physical and Biological Sciences* 27.2 (1997): 237–267.

Huang, Betsy. "Citizen Kwang: Chang-rae Lee's *Native Speaker* and the Politics of Consent," *Journal of Asian American Studies* 9.3 (October 2006): 243–269.

Hungerford, Amy. *Postmodern Belief: American Literature and Religion since 1960*. Princeton, N.J.: Princeton University Press, 2010.

Hurwicz, Leonid. "Game Theory and Decisions," *Scientific American* (February 1955): 78–83.

Hutcheon, Linda. "Beginning to Theorize the Postmodern," in *A Postmodern Reader*, ed. Joseph Natoli and Linda Hutcheon. 1987. Albany: SUNY Press, 1993.

Hutchinson, Stuart. "DeLillo's *Libra* and the Real," *Cambridge Quarterly* 30.2 (2001): 117–131.

Ikard, David. *Breaking the Silence: Toward a Black Male Feminist Criticism*. Baton Rouge: Louisiana State University Press, 2007.

Iversen, Margaret. "The Aesthetics of Chance," in *Chance*, ed. and intro, Iversen. Cambridge, Mass.: MIT Press, 2010.

Jackson, Lawrence. *Ralph Ellison: Emergence of a Genius*. Athens: University of Georgia Press, 2007.

Jackson, Tony. "Postmodernism, Narrative, and the Cold War Sense of an Ending," *Narrative* 8.3 (October 2000): 324–338.

Jacobson, Matthew Frye, and Gaspar González. *What Have They Built You to Do? The Manchurian Candidate and Cold War America*. Minneapolis: University of Minnesota Press, 2006.

James, Alison. "Automatism, Arbitrariness, and the Oulipian Author," *French Forum* 31.2 (Spring 2006): 111–125.

———. *Constraining Chance: Georges Perec and the Oulipo*. Evanston, Ill.: Northwestern University Press, 2009.

James, Henry. *The Ambassadors*. Ed. and Intro. Leon Edel. 1903. Boston: Houghton Mifflin, 1960.

"Japanese Scientist Said Today that Soviet Nuclear Tests Last Month had been Carried out at Novaya Zemlya Island in the Arctic Ocean," *New York Times* (March 9, 1958): 41.

Jarrell, Randall. *Pictures from an Institution*. New York: Farrar, Straus and Giroux, 1954.

Jervis, Robert. *The Illogic of American Nuclear Strategy*. Ithaca, N.Y.: Cornell University Press, 1984.

Johns, Gillian. "Reading for the Comic and the Tragic in Modern Black Fiction; or, Reflections on Richard Wright's Change of Heart from *Lawd Today!* to *Native Son*," *CLA Journal* 49. 3 (March 2006): 249–282.

Johnson, B. S. *The Unfortunates*. London: Secker & Warburg, 1969.

Johnson, David K. *The Lavender Scare: The Cold War Persecution of Gays and Lesbians in the Federal Government*. Chicago: University of Chicago Press, 2004.

Johnston, John. *Carnival of Repetition: Gaddis's The Recognitions and Postmodern Theory*. Philadelphia: University of Pennsylvania Press, 1990.

Jorden, William. "Russians Report 10% Output Rise during Overhaul," *New York Times* (December 20, 1957): 1.

———. "Soviet Science Aide Says Country Still Does Not Lead U.S.," *New York Times* (December 20, 1957): 1.

Kaag, John. "Chance and Creativity: The Nature of Contingency in Classical American Philosophy," *Transactions of the Charles S. Peirce Society* 44.3 (Summer 2008): 393–411.

Kahn, Herman. *On Thermonuclear War*, 2d ed. Princeton, N.J.: Princeton University Press, 1961.

Kakutani, Michiko. "Pynchon Hits the Road with Mason and Dixon," *New York Times* (April 29, 1997): C11.

Kamenish, Paula K. "New Applications of Game Theory: Genet's 'Prisoner's Dilemma,'" *Cincinnati Romance Review* 15 (1996): 184–191.

Kaplan, Amy. "'Left Alone with America': The Absence of Empire in the Study of American Culture," in *Cultures of United States Imperialism*, ed. Amy Kaplan and Donald Pease. Durham, N.C.: Duke University Press, 1993.

Kaplan, Fred. "Truth Stranger than 'Strangelove,'" *New York Times* (October 10, 2004): AR21.

———. *The Wizards of Armageddon*. Stanford, Calif.: Stanford University Press, 1991.

Kaplan, Morton. "Introduction," in *Strategic Thinking and Its Moral Implications*, ed. Morton Kaplan. Chicago: University of Chicago Center for Policy Study, 1973.

Kavanagh, Thomas, ed. *Chance, Culture and the Literary Text, Michigan Romance Studies* 14 (1994).

Keenaghan, Eric. *Queering Cold War Poetry: Ethics of Vulnerability in Cuba and the United States.* Columbus: Ohio State University Press, 2009.

Kercher, Stephen E. *Revel with a Cause: Liberal Satire in Postwar America.* Chicago: University of Chicago Press, 2006.

Kermode, Frank. *The Sense of an Ending: Studies in the Theory of Fiction with a New Epilogue.* Oxford: Oxford University Press, 2000.

———. "Zemblances," *The New Statesman* (November 9, 1962): 671–672.

Kerouac, Jack. *The Subterraneans.* New York: Grove, 1958.

Kharpertian, Theodore. *A Hand to Turn the Time: The Menippean Satires of Thomas Pynchon.* Madison, N.J.: Fairleigh Dickinson University Press, 1990.

Khrushcheva, Nina L. *Imagining Nabokov: Russia between Art and Politics.* New Haven, Conn.: Yale University Press, 2008.

Killens, John O. *Youngblood.* 1954. New York: Trident Books, 1966.

Kim, Daniel. "Do I, Too, Sing America?: Vernacular Representations and Chang-rae Lee's *Native Speaker*," *Journal of Asian American Studies* 6.3 (2003): 231–260.

Kim, Jodi. *Ends of Empire: Asian American Critique and the Cold War.* Minneapolis: University of Minnesota Press, 2010.

———. "From *Mee-gook* to Gook: The Cold War and Racialized Undocumented Capital in Chang-rae Lee's *Native Speaker*," *MELUS* 34.1 (Spring 2009): 117–137.

Kinchy, Abby. "African Americans in the Atomic Age: Postwar Perspectives on Race and the Bomb, 1945–1967," *Technology and Culture* 50.2 (April 2009): 291–315.

Klein, Christina. *Cold War Orientalism: Asia in the Middlebrow Imagination, 1945–1961.* Berkeley: University of California Press, 2003.

Klein, Richard, and William B. Warner. "Nuclear Coincidence and the Korean Airline Disaster," *Diacritics* 16. 1 (Spring 1986): 2–21.

Knight, Peter. "Everything is Connected: *Underworld*'s Secret History of Paranoia," *Modern Fiction Studies* 45.3 (Fall 1999): 811–836.

Kosinski, Jerzy. *Blind Date.* Boston: Houghton Mifflin Company, 1977.

Kraft, Joseph. "RAND: Arsenal for Ideas," *Harpers* (July 1960): 69–76.

Kramish, Arnold. *Atomic Energy in the Soviet Union.* Stanford, Calif.: Stanford University Press, 1959.

Krieger, Leonard. "Marx and Engels as Historians," *Journal of the History of Ideas* 14.3 (June 1953): 381–403.

Kuhn, H. W., and A. W. Tucker, "Preface," *Contributions to the Theory of Games*, Vol. II. Princeton, N.J.: Princeton University Press, 1953.

Langman, Larry. *Encyclopedia of American Film Comedy.* New York: Garland, 1987.

Lardner, Rex. "How to Make a Sucker Out of Your Opponent," *New York Times* (August 27, 1950): BR2.

Lathrop, Kathleen. "Comic-Ironic Parallels in William Gaddis's *The Recognitions*," *The Review of Contemporary Fiction* 2 (Summer 1982): 32–40.

Lears, Jackson. *Something for Nothing: Luck in America.* New York: Viking, 2003.

LeCarré, John. *The Spy Who Came in from the Cold.* New York: Dell, 1963.

Lee, Chang-rae. *Native Speaker.* New York: Riverhead, 1995.

Leites, Nathan. *A Study of Bolshevism.* Glencoe, Ill.: Free Press, 1953.

Lentricchia, Frank. "*Libra* as Postmodern Critique," *South Atlantic Quarterly* 89 (Spring 1990): 431–453.

Leonard, Robert J. "Creating a Context for Game Theory," in *Toward a History of Game Theory*, ed. E. Roy Weintraub. Durham, N.C.: Duke University Press, 1992.

———. *Von Neumann, Morgenstern, and the Creation of Game Theory: From Chess to Social Science, 1900–1960.* Cambridge: Cambridge University Press, 2010.

Lestienne, Rémy. *The Creative Power of Chance*, trans. E. C. Neher. Urbana: University of Illinois Press, 1998.

Lethem, Jonathan. *Amnesia Moon.* New York: Harvest, 1995.

Lewis, Barry. "Postmodernism and Fiction," in *The Routledge Companion to Postmodernism*, ed. Stuart Sim. London: Routledge, 2005.

Liggins, Saundra. "The Urban Gothic Vision of Colson Whitehead's *The Intuitionist*," *African American Review* 40.2 (Summer 2006): 358–369.

Lissner, Will. "Mathematical Theory of Poker Is Applied to Business Problems," *New York Times* (March 10, 1946): 1.
Lodge, David. *The Art of Fiction*. London: Secker & Warburg, 1992.
Luce, Duncan R., and Howard Raïffa. *Games and Decisions: Introduction and Critical Survey*. New York: John Wiley & Sons, Inc., 1957.
Lucretius, *The Nature of Things*. Trans. Frank O. Copley. New York: Norton, 1977.
Lukas, J. Anthony. "Class Reunion: Kennedy's Men Relive the Cuban Missile Crisis," *New York Times* (August 30, 1987): SM22+.
Macdonald, Dwight. "The Now-Non-Conservatism, or Notes on a Career," in *Memoirs of a Revolutionist: Essays in Political Criticism*. 1952. New York: Farrar, Straus and Cudahy, 1957.
———. "Virtuosity Rewarded, or Dr. Kinbote's Revenge," *Partisan Review* 29 (Summer 1962): 437–442.
Maduka, Chidi. "Irony and Vision in Richard Wright's *The Outsider*," *Western Humanities Review* 38. 2 (Summer 1984): 161–169.
Maher, Paul. *Kerouac: The Definitive Biography*. New York: Taylor Trade, 2004.
Mailer, Norman. "The Homosexual Villain," in his *Advertisements for Myself*. 1959. Cambridge, Mass.: Harvard University Press, 1992.
Marcus, Stephen. "The American Negro in Search of an Identity," *Commentary* 56 (November 1953): 456–463.
Marcuse, Herbert. "Dialectic and Logic since the War," in *Continuity and Change in Russian and Soviet Thought*, ed. and intro. Ernest J. Simmons. Cambridge, Mass.: Harvard University Press, 1955.
———. *Soviet Marxism: A Critical Analysis*. New York: Columbia University Press, 1958.
Markson, David. *This Is Not a Novel*. Berkeley: Counterpoint, 2001.
Mathews, Harry. *My Life in CIA: A Memoir of 1973*. Normal, Ill.: Dalkey Archive Press, 2005.
Mathews, Harry, and Alastair Brotchie, ed. *Oulipo Compendium*, rev. ed. Los Angeles: Make Now Press, 2005.
Mattessich, Stephan. *Lines of Flight: Discursive Time and Countercultural Desire in the Work of Thomas Pynchon*. Durham, N.C.: Duke University Press, 2002.
Matthews, Kristin L. "The ABCs of *Mad* Magazine: Reading, Citizenship, and Cold War America," *International Journal of Comic Art* 8.2 (Fall 2006): 248–268.
Maxwell, William. *New Negro, Old Left: African-American Writing and Communism between the Wars*. New York: Columbia University Press, 1999.
May, Elaine Tyler. *Homeward Bound: American Families in the Cold War Era*. New York: Basic Books, 1988.
McCaffery, Larry. *The Metafictional Muse: The Works of Robert Coover, Donald Barthelme, and William H. Gass*. Pittsburgh, Penn.: University of Pittsburgh Press, 1982.
McCaffery, Larry, and Sinda Gregory, "An Interview with Paul Auster," *Contemporary Literature* 33.1 (Spring 1992): 1–23.
McCann, Sean. *A Pinnacle of Feeling: American Literature and Presidential Government*. Princeton, N.J.: Princeton University Press, 2008.
McCann, Sean, and Michael Szalay. "Do You Believe in Magic? Literary Thinking after the New Left," *Yale Journal of Criticism* 18.2 (Fall 2005): 435–468.
———. "Eerie Serenity: A Response to John McClure," *boundary 2*, 36.2. (Summer 2009): 145–153.
McCarthy, Mary. "A Bolt from the Blue," in her *The Writing on the Wall and Other Literary Essays*. New York: Harcourt, 1970.
McClintock, Anne. "Paranoid Empire: Specters from Guantánamo and Abu Ghraib," *Small Axe* 28, 13.1 (March 2009): 50–74.
McClure, John A. "Do They Believe in Magic? Politics and Postmodern Literature," *boundary 2*, 36.2 (Summer 2009): 125–143.
———. *Partial Faiths: Postsecular Fiction in the Age of Pynchon and Morrison*. Athens: University of Georgia Press, 2007.
McDonald, John. "Secret Weapon: Theory of Games," *Science Digest* (December 1950): 7–11.
———. *Strategy in Poker, Business, and War*. New York: Norton, 1950.
———. "A Theory of Strategy," *Fortune* (June 1949): 100–110.
———. "War of Wits," *Fortune* (March 1951): 99–157.

McGurl, Mark. *The Program Era: Postwar Fiction and the Rise of Creative Writing.* Cambridge, Mass.: Harvard University Press, 2009.
McKinsey, J. C. C. *Introduction to the Theory of Games.* New York: McGraw-Hill, 1952.
McNeil, Donald R. *The Fight for Fluoridation.* New York: Oxford University Press, 1957.
Mead, Margaret. *Soviet Attitudes toward Authority: An Interdisciplinary Approach to Problems of Soviet Character.* 1951. New York: William Morrow & Co., Inc., 1955.
Mearsheimer, John. "Why We Will Soon Miss the Cold War" *Atlantic Monthly* 266.2 (August 1990): 35–50.
Medhurst, Martin, et al. *Cold War Rhetoric: Strategy, Metaphor, and Ideology.* East Lansing: Michigan State University Press, 1997.
Medovoi, Leerom. "Cold War American Culture as the Age of Three Worlds," *Minnesota Review* 55–27 (2002): 167–186.
———. *Rebels: Youth and the Cold War Origins of Identity.* Durham, N.C.: Duke University Press, 2005.
Melley, Timothy. *Empire of Conspiracy: The Culture of Paranoia in Postwar America.* Ithaca, N.Y.: Cornell University Press, 2000.
Mendell, David. "Obama Would Consider Missile Strikes on Iran," *Chicago Tribune* (September 25, 2004).
Meriwether, James. *Proudly We Can Be Africans: Black Americans and Africa, 1935–1961.* Chapel Hill: University of North Carolina Press, 2002.
Meyer, Alfred G. *Leninism.* Cambridge, Mass.: Harvard University Press, 1957.
Meyer, Priscilla. *Find What the Sailor has Hidden: Vladimir Nabokov's* Pale Fire. Middletown, Conn.: Wesleyan University Press, 1988.
Milesi, Laurent. "Postmodern Ana-Apocalyptics: Pynchon's V-Effect and the End (of Our Century)," *Pynchon Notes* 42–43 (1998): 213–243.
Miller, D. A. "Secret Subjects, Open Secrets," in his *The Novel and the Police.* Berkeley: University of California Press, 1988.
Mirowski, Philip. "When Games Grow Deadly Serious: The Military Influence on the Evolution of Game Theory," in *Economics and National Security: A History of Their Interaction,* ed. Craufurd D. W. Goodwin. Durham, N.C.: Duke University Press, 1991.
Monk, Leland. *Standard Deviations: Chance and the Modern British Novel.* Stanford, Calif.: Stanford University Press, 1993.
Monod, Jacques. *Chance and Necessity: An Essay on the Natural Philosophy of Modern Biology,* trans. Austryn Wainhouse. New York: Knopf, 1971.
Moore, Steven. *William Gaddis.* New York: Twayne, 1989.
Morgenstern, Oskar. *The Question of National Defense,* 2d rev. ed. New York: Vintage Books, 1961.
Morson, Gary Saul. *Narrative and Freedom: The Shadows of Time.* New Haven, Conn.: Yale University Press, 1994.
Mosley, Nicholas. *Accident.* 1965. Elmwood Park, Ill.: Dalkey Archive Press, 1985.
Motley, Willard. *Knock on Any Door.* New York: Appleton-Century, 1947.
Mottram, Eric. "'Eleusions Truths': Harry Mathews's Strategies and Games," *Review of Contemporary Fiction* 7.3 (Fall 1987): 154–172.
Movius, Geoffrey. "A Conversation with Jerzy Kosinski," *New Boston Review* (Winter 1975): 3–6.
Nabokov, Vladimir. *Ada; or Ardor: A Family Chronicle.* New York: McGraw-Hill, 1969.
———. *The Annotated Lolita.* Revised and Updated. 1955. Ed. Alfred Appel, Jr. New York: Vintage, 1991.
———. *Pale Fire.* 1962. New York: Knopf, 1992.
———. *Pnin.* 1957. New York: Vintage, 1989.
———. *Speak, Memory: An Autobiography Revisited.* New York: Putnam, 1966.
———. *Strong Opinions.* 1973. New York: Vintage, 1990.
Nadel, Alan. *Containment Culture: American Narratives, Postmodernism, and the Atomic Age.* Durham, N.C.: Duke University Press, 1995.
———. *Invisible Criticism: Ralph Ellison and the American Canon.* Iowa City: University of Iowa Press, 1988.
Neff, Heather. *Accident of Birth.* New York: Harlem Moon/Broadway Books, 2004.
"New Soviet Tests of Atom Weapons Disclosed by U.S.," *New York Times* (November 8, 1958): 1.

Newman, James R. "A Moral Tract on Mass Murder," *Washington Post* (February 26, 1961): E7.
———. "Two Discussions of Thermonuclear War," *Scientific American* (March 1961): 197–198+.
Nolan, William A. *Communism Versus the Negro*. Chicago: Henry Regnery Company, 1951.
Noon, David. "Operation Enduring Analogy: World War II, the War on Terror, and the Uses of Historical Memory," *Rhetoric and Public Affairs* 7 (Fall 2004): 339–365.
Novak, Joseph. *The Future Is Ours, Comrade*. 1960. New York: Dutton, 1964.
———. *No Third Path*. Garden City, N.Y.: Double Day, 1962.
O'Connor, Flannery. *The Complete Stories*. New York: Farrar, Straus and Giroux, 1971.
———. *Mystery and Manners*, ed. Sally and Robert Fitzgerald. New York: Farrar, Straus and Giroux, 1962.
Okada, John. *No-No Boy*. 1957. Seattle: University of Washington Press, 1978.
Olderman, Raymond. *Beyond the Waste Land: A Study of the American Novel in the 1960s*. New Haven, Conn.: Yale University Press, 1972.
Olsen, Lance. "Stand by to Crash! Avant-pop, Hypertextuality, and Postmodern Comic Vision in Coover's *The Public Burning*," *Critique* 42.1 (Fall 2000): 51–68.
Olster, Stacey. *Reminiscence and Re-Creation in Contemporary American Fiction*. New York: Cambridge University Press, 1989.
O'Rand, Angela. "Mathematizing Social Science in the 1950s: The Early Development and Diffusion of Game Theory," in *Toward a History of Game Theory*, ed. E. Roy Weintraub. Durham, N.C.: Duke University Press, 1992.
Osborne, Virginia. "'Let's Go to the Woods, Boys': Reading *Deliverance* as a Cold War Novel," *James Dickey Newsletter* 24.2 (Spring 2008): 1–20.
Park, Hyungji. "The Immigrant as Spy," *American Book Review* 31.1 (November/December 2009): 7–8.
Paton, Fiona. "Beyond Bakhtin: Towards a Cultural Stylistics," *College English* 63.2 (November 2000): 166–193.
Paulson, William. "Chance, Complexity, and Narrative Explanation," *SubStance* 74 (1994): 5–21.
Pavel, Thomas. *Fictional Worlds*. Cambridge, Mass.: Harvard University Press, 1986.
Payne, Kenneth. "McCarthyism and Cold War America in Patricia Highsmith's *The Blunderer*," *McNeese Review* 41 (2003): 76–84.
Pease, Donald. *Visionary Compacts: American Renaissance Writings in Cultural Context*. Madison: University of Wisconsin Press, 1987.
Peirce, Charles S. *Selected Writings (Values in a Universe of Chance)*, ed. with intro. and notes by Philip P. Wiener. New York: Dover, 1966.
Petry, Ann. *The Narrows*. 1953. New York: Dafina Books, 2008.
Piette, Adam. *The Literary Cold War: 1945 to Vietnam*. Edinburgh: Edinburgh University Press, 2009.
Pitzer, Andrea. "Memory Speaks: History and Witnessing in Nabokov's *Pale Fire*," *Nabokov Studies*, forthcoming.
"Planned Chance," *Newsweek* (May 21, 1951): 58.
Platt, Anthony. *E. Franklin Frazier Reconsidered*. New Brunswick, N.J.: Rutgers University Press, 1991.
Plimpton, George. "The Whole Sick Crew," *New York Times* (April 21, 1963): BR3.
Plummer, Brenda Gayle. *Rising Wind: Black Americans and U.S. Foreign Affairs, 1935–1960*. Chapel Hill: University of North Carolina Press, 1996.
Poiger, Uta. *Jazz, Rock, and Rebels: Cold War Politics and American Culture in a Divided Germany*. Berkeley: University of California Press, 2000.
Pollard, William. *Chance and Providence*. New York: Scribner, 1958.
Popper, Karl. *The Open Universe: An Argument for Indeterminism*. 1956. Totowa, N.J.: Rowman and Littlefield, 1982.
———. *The Poverty of Historicism*. 1957. New York: Routledge, 2002.
Powers, Richard. *The Gold Bug Variations*. 1991. New York: Harper Perennial, 1992.
———. *Prisoner's Dilemma*. 1988. New York: Perennial, 2002.
Puskar, Jason. "Risking Ralph Ellison," *Daedalus* 138.2 (Spring 2009): 83–93.
Pynchon, Thomas. *Against the Day*. New York: Penguin, 2006.
———. *The Crying of Lot 49*. 1966. New York: Harper Perennial, 2006.

———. *Gravity's Rainbow*. 1973. New York: Penguin, 2006.
———. "Togetherness," *Aerospace Safety* (December 1960): 6–8.
———. *V.* 1963. New York: Harper Perennial, 2005.
Raney, David. "Culture of Contagion: Germs, Aliens, and American Identity," *Popular Culture Review* 14 (February 2003): 55–66.
Rapoport, Anatol. *Strategy and Conscience*. New York: Harper & Row, 1964.
———. "The Use and Misuse of Game Theory," *Scientific American* (December 1962): 108–118.
Raymond, Jack. "Pentagon Seeks an Extra Billion to Spur Weapons," *New York Times* (December 20, 1957): 1.
Rea, John. "And a Nearctic Zembla," *The Nabokovian* 42 (Spring 1999): 9–10.
Redding, Arthur. *Turncoats, Traitors, and Fellow Travelers: Culture and Politics of the Early Cold War*. Jackson: University Press of Mississippi, 2008.
Redfield, Marc. "Pynchon's Postmodern Sublime," *PMLA* 104.2 (March 1989): 152–162.
Reilly, John. "Thinking History in *The Man Who Cried I Am*," *Black American Literature Forum* 21. 1–2 (Spring–Summer 1987): 25–42.
Relyea, Sarah. *Outsider Citizens: The Remaking of Postwar Identity in Wright, Beauvoir, and Baldwin*. New York: Routledge, 2006.
———. "The Vanguard of Modernity: Richard Wright's *The Outsider*," *Texas Studies in Literature and Language* 48. 3 (Fall 2006): 187–219.
Richardson, Brian. *Unlikely Stories: Causality and the Nature of Modern Narrative*. Newark: University of Delaware Press, 1997.
Rigby, Sherman. "Tit for Tat," *New York Times* (January 3, 1965): SM 2; SM 4.
Rogin, Michael. "Kiss Me Deadly: Communism, Motherhood, and Cold War Movies," *Representations* 6 (1984): 1–36.
Roosevelt, Eleanor. "My Day" (December 20, 1957), archived at: http://www.gwu.edu/~erpapers/myday/displaydoc.cfm?_y=1957&_f=md003991>.
Roth, Phyllis. "The Psychology of the Double in Nabokov's *Pale Fire*," *Essays in Literature* 2 (1975): 209–229.
Roubaud, Jacques. "The Oulipo and Combinational Art," in *Oulipo Compendium*, ed. Harry Mathews and Alastair Brotchie. Los Angeles, Calif.: Make Now Press, 2005.
Rowley, Hazel. *Richard Wright: The Life and Times*. New York: Henry Holt, 2001.
Russell, Alison. "Recalibrating the Past: Colson Whitehead's *The Intuitionist*," *Critique* 49.1 (Fall 2007): 46–60.
Sampson, Harold. "An Investigation of the Relationship of Chance-Taking Behavior to Authoritarianism and Impulsivity." Ph.D. Diss., University of California, 1953.
Saporta, Marc. *Composition No. 1*, trans. Richard Howard. New York: Simon and Schuster, 1963.
Saunders, Frances Stonor. *The Cultural Cold War: The CIA and the World of Arts and Letters*. New York: New Press, 2000.
Savran, David. *Communists, Cowboys, and Queers: The Politics of Masculinity in the Work of Arthur Miller and Tennessee Williams*. Minneapolis: University of Minnesota Press, 1992.
Schaub, Thomas. *American Fiction in the Cold War*. Madison: University of Wisconsin Press, 1991.
———. *Pynchon: The Voice of Ambiguity*. Urbana: University of Illinois Press, 1981.
Scheer, Robert. *With Enough Shovels: Reagan, Bush and Nuclear War*. New York: Random House, 1982.
Schlesinger, Jr., Arthur. *The Vital Center: The Politics of Freedom*. Boston: Houghton Mifflin, 1949.
Schrecker, Ellen, ed. *Cold War Triumphalism: The Misuse of History after the Fall of Communism*. New York: The New Press, 2004.
Schreiber, Rebecca M. *Cold War Exiles in Mexico: U.S. Dissidents and the Culture of Critical Resistance*. Minneapolis: University of Minnesota Press, 2008.
Sell, Jonathan. "Chance and Gesture in Zadie Smith's *White Teeth* and *The Autograph Man*: A Model for Multicultural Identity?" *Journal of Commonwealth Literature* 41.3 (September 2006): 27–44.
Shapiro, Gavrilo. "Nova Zembla Revisited Once Again," *The Nabokovian* 26 (Spring 1991): 49–51.
Shaw, Lytle. "An Interview with Harry Mathews," *Chicago Review* (Spring 1997): 36–52.
Shepheard, David. "Nuclear Strategy/Nuclear Politics," *Paragraph* 9 (March 1987): 31–48.
Sherif, Ann. *Japan's Cold War: Media, Literature, and the Law*. New York: Columbia University Press, 2009.

Shiff, Stacy. *Véra (Mrs. Vladimir Nabokov)*. New York: Random House, 1999.
Shiloh, Ilana. "A Place Both Imaginary and Realistic: Paul Auster's *The Music of Chance*," *Contemporary Literature* 43.3 (Fall 2002): 488–517.
Shute, J. P. "Nabokov and Freud: The Play of Power," *Modern Fiction Studies* 30 (1984): 637–650.
Siegel, Greg. "The Accident is Uncontainable/The Accident Must Be Contained: High-Speed Cinematography and the Development of Scientific Crash Testing," *Discourse* 30.3 (Fall 2008): 348–372.
Silk Stockings, DVD, directed by Rouben Mamoulian. 1957. Warner Home Video, 2003.
Singh, Nikhil Pal. *Black Is a Country: Race and the Unfinished Struggle for Democracy*. Cambridge, Mass.: Harvard University Press, 2004.
———. "Cold War Redux: On the 'New Totalitarianism,'" *Radical History Review* 85 (Winter 2003): 171–181.
Sklyarenko, Alexey. "Addendum to '*Ada* as a Triple Dream,'" *The Nabokovian* 53 (Fall 2004): 22–24.
Sloan, James Park. *Jerzy Kosinski: A Biography*. New York: Dutton, 1996.
Smith, Bruce. *The RAND Corporation: Case Study of a Nonprofit Advisory Corporation*. Cambridge, Mass.: Harvard University Press, 1966.
Spanos, William. *The Errant Art of* Moby-Dick: *The Canon, the Cold War, and the Struggle for American Studies*. Durham, N.C.: Duke University Press, 1995.
Spiegel, Irving. "Facts on Shooting Sought by Byrnes," *New York Times* (November 25, 1946): 11.
Stearn, Jess. *The Sixth Man*. New York: Doubleday, 1961.
Stegner, Page. *Escape into Aesthetics: The Art of Vladimir Nabokov*. New York: Dial, 1966.
Sterne, Laurence. *The Life and Opinions of Tristram Shandy, Gentleman*, ed. Ian Watt. Boston: Houghton Mifflin, 1965.
Stevens, Jason W. *God-Fearing and Free: A Spiritual History of America's Cold War*. Cambridge, Mass.: Harvard University Press, 2010.
Swirski, Peter. "Game Theory in the Third Pentagon: A Study in Strategy and Rationality," *Criticism* (1996): 303–330.
———. "The Role of Game Theory in Literary Studies," in *Empirical Approaches to Literature*, ed. Gebhard Rusch. Siegen: LUMIS-Publications, 1994.
Szalay, Michael. *New Deal Modernism: American Literature and the Invention of the Welfare State*. Durham, N.C.: Duke University Press, 2000.
Tanner, Tony. *City of Words: American Fiction, 1950–1970*. New York: Harper, 1971.
———. *Thomas Pynchon*. New York: Methuen, 1982.
Taras, Ray. "Kosinski as Kremlinologist: Soviet Studies or Spoof?" *Polish Review* 49.1 (2004): 621–640.
Theobald, D. W. "Accident and Chance," *Philosophy* (April 1970): 106–113.
"Theory of Games," *Washington Post* (September 3, 1950): B7.
Tietchen, Todd. *The Cubalogues: Beat Writers in Revolutionary Havana*. Gainesville: University Press of Florida, 2010.
"Valuable Batch of Brains," *Life* (May 11, 1959): 101–107.
Vidal, Gore. *Dark Green, Bright Red*. New York: Dutton, 1950.
———. "In the Lair of the Octopus," in his *Dreaming War: Blood for Oil and the Cheney-Bush Junta*. New York: Thunder's Mouth Press, 2002.
Villa, Dana. "Genealogies of Total Domination: Arendt, Adorno, and Auschwitz," *New German Critique* (Winter 2007): 1–45.
Virilio, Paul. *The Original Accident*, trans. Julie Rose. Cambridge: Polity Press, 2007.
Vizenor, Gerald, ed. *Narrative Chance: Postmodern Discourse on Native American Indian Literatures*. Norman: University of Oklahoma Press, 1993.
Von Eschen, Penny. *Race Against Empire: Black Americans and Anticolonialism, 1937–1957*. Ithaca, N.Y.: Cornell University Press, 1997.
Von Neumann, John, and Oskar Morgenstern. *Theory of Games and Economic Behavior*. 1944. Princeton, N.J.: Princeton University Press, 1980.
Vonnegut, Kurt. *Player Piano*. 1952. New York: Dial Press, 1999.
W.K., "Poker in the Interest of Science," *New York Times* (February 1, 1953): E9.
Walker, David. "'The Viewer of the View': Chance and Choice in *Pale Fire*," *Studies in American Fiction* 4 (1976): 203–222.
Wallace, David Foster. *Infinite Jest*. New York: Back Bay Books, 1996.

Walsh, Richard. "Fictionality and Mimesis: Between Narrativity and Fictional Worlds," *Narrative* 11 (January 2003): 110–121.
Walther, Malin LaVon. "Re-Wrighting Native: Gwendolyn Brooks's Domestic Aesthetic in *Maud Martha*," *Tulsa Studies in Women's Literature* 13. 1 (Spring 1994): 143–145.
Walton, Jean. "Dissenting in an Age of Frenzied Heterosexualism: Kinbote's Transparent Closet in Nabokov's *Pale Fire*," *College Literature* 21.2 (June 1994): 89–105.
Washington, Mary Helen. "'Taming All That Anger Down': Rage and Silence in Gwendolyn Brooks' *Maud Martha*," *Massachusetts Review* 24. 2 (Summer 1983): 453–466.
Weart, Spencer. *Nuclear Fear: A History of Images*. Cambridge, Mass.: Harvard University Press, 1988.
Weisenburger, Stephen. "An Afterword," in Mosley, *Accident*.
Welsen, Peter. "Kinbote's Psychosis—a Key to Vladimir Nabokov's *Pale Fire*," in *Russian Literature and Psychoanalysis*, ed. Daniel Rancour-Laferriere. Amsterdam: John Benjamins Publishing Co., 1989.
Westad, Odd Arne. *The Global Cold War: Third World Interventions and the Making of Our Times*. Cambridge: Cambridge University Press, 2005.
Westwood, Gordon. *Society and the Homosexual*. New York: Dutton, 1953.
Wetmore, Kevin. "1954: Selling Kabuki to the West," *Asian Theatre Journal* 26.1 (Spring 2009): 78–93.
White, Hayden. "The Value of Narrativity in the Representation of Reality," *Critical Inquiry* 7 (Autumn 1980): 5–27.
Whitehead, Colson. *The Intuitionist*. New York: Anchor, 1999.
Whitfield, Stephen. *The Culture of the Cold War*. Baltimore, Md.: Johns Hopkins University Press, 1991.
Widmer, Kingsley. "The Existential Darkness: Richard Wright's *The Outsider*," *Wisconsin Studies in Contemporary Literature* 3 (Fall 1960): 13–21.
Williams, J. D. *The Compleat Strategyst: Being a Primer on the Theory of Games of Strategy*. New York: McGraw Hill, 1954.
Williams, John A. *The Man Who Cried I Am*. 1967. New York: Thunder's Mouth Press, 1985.
Wilson, Robert Rawdon. "In Palamedes' Shadow: Game and Play Concepts Today," *Canadian Review of Literature* (June 1985): 177–199.
Winkler, Carol. "Parallels in Preemptive War Rhetoric: Reagan on Libya; Bush 43 on Iraq," *Rhetoric & Public Affairs* 10.2 (Summer 2007): 303–334.
Wiskari, Werner. "Khrushchev Calls Off Plan for a Visit to Scandinavia; KHRUSHCHEV TRIP TO NORTH PUT OFF," *New York Times* (July 21, 1959): 1–2.
Wisnicki, Adrian. "A Trove of New Works by Thomas Pynchon?: Bomarc Service News Rediscovered," *Pynchon Notes* 46–49 (Spring–Fall 2000–2001): 9–34.
Wolf, Werner. "Chance in Fiction as a Privileged Index of Implied World-views: A Contribution to the Study of the World Modelling Functions of Narrative Fiction," in *Theorizing Narrativity*, ed. John Pier and José Ángel García Landa. Berlin: Walter de Gruyter, 2008.
Wolfe, Jesse. "'Ambivalent Man': Ellison's Rejection of Communism," *African American Review* 34.4 (Winter 2000): 621–637.
Woods, Tim. "The Music of Chance: Aleatorical (Dis)harmonies within 'The City of the World,'" in *Beyond the Red Notebook: Essays on Paul Auster*, ed. Dennis Barone. Philadelphia: University of Pennsylvania Press, 1995.
Wright, Richard. "I Tried to Be a Communist," in *The God That Failed*, ed. Richard Crossman. New York: Bantam, 1950.
———. *Lawd Today!* 1963. Boston: Northeastern University Press, 1993.
———. *The Outsider*. New York: Harper & Brothers, 1953.
———. *Native Son*. 1940. New York: Harper Perennial, 1996.
Young, La Monte, and Jackson Mac Low, ed. *An Anthology of Chance Operations*. New York: La Monte Young & Jackson Mac Low, 1963.
Young-Bruehl, Elisabeth. *Why Arendt Matters*. New Haven, Conn.: Yale University Press, 2006.
Žižek, Slavoj. *Did Somebody Say Totalitarianism? Five Interventions in the (Mis)use of a Notion*. London: Verso, 2001.
Zweig, Ellen. "Jackson Mac Low: The Limits of Formalism," *Poetics Today* 3.3 (Summer 1982): 79–86.

Index

absolute chance. *See* chance
accident
  Aristotelian theories of, 21–23, 45, 161n80
  science as progenitor of, 45–46, 47, 48
  as source of fear in Cold War, 19, 21, 45–46, 106
  suppression by Soviet Union, 16, 48, 59, 142
  use of term by author, 158n48
  See also chance
Adam, Ken, 114
Adorno, Theodor, 40–41, 165n28
African-American literature
  and African trickster figure, 87
  chance linked to self-definition in, 33, 81, 83, 85, 91, 92–93, 94–95
  dramatizations of being caught between two worlds, 33, 82–83, 99–100
  "Wright School," 84–85
  See also specific novels
African Americans
  relationship with Communism, 33, 82–83
  and self-definition, 81, 173n26
  See also African-American literature
Anthology of Chance Operations, An (Young and Mac Low), 30–31
Appel, Alfred, 68
Appy, Christian, 157n38
Arendt, Hannah, *Origins of Totalitarianism*, 48–50, 52, 57
Aristotle
  Poetics, 22–23
  theories of accident, 21–23, 45, 161n80
Ashbery, John, 140
Auster, Paul
  chance as theme in works of, 34, 130, 131, 132, 133, 135
  Works:
  In the Country of Last Things, 131
  The Invention of Solitude (memoir), 131
  Invisible, 131–132

Moon Palace, 131
The Music of Chance, 130, 131, 132–135, 140
The New York Trilogy, 131

Bacon, Jon Lance, 163n99
Baldwin, Hanson W., 71, 72
Baldwin, James, 96, 173n26, 175n49
Baldwin, Kate, 172n3
Barrett, William, 20–21
Barthelme, Donald, "Game," 115–116, 179n50
Bauer, Raymond, 159n62
Beautiful Mind, A (film), 102
Belgrad, Daniel, 160n72, 161n76, 183n13
Bell, Daniel, 15–16, 158n43, 159n62
Bell, David, 158n43
Belletto, Steven, 157n32, 161n76, 167n3, 183n10
Bergler, Edmund, 66, 67, 170n17, 170n21
Berkeley, Edmund C., 45
Berlin, Isaiah, 6
Berlin Wall, fall of, 129, 131
Blade Runner (film), 107
Blind Date (Kosinski)
  critiques of Marxism in, 7, 8
  explorations of chance in, 9–10, 156n30
  Monod's appearance in, 9
Boehmer, Konrad, 31
Bone, Robert, 84
Book of Common Prayer, A (Didion), 122–124, 180n71–72
Boyd, Brian, 69, 73, 168n6–7, 168n11, 169n11, 170n25, 171n34
Boyer, Paul, 165n24, 175n3
Brill, John, 17–18
Brooks, Gwendolyn, *Maud Martha*, 85–86
Bruhm, Steven, 168n11
Buckley, William F., *God and Man at Yale*, 7
Bukharin, Nikolai, 6, 16

Bunge, Mario, "What is Chance?," 156n17
Burn After Reading (film), 129
Burroughs, William S.
  cut-up method, 30, 106, 163n114
  explorations of chance, 29–30, 163n115
  Naked Lunch, 30, 106

Cage, John, 30–31
Campbell, John W., Jr., 106–107, 108
Cannif, Milton, 106
Carruthers, Susan L., 158n41
Casino Royale (film), 129
Caute, David, 157n33
Celmer, Paul, 38
chance
  and chaos theory, 161n79
  denial by Soviet/Marxist ideology, 4–5, 6–7, 8–9, 10, 15–21, 24, 37, 160n74
  distinguished from narrative chance, 23, 24–28, 36–37, 132, 161n87, 162n91
  in evolution, 7–8, 17–18, 147–148
  inability of science to explain, 35–36, 46, 60, 164n1
  as marker of American democratic freedom, 4–5, 10, 14–15, 19–21, 160n72
  as marker of objective reality, 4, 5–6, 8–9, 15, 19, 25, 28, 35, 36, 48–49, 156n30
  politicization during Cold War, 4–5, 37
  and postmodernism, 164n3
  and providence, 27, 163n101
  in quantum realm, 13–14
  as source of fear in Cold War, 19, 21, 45–46
  use of term by author, 14, 158n48
  See also accident; narrative chance
Chance and Necessity: An Essay on the Natural Philosophy of Modern Biology (Monod), 7–10, 15, 156n22
Chance Character of Human Existence, The (Brill), 17–18
Charters, Ann, 183n9
Chen, Tina, 182n19
Choi, Susan, *The Foreign Student*, 182n21
CIA (Central Intelligence Agency), 4, 29, 59, 183n31
  See also My Life in CIA (Mathews)
Clark, Suzanne, 103, 170n20, 176n8, 179n47
Cold War
  dates of, 158n41
  as global phenomenon, 11–12, 119
  persistence of themes and concerns today, 34, 129–131, 148, 181n4
  politicization of chance in, 4–5, 34, 37
  role of language in, 10
  See also chance; Cold War culture; Cold War literature; Marxism; Soviet Union
Cold War culture
  "agency panic," 29
  containment narrative in, 11–12, 62
  culture of spontaneity, 160n72
  homophobia of, 62, 63, 64, 65, 66, 67, 167n4, 170n21–22
  hypermasculinity in, 102, 176n8
  interest in chance, 4–5, 10, 14–15, 60, 102, 158n50
  "no accident" parody, 7
  paranoia, 29
  perceptions of Soviet system, 3–4, 6, 7, 14–21, 156n15
  role of language in shaping objective reality, 10–12, 156n31
  See also chance; Cold War literature; films; game theory narrative; music; nuclear weapons/war
Cold War literature
  current literary studies, 10–12, 147–154, 158n43, 184n23
  examined through chance, 4–5, 10, 12, 158n43
  experiments in creating absolute chance, 30–31, 161n87
  explorations of chance in, 21, 23–24, 25, 26–31, 37, 58–59, 60, 161n87, 162n92–93
  individual agency as political in, 150–153
  politics embedded in, 10–12, 28–31, 150–154
  See also homophobic narrative; *individual works*
Communism
  African-American interest in, 33, 82–83, 88
  literary critiques of, 33, 83, 88, 91, 92, 93–94, 99
Communist Party of the United States (CPUSA), 82–83, 88, 91, 174n46
Condon, Richard, *The Manchurian Candidate*, 11
containment narrative
  in Cold War culture, 11–12, 62
  See also Pale Fire (Nabokov)
Conte, Joseph M., 161n79
Continuity and Change in Russian and Soviet Thought, 18
Cooley, Ronald, 55–56
Coover, Robert
  The Public Burning, 58–59
  "The Second Son," 109
  The Universal Baseball Association, 34, 109–111, 119
Cornis-Pope, Marcel, 164n7, 184n21
Cory, Donald Webster, 170n21
Culler, Jonathan, on puns, 62–63, 68, 78

Darwin, Charles, 22, 147
Dawahare, Anthony, 172n5
de la Durantaye, Leland, 167n3, 169n16
DeLillo, Don
  paranoid sensibility of, 29
  Works:
    End Zone, 178n33
    Libra, 58, 59
    The Names, 180n81
    Underworld, 101, 130, 136

Demby, William, *Beetlecreek*, 85
Dickey, James, *Deliverance*, 11
Dick, Philip K., *Solar Lottery*, 34, 103, 107–109, 111, 177n27, 178n29
Dickstein, Morris, 157n37
Didion, Joan
  critiques of game theory narrative, 34, 103, 136
  as political and cultural critic, 122
  Works:
  A Book of Common Prayer, 122–124, 180n71–72
  Democracy, 124, 125
  The Last Thing He Wanted, 103, 124, 125–127, 180n80, 180n82
Douglas, Ann, 151, 183n14
Dr. Strangelove, or: How I Learned to Stop Worrying and Love the Bomb (film), 19, 34, 103, 111–112, 113–115, 116
Drury, Allen, *A Shade of Difference*, 11
Dudziak, Mary L., 172n3

Edelman, Lee, 170n20
Eisenhower, Dwight, 3–4, 108
Ellison, Ralph
  interest in Communism, 88
  See also Invisible Man (Ellison)
End of Ideology: On the Exhaustion of Political Ideas in the Fifties (Bell), 15
Engels, Friedrich, 6, 16, 18
Engerman, David, 159n51, 159n62
Evans, Richard, 6

Fail-Safe (film), 19, 113, 178n43
Fail-Safe (novel), 178n43
Fainsod, Merle, 160n62
Field, Andrew, 167n3, 168n6
films
  accident in, 44, 165n20
  critiques of Communism, 94
  recent films on Cold War, 129
  See also Dr. Strangelove; Fail-Safe
Fluxus, 30
Foley, Barbara, 88, 173n30, 174n31–32
foreshadowing, 25, 162n91
Frazier, E. Franklin, 83
Frazier, Valerie, 85, 87
Future is Ours, Comrade, The (Kosinski)
  Aliosha's tale, 5–6, 8, 9
  American embrace of, 4
  author's pseudonym, 155n2
  chance as marker of democratic freedom in, 4–5, 10
  chance as marker of objective reality in, 5, 6
  as critique of Soviet/Marxist denial of chance, 4–6, 10, 26, 155n11
  publication, 3

Gaddis, William
  in *This is Not a Novel* (Markson), 149–150
  See also Recognitions, The (Gaddis)
Gaines, Kevin, 172n10
"Game" (Barthelme), 115–116, 179n50
Games and Decisions: Introduction and Critical Survey (Luce and Raïffa), 110, 179n57
game theory
  and fantasies of control, 103–106, 179n57
  popularization of, 34, 102, 104–105, 175n5
  use by U.S. military, 33–34, 103–105
  See also game theory narrative
game theory narrative
  and fantasies of control, 33–34, 101–103, 110–111, 119, 128
  interactions of state and non-state actors, 119–127
  as irrational rationality, 34, 111–119
  literary and cultural treatments of, 34, 103, 106–111, 113–116, 117–127, 176n7, 178n33
  predictive pretensions, 125–127, 180n81
  promulgation of, 34, 102
  waning of, 116–117
Gates, Henry Louis, 87
Ghamari-Tabrizi, Sharon, 177n24, 178n37, 178n42
Gilroy, Paul, 174n44
Ginsberg, Allen, *Kaddish*, 11
González, Gaspar, 157n33
Gornick, Vivian, 7, 156n21
Grausam, Daniel, 161n76, 167n51, 178n32, 181n3
Gregory, Sinda, 132, 181n5
Gysin, Brion, 30

Hacking, Ian
  on emergence of chance in science, 13, 14
  The Taming of Chance, 31, 35, 36, 46
Hamilton, Ross
  history of accident, 21–23, 158n43, 161n80
  on slapstick, 42, 43, 44
Hammond, Andrew, 152, 157n39, 183n15
Hassan, Ihab, 164n3
Hayles, N. Katherine, 161n79, 164n119
Henriksen, Margot, 178n37
Highsmith, Patricia, *The Blunderer*, 11
Himes, Chester
  If He Hollers Let Him Go, 175n46
  Lonely Crusade, 174n46
Hinds, Lynn Boyd, 156n31
historical determinism. *See* Marxism
Hite, Molly, 166n45
Hoberek, Andrew, 152, 183n16
Hofstadter, Richard, 38
Holocaust, 47–48

Holton, Robert, 165*n*14, 165*n*31, 166*n*45
homophobia
  in Cold War culture, 62–67, 170*n*21–22
  in Cold War literature, 65, 66, 169*n*15
  1951 Senate subcommittee report, 67
  See also homophobic narrative
homophobic narrative
  defined, 33
  See also Pale Fire (Nabokov)
Hook, Sidney, 20, 160*n*74, 161*n*75, 161*n*77
Horkheimer, Max, 40–41, 165*n*28
Horne, Gerald, 172*n*3
Howard, Leslie, 149, 150
Hungerford, Amy, 183*n*2
Hutcheon, Linda, 164*n*3

Ikard, David, 173*n*19
imperialism
  as roots of totalitarianism, 48, 51
  of United States, 11–12
Inkeles, Alex, 159*n*62
Institute of International Education, 4
International Spy Museum, 129
Intuitionist, The (Whitehead)
  explorations of race, 33, 80–81
  nostalgia for Cold War, 81, 136
  role of accident/chance in, 33, 81–82
Invasion of the Body Snatchers (film), 94
Invisible Man (Ellison)
  critique of American democratic system, 86, 89–90, 95, 99–100
  critique of Communism, 33, 83, 86, 88–90, 91, 94, 99
  linking of chance to self definition, 87, 90–91
  relationship between race and chance, 86–87, 90–91
  trope of game-playing in, 86, 88
Iversen, Margaret, 164*n*20, 164*n*116

Jackson, Lawrence, 174*n*35
Jackson, Tony, 19, 70, 160*n*71
Jacobson, Matthew Frye, 157*n*33
James, Alison, 158*n*43
James, Henry, *The Ambassadors*, 162*n*92
Jarrell, Randall, *Pictures from an Institution*, 7
Jervis, Robert, 117
Johnson, B.S., *The Unfortunates*, 161*n*87
Johnson, David K., 170*n*20
Johnston, John, 164*n*3

Kahn, Herman
  On Thermonuclear War, 111–113, 114, 178*n*42, 179*n*48
  work with RAND, 178*n*35
Kakutani, Michiko, 57
Kaplan, Amy, 11, 157*n*38

Kaplan, Fred, 105
Kavanagh, Thomas, 161*n*86
Keenaghan, Eric, 157*n*39
Kercher, Stephen E., 178*n*37, 179*n*49
Kermode, Frank, 160*n*71, 163*n*115, 167*n*3, 171*n*35
Kerouac, Jack
  mentioned in Markson's works, 149–150
  as political writer, 150–152, 183*n*10, 183*n*14
  Works:
  Doctor Sax, 11
  The Subterraneans, 150, 151
Killen, John O., *Youngblood*, 91
Kim, Daniel, 182*n*20
Kim, Jodi, 153, 157*n*39, 182*n*20, 184*n*25
King Creole (film), 11
Klein, Christina, 119, 153, 157*n*39, 179*n*64, 184*n*20
Kluckhohn, Clyde, 159*n*62
Knight, Peter, 167*n*50
Kosinski, Jerzy
  critiques of Marxist ideology, 4–6, 7, 8, 26, 155*n*11
  explorations of chance in works of, 9, 10, 26, 156*n*30
  immigration to U.S., 3–4
  Jacques Monod as friend and influence, 7, 8, 9
  Works:
  Being There, 3
  Blind Date, 7–10, 156*n*30
  No Third Path, 155*n*2
  The Painted Bird, 3
  See also Future is Ours, Comrade, The (Kosinski)
Kubrick, Stanley
  Dr. Strangelove, 19, 34, 103, 111–116
  study of nuclear strategy, 112

Langman, Larry, 40
Last Thing He Wanted, The (Didion), 103, 124, 125–127, 180*n*80, 180*n*82
Lears, Jackson, 19, 86, 177*n*27
LeCarré, John, *The Spy Who Came in from the Cold*, 11, 169*n*15
Lee, Chang-rae. *See Native Speaker* (Lee)
Legba, 87
Leites, Nathan
  Study of Bolshevism, A, 16–17, 19, 159*n*58–59
  The Operational Code of the Politburo, 16
Lenin, Vladimir, 56, 159*n*59
Lentricchia, Frank, 167*n*53
Leonard, Robert J., 176*n*10
Luce, Duncan R., 110, 179*n*57
Lucretius, *De Rerum Natura*, 13, 14
Lumet, Sidney, *Fail-Safe* (film), 19, 113

Macdonald, Dwight, 7, 156n20, 167n3, 171n35
Mac Low, Jackson, *An Anthology of Chance Operations*, 30–31
Mad magazine, 11
Mad Men (television program), 129
Maher, Paul, 183n8
Mailer, Norman, 65, 170n21, 171n35
Man Who Cried I Am, The (Williams)
  Africa as symbol of freedom in, 99
  critique of American government, 33, 96–100, 175n48
  role of chance/accident in, 86, 98, 99, 175n48
Marcuse, Herbert, 18–19, 20, 160n66–68, 160n68
Markson, David, 149–150
Marxism
  Cold War American perceptions of, 6, 7, 14–21, 156n15
  denial of chance by, 6–7, 15–21, 37, 156n17, 160n74
  and dialectical materialism, 8, 19, 156n17
  historical determinism of, 6, 19, 20, 160n74
  orthodox vs. Soviet-style, 18–19, 20, 160n68
Mathews, Harry
  as expatriate, 34, 140
  trope of game playing in works of, 140
  Works:
    The Conversions, 140
    See also My Life in CIA (Mathews)
Matthews, Kristin L., 157n34
Mauldin, Bill, 120
Maxwell, William, *New Negro, Old Left*, 83, 172n8
May, Elaine Tyler, 157n35
McCaffery, Larry, 132, 178n32, 181n5
McCann, Sean, 152, 162n93, 183n18–19
McCarthy, Mary, 71, 171n30, 171n35
McClintock, Anne, 181n4
McClure, John A., 183n2, 183n19
McDonald, John
  work used as epigraph to *Solar Lottery* (Dick), 107
  popularization of game theory, 102, 104–105
  Works:
    Strategy in Poker, Business and War, 104, 105–106, 107, 176n13
    "A Theory of Strategy," 104–105
McGurl, Mark, 167n53, 184n23
Mead, Margaret, *Soviet Attitudes Toward Authority*, 17
Mearsheimer, John, 130
Medhurst, Martin, 156n31
Medovoi, Leerom, 12, 119, 152, 157n34, 157n39, 179n64–65, 183n17
Melley, Timothy, 29, 163n110, 165n11, 175n2
Meriwether, James, 175n50
Meyer, Priscilla, 167n3
Milesi, Laurent, 47–48
Mirowski, Philip, 103, 115
Monk, Leland, 24, 158n43, 161n85, 163n108

Monod, Jacques
  critiques of Marxist ideology, 8–9
  on evolution, 7–8
  as friend and influence on Kosinski, 7, 8, 9
  on "pure chance," 13
  Works:
    Chance and Necessity, 7–10, 15, 156n22
Morgenstern, Oskar, 104–105, 179n50
Morson, Gary Saul, 25–26, 162n88, 162n91–92
Mosley, Nicholas, *Accident*, 28
Motley, Willard, *Knock on Any Door*, 85
music
  and "culture of spontaneity," 160n72
  experiments with chance, 30–31
Music of Chance, The (Auster), 130, 131, 132–135, 140
My Life in CIA: A Chronicle of 1973 (Mathews), 34, 130–131, 140–145, 182n30

Nabokov, Vladimir
  attitude toward homosexuality, 61, 168n11
  on coincidence, 68, 170n24
  fictional worlds in novels of, 168n9
  hiding places, interest in. See *Pale Fire*, crown jewels
  political critique in works of, 32, 64, 78
  relationship with brother Sergey, 61, 79, 168n11
  and Sigmund Freud, 66
  Works:
    Ada, 171n38
    Lolita, 27–28, 78, 162n93
    Speak, Memory (autobiography), 61, 167n1, 169n11, 171n30
    See also Pale Fire (Nabokov)
Nadel, Alan, 11, 12, 157n35–36, 157n40, 173n29, 175n48
narrative chance
  in Cold War writing, 21, 23–24, 25, 26–31, 37, 58–59, 60, 162n92–93
  defined, 23
  distinguished from absolute chance, 23, 24–28, 36, 132, 161n87, 162n91
  and role of puns, 68
  tied to interpretation, 21–23, 24, 36, 68
  writers' awareness of, 23–24
  See also chance; Cold War literature; *specific literary works*
Nash, John, 102, 132
Native Son (Wright), 33, 84, 85, 88, 91
Native Speaker (Lee)
  chance/accident as matter of interpretation, 137–140
  critique of Cold War causal logic, 34, 135, 137–139, 140, 182n20
  nostalgia for Cold War concerns, 135–137
  on post–Cold War racial norms, 130, 135, 136–137, 138–139, 182n20–22
NATO, 3–4

Newman, James R., 112–113
New York University Institute of Philosophy, 20
"no accident" (phrase), 7, 15
Nolan, William, 82–83
Novaya Zemlya (Nova Zembla), 71, 72, 171n30, 171n32-33
   See also Pale Fire (Nabokov)
nuclear weapons/war
   American apprehensions about, 19, 21, 45–46, 70, 71, 106, 119
   Soviet testing of, 71, 72, 171n32-33
   See also films; game theory narrative

Obama, Barack, 101
O'Connor, Flannery
   Christian beliefs, 26, 27, 163n98
   Cold War dissent, 27, 163n99
   Works:
   "A Good Man Is Hard to Find," 26–27
Okada, John, 173n27
On the Origin of Species (Darwin), 147
On Thermonuclear War (Kahn), 111–113, 114, 178n42, 179n48
Origins of Totalitarianism, The (Arendt), 48–50, 52, 57
Oulipo, 34, 140, 182n27
Outsider, The (Wright)
   as critique of American democratic system, 33, 86, 93, 94–95
   as critique of Communism, 86, 91, 93–94, 95
   linking of chance to self-definition in, 91, 92–93, 94–95
   links with Invisible Man, 91, 174n37
   plot, 174n42

Pale Fire (Nabokov)
   containment narrative, 62, 67, 71
   crown jewels in. See Nabokov, hiding places
   fictional world of, 168n9
   homophobic narrative, 28, 32, 33, 61–62, 63, 64–70, 71, 73–74, 78, 167n4, 168n11, 170n22
   Kinbote's attempts to manage chance, 62, 64, 65, 68–69, 73–77, 171n37
   Kinbote's Zembla narrative, 32–33, 61–62, 63–64, 65, 68–69, 71–73, 168n10, 170n26, 171n28, 171n30
   Nabokov's biography as influence on, 61, 79, 168n11
   plot synopsis, 32–33, 63–64
   as political critique, 32–33, 62–63, 64, 66–67, 70–73, 78–79, 167n3, 169n13, 171n35
   and real Nova Zembla, 71, 72, 171n30, 171n32-33
   role of chance in, 28, 32–33, 62, 64, 65, 67–69, 73–79
   role of coincidence in, 63, 67–68, 78, 168n7, 172n38

role of puns/wordplay, 32, 33, 62–63, 68, 69–70, 78, 170n26
Shade's "Pale Fire" poem, 32, 63, 69–71, 74, 77–78
as single-author vs. dual-author, 63, 168n6
structure, 32, 62
Paranoid Style in American Politics (Hofstadter), 38
Paulson, William, 24, 161n84
Pavel, Thomas, 168n9
Pease, Donald, 157n35, 157n38
Peirce, Charles Sanders, "The Doctrine of Necessity," 13
Petry, Ann, The Narrows, 85
Piette, Adam, 153, 157n34, 167n3, 181n3, 184n22, 184n24
Pitzer, Andrea, 171n33
Plath, Sylvia, The Bell Jar, 11
Platt, Anthony, 172n10
Pletsch, Carl, 119
Pnin (Nabokov), 67–68, 69, 70
Poiger, Uta, 157n39
Popper, Karl, 13–14
postmodernism
   first novels of, 32, 57, 164n3
   interest in chance, 57–60, 164n3
Powers, Richard
   on waging randomness, 101
   Works:
   The Gold Bug Variations, 58, 59–60
   Prisoner's Dilemma, 34, 117–119
Prisoner's Dilemma (Powers), 34, 117–119
puns
   role in narrative, 62–63, 68
   See also Pale Fire (Nabokov); Pnin
Puskar, Jason, 173n23
Pynchon, Thomas
   paranoid sensibility of, 29
   themes of chance in works of, 46, 57–58
   Works:
   Against the Day, 58
   Crying of Lot 49, The, 47–48, 57–58, 140
   Gravity's Rainbow, 47–48, 51, 52, 57, 166n39
   "Togetherness," 46, 166n42
   Vineland, 57
   See also V. (Pynchon)

race
   as accident of birth, 86–87, 173n26-27
   See also African-American literature; Intuitionist, The (Whitehead); Invisible Man (Ellison); Native Speaker (Lee)
Raïffa, Howard, 110, 179n57
RAND Corporation, 16, 105, 113, 114
Raney, David, 169n13
Rapoport, Anatol, 116, 179n57

Reagan administration, 117
Recognitions, The (Gaddis)
  chance events in, 35–37
  noted in other works, 149, 150
  and postmodernism, 164n3
  on science's inability to explain chance, 35–36, 46, 60, 164n1
Redding, Arthur, 157n33–34, 172n3
Redfield, Marc, 165n9
Relyea, Sarah, 92, 174n41
Richardson, Brian, 161n86
Rogin, Michael, 169n13
Roosevelt, Eleanor, 4
Rowley, Hazel, 174n37

Saunders, Frances Stonor, 155n5
Savran, David, 170n20, 176n8
Schaub, Thomas, 53, 161n75, 163n99, 166n43, 174n30
Schlesinger, Arthur, Jr., 19–20
Schrecker, Ellen, 181n3
Schreiber, Rebecca M., 157n39
science
  inability to explain chance, 35–36, 46, 60, 164n1
  as progenitor of accidents, 45–46, 47, 48
  as tamer of chance, 36, 46
Shaw, Irwin, *The Troubled Air*, 11
Sherif, Ann, 157n39
Shiff, Stacy, 169n11
sideshadowing, 25
Sigmund Freud, 66, 67
Silk Stockings (film), 94
Simmons, Ernest, 18
Singh, Nikhil Pal, 172n3, 181n4
slapstick
  violence of, 40–41, 43
  See also V. (Pynchon)
Sloan, James Park, 4
Smith, Zadie, *White Teeth*, 182n22
Solar Lottery (Dick), 34, 103, 107–109, 111, 177n27, 178n29
Soviet Attitudes Toward Authority (Mead), 17
Soviet Union
  Cold War American perceptions of, 3–4, 6, 14–21
  collapse of, 129
  compulsion for political control and planning, 4, 17–18, 159n62
  crash of Tupolev-144, 142
  denial and manipulation of chance, 4–5, 6–7, 8–9, 10, 15–21, 24, 37, 160n74
  denial of accidents/disasters, 16, 48, 59, 142
  and historical determinism, 6
  and Korean Airlines Disaster, 159n56
  nuclear testing by, 71, 72, 171n32–33
  Stadnik affair, 15–16, 17
  See also Marxism; Novaya Zemlya

Spanos, William, 157n35
Stadnik, Gregory, 15–16
Stalin, Joseph, 16, 159n59
Stearn, Jess, *The Sixth Man*, 66
Sterne, Laurence, *Tristram Shandy*, 162n92
Steve Canyon (cartoon), 106, 177n24
Stevens, Jason W., 163n99, 183n2
Strategy in Poker, Business and War (McDonald), 104, 105–106, 107, 176n13
Study of Bolshevism, A (Leites), 16–17, 159n59
Swirski, Peter, 176n7
Szalay, Michael, 152, 173n20, 174n44, 183n18–19

Taming of Chance, The (Hacking), 31, 35, 36, 45, 46
Tanner, Tony, 29, 38, 163n109, 164n6, 164n8, 167n3
Theory of Games and Economic Behavior (Von Neumann and Morgenstern), 104–105, 106, 176n11
This is Not a Novel (Markson), 149–150
Tietchen, Todd, 183n10
Tillich, Paul, *The Courage to Be*, 19
"Togetherness" (Pynchon), 46
Tolstoy, Leo
  sideshadowing by, 25
  War and Peace, 170
totalitarianism
  roots of, 48–50, 51
  U.S. state control reminiscent of, 10, 33–34, 58–59, 165n28
  See also Origins of Totalitarianism (Arendt)

United States
  chance as marker of democratic freedom, 4–5, 10, 14–15, 19–21, 160n72
  imperialism of, 11–12
  state control reminiscent of totalitarianism, 10, 33–34, 58–59, 165n28
  See also Cold War culture; United States military
United States Information Agency (USIA), 4
United States military
  and end of Cold War, 181n4
  use of game theory, 33–34, 103–105
Universal Baseball Association, The (Coover), 34, 109–111, 119

V. (Pynchon)
  Benny Profane, 38, 39–40, 41–43, 44, 47, 55, 164n7
  Cold War frame for, 37, 57, 60
  as critique of totalitarianism, 32, 40, 44, 47–56, 94, 165n31
  Esther Harvitz's nose job, 33, 55–57, 166n45
  genocidal imagery as political critique, 44, 47–48, 50–52, 53–56, 165n28, 166n45
  Herbert Stencil, 32, 38–39, 49, 50–51

V. (Pynchon) (continued)
  introduction to, 38
  Mondaugen, 50–52, 54–55
  role of slapstick in, 40–44, 165n14, 165n19
  tensions between chance and design, 31–32, 37–39, 43, 49–51, 56–57
  on violent potential of narrative chance, 37, 40–43, 48, 57, 134–135
Vidal, Gore
  The City and the Pillar, 120
  Dark Green, Bright Red, 120–122
Virilio, Paul
  on science as progenitor of accidents, 45–46, 47, 48
  on Soviet treatment of accident, 16
Vishinsky, Andrey, 15, 16
The Vital Center: The Politics of Freedom (Schlesinger), 19–20
Vizenor, Gerald, 158n43
Von Eschen, Penny, 172n3
Vonnegut, Kurt, *Player Piano*, 106
Von Neumann, John, 104–105, 106, 108, 177n28

Wallace, David Foster, *Infinite Jest*, 43–44
Walsh, Richard, 168n9
Walther, Malin LaVon, 173n22
Washington, Mary Helen, 173n22
Weart, Spencer, 160n70, 165n24
Weisenburger, Steven, 28
Westad, Odd Arne, 157n38, 180n69

Westwood, Gordon, 66
Wetmore, Kevin, 157n34
White, Hayden, 168n10
Whitehead, Colson. *See The Intuitionist*, 33
Whitfield, Stephen, 178n37
Widmer, Kingsley, 92
Williams, John A.
  as expatriate, 96
  explorations of race in works of, 83
  See also Man Who Cried I Am, The (Williams)
Windt, Theodore Otto, Jr., 156n31
Wolfe, Jesse, 174n33
Wolf, Werner, 161n86
Woods, Tim, 134, 181n7, 181n16
Wright, Richard
  as expatriate, 96
  explorations of race in works of, 83
  interest in Communism, 82, 91, 92
  Works:
    "I Tried to Be a Communist," 82, 91
    Lawd Today!, 174n42
  See also Native Son (Wright); *Outsider, The* (Wright)

Young-Bruehl, Elisabeth, 166n34
Young, La Monte, 30

Žižek, Slavoj, 166n34
Zweig, Ellen, 30